12.00

Heterosexism

Heterosexism

An Ethical Challenge

Patricia Beattie Jung
and
Ralph F. Smith

8/2-

STATE UNIVERSITY OF NEW YORK PRESS

Published by
State University of New York Press, Albany

© 1993   State University of New York

For information, address State University of New York Press,
State University Plaza, Albany, N.Y., 12246

Production by Bernadine Dawes
Marketing by Nancy Farrell

Library of Congress Cataloging-in-Publication Data

Jung, Patricia Beattie.
    Heterosexism : an ethical challenge / Patricia Beattie Jung, Ralph
F. Smith.
        p.   cm.
    Includes bibliographical references (p.   ) and index.
    ISBN 0-7914-1695-X (hc. : alk. paper) : — ISBN
0-7914-1696-8 (pbk. : alk. paper) :
    1. Homophobia—United States—Moral and ethical aspects.
    2. Homosexuality—United States—Moral and ethical aspects.
    3. Sexism—United States—Moral and ethical aspects.   I. Smith,
Ralph F., 1950-. II. Title.
    HQ76.3.U5J86   1993
    306.76'6—dc20   92-43405
                                                           CIP

10 9 8 7 6 5 4 3 2

For B. J. and D. J.,
whose commitment and work for justice
are both delight and inspiration

Contents

Preface

People in every age like to assume that they live at a turning point in history. Events seem to signal a movement from old to new that makes contemporary decisions part of a larger process of transition. In the midst of the changes some consider themselves reformers, others preservers of tradition. A degree of personal and cultural hubris often contributes to such assumptions, but they are rarely without at least a measure of truth.

Many have argued that in the mid-twentieth century North American culture began a period of transition broadly termed the *sexual revolution*. Some consider the decades since then to have been a period of enlightenment. Others question whether a revolution ever occurred and sadly conclude that we have deceived ourselves in thinking that we have learned anything new about human sexuality.

We believe that those who argue for sexual enlightenment are closer to the truth. The explosion of knowledge, especially in biology, anthropology, psychology, and sociology has altered forever our understanding of human sexuality. We know more about its complexity than any other generation. The question, of course, is whether that wealth of knowledge has made us any wiser.

We are willing to risk the hubris that says it has made us wiser and that we are at a critical turning point in our culture. We must either embrace or reject the wisdom available to us. To embrace it is to let go of the prejudices spawned by a heterocentric vision of human sexuality. To reject it is to cling to those prejudices. We intend this book as an invitation to the embrace.

Our gratitude to those who have supported, challenged, and nurtured us in our work is deep and heartfelt. We thank our families and friends, knowing that their sacrifices on our behalf cannot be repaid. We acknowledge as well the support of our colleagues at Wartburg Theological Seminary. They have been gracious partners in dialogue and offered us the kind of critical reflection that takes disagreement seriously by seeing it as an invitation to growth and using it as a tool of discernment.

We especially thank people in the gay community who welcomed us as friends, honored our work, patiently suffered our ignorance and endless inquiry, and shared our hope and vision. We dedicate our labor to them.

Introduction

One question has been asked repeatedly as we have worked on this project: "Why are you writing this book?" Other questions usually followed quickly on that first one. Two of them are substantive: "What motivates you personally to devote time and energy to this?" and "Why are you willing to risk speaking publicly on such controversial issues?" Honesty in exploring and assessing the relationship between one's own faith convictions and sexual values is essential for dialogue in sexual ethics. We want to be clear about both the personal and public issues that led to our collaboration and resulted in the perspectives articulated in the following chapters.

Our collaboration grew out of our initially independent work with students at the Lutheran seminary where we teach. Seminarians were questioning developments in the Evangelical Lutheran Church in America (ELCA) regarding ministry, call, ordination, and sexuality. Between 1987 and 1991 events in the ELCA and other church bodies brought the issue of homosexuality to the forefront of many denominational discussions of sexual ethics.

We found ourselves responding to these events personally and as a consequence of our teaching roles also being asked to define and interpret the issues for others from the perspectives of the theological traditions of the Church. We discovered that we were ready to deal faithfully with ecclesiastical, historical, and broader theological traditions on these matters, but that neither the Church nor society was fully open to dialogue. People either stifled it or could not get past debates that shed more heat than light on the subject.

Our pastoral involvement with gay and lesbian support groups also forced us to struggle with the witness of Christians who were at the margins of the Church's life. They raised critical questions for the Church that could no longer be ignored. We found ourselves living in two worlds of discourse, and the voices in one were not being heard in the other. As we explored with each other how we thought and felt about the issues, we came to the conclusion that together we might contribute to clarifying some of the concerns that were blocking fruitful dialogue and faithful attempts to reform Church teaching. Collaborating to write this book is our attempt to make that contribution. Throughout the process we have stayed in dialogue with the gay community to ensure that our efforts to bridge the gap between these two worlds of discourse were not unduly distorted by our own biases.

We arrived at the common ground we share regarding our views on heterosexism by radically different routes. We are not in complete agreement about every issue, nor do we see the need to be. But we are mutually convinced of the foundational principles that eventually put us at odds with traditional theological conclusions about homosexuality. Thus in coauthoring this book we attempt to speak with a common voice.

Little of what we say here is new. We rehearse basic information about homosexuality that ought to be taken for granted today, yet continues to be viewed with undue suspicion or is ignored in much theological debate. We draw on traditional questions and theological issues to contextualize our argument for change. We see ourselves as standing firmly within the Christian tradition in terms of our methodology, our commitment to the authority of Scripture, and our faithfulness to doctrine. We write ecumenically and address our argument to fellow Christians, but we see this as an asset in generating dialogue with other religious and nonreligious traditions.

Working and writing together has of course broadened our horizons. We began with the expectation that our task would be to present a challenging but moderate reinterpretation of the data relevant to understanding homosexuality. Initially our invitation to reform called for reinterpreting teachings on homosexuality. About midway through the process we discovered that we were moving toward the adoption of a new paradigm. This new paradigm shifted the focus of the whole enterprise from homosexuality to heterosexism. Describing that new paradigm and sketching some of its implications for Christian faith and life is the overarching purpose of this book.

If we are to become a people who can debate with charity about potentially divisive matters, we must mutually equip each other for such graceful learning. We develop a five-part typology in chapter 1 for the sake of facilitating inclusive deliberation. The purpose of a typology such as this is to engender conversation across a wide spectrum of views. We hope that this chapter gives voice to and identifies salient aspects of readers' positions in a way that orients us toward real dialogue with others.

In developing the typology we have tried to be fair to positions not our own and to present them at their strengths. Like all typologies, it obscures some significant nuances in complex positions. This is a cost associated with such categorizing of moral arguments. We believe, of course, that the benefit of such work outweighs its inevitable costs.

Some of those who are gay among us feel demeaned, if not infuriated by the debate about the morality of homosexuality. Others welcome the opportunity to explore their own reservations about their sexual orientation, recognizing that their concern may be the consequence of internalized ecclesial and social prejudice. The moral debate about whether or not gay people are by their very orientation imperfect, defective, diseased, evil, or good continues to be necessary. It must simply be joined with identical inquiry regarding straight people. Questions about what causes our sexuality in all its diversity may not be finally or fully answerable, but the scientific debate about etiology is always relevant. We hope that perseverance in both realms of debate will lead to the upbuilding and eventual reform of the Church.

To expect of even devoutly faithful gay people, and in some cases their families and friends, that they will be able to detach themselves from the insult inherent in the debate when it is restricted to homosexuality is to ask them to go above and beyond the call of duty. John Fortunato puts the matter sharply: "Imagine, if you will, asking black clergy to sit on a 'Committee on Race' and listen open-mindedly to a discussion of whether or not black people are by nature intellectually inferior to white people (discussions that have not been unknown in South Africa). . . . The appropriate response to injustice is outrage and protest—not polite dialogue."[1] Such persons if they are willing to participate in and contribute to this process of moral deliberation do so at great personal cost. We trust that all readers will keep this in mind as we work through the typology.

Chapter 2 examines the relevance and relative authority of various sources of moral wisdom for our deliberations on homosexuality and heterosexism. It opens with a discussion of how our approach in this book and our defining of the problem shape the conversation. We argue that those who sustain heterosexism must defend their point of view in light of the erosion of its credibility. Recognition of this erosion stems from an extended analysis of the consistency, comprehensiveness, coherence, and faithfulness of heterosexist traditions. We close the chapter with a review of the bibli cal warrants for the use of other sources of wisdom and for the primacy of Scripture in a faithful reformation of our tradition.

The first two chapters seek to provide sufficient common understanding so that the arguments about Scripture explored in chapter 3 have a clear context. We hear the voice of Scripture with ears that are attuned both to its word to us and the concerns of the world to which it speaks. Scripture cannot speak in a vacuum because there is no vacuum. Our task in every time and place as faithful stewards of God's Word is to be as clear as we can about the context in and to which Scripture speaks.

In chapter 3 we evaluate the few scriptural passages that mention same sex behaviors and the traditional interpretation of each. This includes assessing why these texts are clustered rather than treated in context and how such clustering affects their interpretation. In addition, the few texts that are traditionally used to support heterocentrism are discussed in light of contemporary debate about human sexuality.

The biblical focus of chapter 3 is crucial for a number of reasons. One could attempt to mount a case against heterosexism by using only nonbiblical evidence. Our primary audience, however, is the Church. We speak as Christians to Christians in order to call the Christian community to a reform that can in turn inform the larger society. No Christian denomination will succeed in fostering a change in its teaching and institutional practices without making a biblical case for the proposed change, because Scripture has a normative and authoritative role in all churches.

Furthermore, the wider, culturally formative influence of Scripture in the West, especially in issues of morality, cannot be denied. Thus for purely historical reasons everyone must deal with the biblical data when tackling ethical issues in human sexual behavior. We also develop other kinds of arguments; for example, social and more generally theological ones. The scriptural focus of this chapter is foundational to but not exhaustive of our work.

Only faithfulness to biblical authority can make the arguments offered here of value to people who are not Christian. In a pluralistic culture, religions are taken seriously by paying attention to and respecting the paradigms within which they function as living traditions. For Christians to ignore biblical data would be like Muslims ignoring the Koran or Jews the Torah. It is not useful for interreligious dialogue to adopt a reductionistic approach in discussing only "what we have in common." The distinctiveness of each tradition's life enriches the common store of human experience.

We believe that our approach can serve a variety of audiences precisely because it takes the internal evidence of Christian tradition seriously while treating it critically. Audre Lorde once commented that the master's tools will never dismantle the master's house. The history of Christianity reveals that Lorde's comment is not always fitting. For Christians it is precisely the master's tools that can dismantle whatever obscures the foundation and structure. The Scriptures have served as the basis for many reformations. They can serve today to challenge heterosexism.

We turn in chapter 4 to the examination of fears that perpetuate heterosexism. There is no question that people are threatened by this topic. Some of these perceived threats disappear when we uncover the false information that informs them. We examine such perceived threats both to society and the Church to add our voices to those who call us to put unfounded fears to rest. Yet challenging heterosexism will produce real and significant threats to some aspects of church life (for example, biblicism) and society (for example, sexism). The analysis in chapter 4 also addresses these threats. We argue that they are the legitimate and necessary consequence of reform.

Chapters 5 and 6 represent a shift of focus. The first four chapters seek to persuade readers that heterosexism is real and that it is both reasonable and necessary to challenge it. In these next two chapters we confront heterosexism in the Church's own life and suggest theological moves that begin the task of confronting and dismantling it. In chapter 5 we explore the foundations for reform that arise from within the Church's own historical structures. We evaluate the Church's understanding of the phrase *active gay lifestyle* and the ways in which it has shaped Church teaching. The current climate in many denominations calls for a "conservative but compassionate" response to gays and lesbians in our midst. We examine how and why this stance inhibits reform.

A key point of chapter 5 is the call for a paradigm shift in the Church's sexual ethic. We can expect little progress in overcoming the barriers erected by heterosexism if we continue to talk only about homosexuality. We must acknowledge heterosexism as sin if we are to develop a holistic sexual ethic within which expressions of homosexuality can be reevaluated. Such an approach allows us to honor the claim that heterosexuality is among God's intentions for human sexuality. To maintain, however, that a heterosexual orientation is *better* than other expressions of God's intention is precisely the conclusion that we challenge. Chapter 5 closes with an extended analysis of the symbolic weight carried by the ordination of gays and lesbians in challenging heterosexism.

In chapter 6 we explore the foundations for a changed theology of sexuality. What we say is not new, but we make the argument in light of the shifts for which we have argued in the preceding chapters. We then use marriage as a ritual test case that allows us to follow one example of the implications of our suggestions to a logical conclusion. We review the traditional interpretations of marriage within a heterocentric worldview. We argue that in the history of marriage there is ample room for expanding our understanding without violating Scripture or tradition. We also acknowledge that the Church may develop a variety of blessing rites that create other directions for its life and witness. Whether the Church reforms traditional rites or creates new ones, taking paths that find their source in its own history affords it the opportunity both to be faithful and to begin dismantling heterosexist structures.

We close our analysis of heterosexism as an ethical challenge with a study of largely unexamined moral questions about sexual authenticity and sexual fidelity in chapter 7. They serve as examples of how individuals might proceed in moving beyond heterosexism. The chapter also serves as a reminder that the personal and public facets of sexual identity cannot be separated.

Readers will quickly notice a lack of uniformity in the terminology used throughout the book. This is deliberate. Conversations with people in the gay community have convinced us that there is no standard or even broadly accepted vocabulary for identifying or differentiating homosexual, bisexual, transgender, and heterosexual people. We have tried to avoid abstractions by using the words *heterosexual* and *homosexual* only as adjectives (homosexual person, homosexual man, heterosexual woman, etc.). Obviously we reject all slang that intends to denigrate gay and lesbian people. Our approach has been to adopt a pluriform rather than uniform terminology to reflect current diversity.

Despite the intentional ambiguity regarding terminology, we use the following working definitions.[2] A heterosexual person is someone who has most or all of his or her erotic needs met in interactions with persons of the other sex. In all other respects they are just like everyone else. A bisexual person is someone who has most or all of his or her erotic needs met in interactions with persons of either sex. In all other respects they are just like everyone else. A homosexual person is someone who has most or all of his or her erotic needs met in interactions with persons of the same sex. In all other respects they are just like everyone else.

A transgender (transsexual) person is someone whose physiological sexual identity is at odds with his or her psycho-social sexual identity (preoperative) or someone who has undergone surgery to bring these into closer conformity (postoperative). This person's erotic needs in either case may make him or her heterosexual, bisexual, or homosexual. Thus the preceding descriptions are applicable to transgender persons.

These definitions have three significant features. First, they are objective and descriptive. They assume no particular cause or purpose for human sexuality. Second, they presume that because human beings are sexual rather than asexual it is appropriate to discuss erotic needs as distinct from, although related to, wants and desires. Third, they acknowledge that human sexuality is central to human identity but does not exhaust all that must be said about why we are who we are.

We use the words *gay* and *lesbian* most frequently because this book focusses on the dichotomy between homosexuality and heterosexuality created by heterosexism. Unlike other terms, *gay* and *lesbian* seem to enjoy general acceptance as nonderogatory ways to designate the sexual orientation of homosexual men and women. Ideally the labeling implicit in such terminology will someday be unnecessary. These language issues necessarily enmesh us in the political agenda associated with them.

In some ways the choices we have made here will please no one. Gay and lesbian activists will chide us for not going far enough toward overcoming the heterosexist biases the book purports to address. Bisexual and transgender persons will accuse us of ignoring their plight. Heterosexists of various sorts (see the typology in chapter 1) will accuse us of adopting uncritically "pro-gay apologetics." We can ask only that such charges take into account the purpose of this book and the contemporary cultural climate regarding homosexuality. We must describe the latter briefly to underscore the former.

Assessment of gay and lesbian history is in a state of flux. Some argue that the gay community has moved from concern with "homosexuality" (considered abstractly and "objectively") to "homosexual consciousness," especially since the 1969 Stonewall riot, and most recently to "queer consciousness." Homosexual consciousness describes a framework in which heterosexual expectations still define gay and lesbian self-acceptance, yet it indicates a move beyond the medical model for defining homosexuality that dominated the nineteenth and most of the twentieth centuries. Queer consciousness represents a move toward reappropriation of the distinctive character of being a gay, lesbian, bisexual, or transgender person. It refuses to accept heterosexist norms for interpreting sexuality and often works from a more militant stance over against the heterocentric majority culture. The use of the word *queer* by the gay community is, of course, an example of the coopting of a traditionally derogatory epithet in order to disarm its power.

The gay and lesbian community itself argues about its social history, the overlapping of these forms of consciousness, and the direction in which gay culture is moving. We grant that we ourselves write within the context of homosexual consciousness, in part because much of the Church for which we write has not moved beyond an abstract treatment of "homosexuality" as *the* problem "out there." In other words, it is partly a matter of strategy. It also results from our personal convictions that writing in the context of queer consciousness would hinder rather than help the purpose of this book—to invite heterosexist Christians to reexamine their biases and the complex character of their own sexual identity and to foster ecclesial and social reform.

We want to state clearly that we recognize the danger in operating out of the context of homosexual consciousness. We do not wish to reinforce heterosexist modes of accepting gay, lesbian, bisexual, or transgender people only as they are willing to pretend to be "just like us." It is precisely seeing them without the lens of heterosexism that can eliminate the "we'll accept them if they act like us" prejudice that undergirds so much of the liberal, yet still heterosexist, understanding of the issues. Furthermore, we focus on gay and lesbian concerns to the near exclusion of questions unique to bisexual and transgender persons for two reasons. Our focus is partly a consequence of the relatively recent emergence of bisexuality and transsexuality as distinct examples of sexual identity. Also, this focus results from our need to deal as fully as possible with the antihomosexual bias that constitutes most of Christian history. We hope that the limited work we do here provides an adequate context for future exploration of the ethical questions raised by the experience of bisexual and transgender men and women.

We want to emphasize as strongly as possible that our overarching purpose is to make a positive biblical and theological case for a paradigm shift in Christian sexual ethics. We cannot rehearse all the arguments against making such a shift. In that sense ours is not a balanced approach. Indeed we believe that our heterocentric tradition has clearly and repeatedly articulated the case *against* reform. The reader must weigh the evidence we offer in that wider context to have a full hearing of the issues and arguments.

We want to stress another point. Faithfulness to the gospel requires critical reflection and openness to radical change. This is true for Christians personally as well as for churches institutionally. Such conversion will entail shifts in our vision of, attitudes toward, teachings about, and treatment of gay and lesbian people. Each of us exercises various roles in the life of the Church. We have specific charisms that contribute to the upbuilding of the body, to its wholeness, and to its healthy functioning. But our roles are not absolutely discrete. The openness to conversion required by faithfulness affects all of these roles.

A primary task of biblical scholars, for example, is to lead us to the sound exegesis of Scripture. Church historians help us to see how we are shaped by the traditions we inherit. Theologians assist us in reflecting critically on the meaning of our faith. Bishops symbolize and foster the unity of the Church. Pastors and laity in all their vocations link faith and action in their daily mission to serve the world. We must be faithful to the ministry that characterizes various roles. We must be extremely cautious, however, about equating faithfulness to our roles with preservation, or assuming that we alone can exercise the functions of that role.

Even bishops called by their office to work for the unity of the Church must be willing to risk disunity for the sake of the gospel. To claim that the divisiveness of any issue makes it a priori beyond reform denies the resurrection witness that God and faith are living realities. This is particularly true of an issue so central as human sexuality in a faith community that worships God Incarnate. Reform does not represent a threat to the substantive and identity-producing historical claims of the Church. It simply honors the fact that God reveals truth; we do not possess it.

As teaching theologians we understand one of our responsibilities to be to highlight for the Church the alternatives it faces on a given issue. To return to the questions with which we began this introduction, we have been motivated to devote time and energy to this issue because we believe that faithful reformation of the prevailing paradigm in Christian sexual ethics will result in enrichment for Church and society.

In our view the alternatives are clear, and they are analogous to those the Church has faced in confronting racism and sexism. Either we engage the task of reforming our heterocentric world-view or we continue to live with the intractable and destructive pastoral and ethical dilemmas that have emerged from it.

The second question, "Why are you willing to risk speaking publicly on such controversial issues?" is deeply personal for each of us.

Speaking publicly on homosexuality in the present climate means facing on occasion the kind of condemnation and ostracism that gay men and lesbian women face daily. The personal and professional risks borne by others who have taken this path before us are plain to see. If we risk personal or professional security, both compassion and theological integrity motivate us. With this book we acknowledge that the life stories of gays and lesbians, like the life stories of women and people of color, have helped to persuade our hearts and minds that we cannot stand by while injustice reigns.

We are also clear about the need to speak as objectively as possible on the issues that divide us in a pluralistic Church and world. We must be informed by our hearts but we cannot be ruled by them. To say this may imply the acceptance of an unfortunate head-heart dichotomy that plagues us generally in North American culture and particularly in the academic world. Perhaps so. Nevertheless our personal work in the two academic disciplines we represent, moral theology and liturgics, reinforces our persuasion that the Church must change. We do not believe that we have confused compassion and objectivity or compromised the value and integrity of either.

For a theological ethicist, dealing with questions about sexuality is part of one's daily professional life. For a liturgical theologian, the controversies surrounding marriage and ordination rites for gays and lesbians raise difficult historical and systematic questions. The links between the two sets of questions are obvious. We found it especially energizing to explore these connections from the perspectives of our disciplines.

As heterosexual persons of different genders, each married with children, each teaching in a graduate school, each representing a distinct Christian tradition (Lutheran and Roman Catholic), each involved in a community of faith, and each inclined by upbringing to a heterocentric understanding of sexuality, we are now unwilling but still unwitting participants in a system of illegitimate prejudice. As a system of prejudice, heterosexism remains largely unchallenged. This book asks the Church to both challenge and help dismantle it.

Heterosexism is not the result of evil actions perpetrated by malevolent people. None of the things we said in the brief list of characteristics about us individually is the cause of heterosexism or is in any way evil in itself. Yet individually and collectively these social roles and institutions are part of a larger whole that sustains heterosexism. Their perpetuation of heterosexism results in injustice and impoverishes humanity's ability to appropriate its sexual being fully and in ethically responsible ways.

We did not arrive at this conclusion easily. In the following chapters we try to communicate the process of theological reflection that led us to the positions for which we argue. We share along with our conclusions the substantive arguments that support them. We hope that the result is an invitation to dialogue rather than the mere presentation of a fait accompli.

We also hope that we have achieved a useful synergy between critical analysis of relevant data and sensitive assessment of the human story. Human beings are not, after all, creatures who live on the basis of accumulating and rearranging facts. Knowledge as information does not lead automatically to wisdom. The perplexing mix of thought, feeling, and circumstance that produces sexual love in human beings cannot be calculated or reduced to mere facts of biological instinct or social theory. We truly must listen to one another, Scripture, and tradition if God's invitation to live in communion with one another is to be more than words.

Often in dialogue about human sexuality the arguments become attacks against the person (*ad hominem*) rather than to the point (*ad rem*). Thomas Carlyle reminded us that when anger takes over in debate we can be sure that we have ceased arguing for the truth and have begun arguing for ourselves. We hope that this book represents a clear and consistent, yet not dispassionate, argument *ad rem*. We also hope that it represents a lively example of faith seeking understanding (*fides quaerens intellectum*.)

1

Defining Heterosexism

I had lived at the same address behind the drugstore for six years. I made it a point to use local businesses whenever possible, and had been a regular customer at that drugstore. After my partner and I had opened a joint checking account, I stopped at the drugstore to have a prescription filled. I wrote out a check for the amount of the prescription, but the clerk refused to accept my check; not because of any problem with my account, but because there were two female names on the check. In the clerk's words, "Two female names on the account just couldn't be right." Not only was it embarrassing to have my check turned down, and to stand there among other customers and explain my living situation, but I also ended up having to drive to another drugstore some distance away to purchase the drugs prescribed for me.[1]

The purpose of this chapter is to describe and define *heterosexism*. The preceding story illustrates one experience of heterosexism in North America. It depicts neither an especially heinous nor a particularly benign instance of this reality. Although obviously unique, it represents the experience of uncloseted gay men and lesbians in our world today. This brief vignette puts a face on the heterosexism endured on a daily basis by openly homosexual persons.

A REASONED SYSTEM OF PREJUDICE

Heterosexism is a reasoned system of bias regarding sexual orientation. It denotes prejudice in favor of heterosexual people and connotes prejudice against bisexual and, especially, homosexual people. By describing it as a *reasoned* system of prejudice we do not mean to imply that it is rationally defensible. Subsequent chapters will develop arguments against such a conclusion. Rather we mean to suggest that heterosexism is not grounded primarily in emotional fears, hatreds, or other visceral responses to homosexuality. Instead it is rooted in a largely cognitive constellation of beliefs about human sexuality.

13

Although heterosexism is often accompanied by *homophobia*, no logical or necessary connection exists between the two. People who are homophobic may not be heterosexist; those who are heterosexist may not be homophobic. Heterosexism is analogous to racism and sexism. Homophobia finds appropriate analogies in racial bigotry and misogynism. Whether gay or straight, people might be homophobic because they cannot think of male same-sex activity without also imaging men as physically vulnerable, as potentially subject to rape. They cannot think of female same-sex activity without imaging women as powerful, as potentially free of male control. Such images of male vulnerability and female strength challenge the heterosexist myth to which we have all grown accustomed.

As a pattern of discrimination heterosexism pervades most dimensions of our cultural life. This "system" shapes our legal, economic, political, social, interpersonal, familial, historical, educational, and ecclesial institutions.[2] *Heterocentrism* lies at the heart of this system of prejudice. Heterocentrism leads to the conviction that heterosexuality is *the* normative form of human sexuality. It is the measure by which all other sexual orientations are judged. All sexual authority, value, and power are centered in heterosexuality.

We can best understand these definitions in the context of a specific history. The term *heterosexuality* was coined in the nineteenth century and first gained currency in the field of medical science. It is an abstract construction that derives its meaning in part from its contrast with "homosexuality."[3] Neither word has an objective referent; that is, they do not refer to a person or thing. Each constitutes a shorthand way to label certain aspects of human sexuality.

We might logically suppose that bisexual and homosexual people could have a "place" in a heterocentric culture. After all, in patriarchal cultures even a woman has a rightful, albeit private, place of activity in her father's or husband's home. Of course, we would need to circumscribe carefully a similar place for gay men and lesbians as we have for our racial and economic ghettos. They would need to recognize, even while in such a place, their obvious subservience and inferiority to the heterocentric norm. Culturally we have developed structures to keep people "in place" in various dimensions of their lives. Such structures link most, if not all, of the "isms" we experience. In this regard heterosexism is deeply connected to sexism, racism, and classism. Our focus on heterosexism provides illumination of the power of these paradigmatic structures to "place" people.

Even within families the only acceptable place for most persons who are not heterosexual is their "closet." Gay people have no safe haven in our culture, not even in the private world of their homes. We ask them to be invisible in our public institutions. Those few places we commonly associate with homosexuality—openly gay neighborhoods and bars—routinely experience all manner of violence, from trashings to bombings. We demand that gay people keep their homosexual orientation private. Why? Because, so the ideology argues, one should not publicly parade or celebrate what is not fully or normatively human (natural!).

We do not offer gay people the protection and safety usually associated with the private sphere. We deprive them not only of a public life but of a private life as well. Apparently it is not enough to confine them to a generally invisible and certainly ignorable private world. We also silence them in our homes and other spheres (such as our churches). In a heterosexist world, a gay person has no safe place to go except into the closet. That is where heterosexist prejudices force such a "scandalous skeleton" to live.

One night I took a walk in a park. The neighborhood surrounding this park was a safe place, so I was not worried. This particular area is also known as a gay cruising area. Unfortunately I was unconscious of that reputation.

As I was walking back to my car after my walk I was physically attacked from behind by a male who was part of a gang hanging out in the park. I was assumed to be gay by this gang and I was beaten for it. Luckily I was able to get away with only a bruised kidney, a slightly fractured jaw and a bloody shoulder and hand. It could have been worse!

When the police arrived on the scene I pointed out my attacker. The officer let the attacker go when he assumed it was a hate crime. I went to the police station and pressed charges against the attacker. Nine months later my assailant went to prison for one month. Being a victim of a violent attack was very difficult for me. What I needed was lots of support. I could not go to the gay community and risk blowing my cover. I had to remain in a tight closet if I wished to continue serving as a pastor. So I tried to get support from my church. When I told the senior pastor about the attack he asked me: "Why are you telling me this?" Apparently he knew the reputation of the park and blamed me for being there. Another "support group" in the church told me I should have known better.

When I told them I was assumed to be gay by my attacker, and that the assault was an incident of "gay bashing," they quickly dismissed that information as not important. They gave me clear sig-

nals not to bring *that* fact up again. They began to distance themselves from me from that time on. The attack itself was quickly dismissed as an insignificant event.

Such is the conflict and rejection endured by a closeted gay person.
Life in such solitary confinement threatens to break even the
strongest of spirits.

We will return to the impact of heterosexism on our life
together at the close of this chapter (and again in chapter 4). At this
juncture we must enflesh our preliminary definitions of heterosexism. We propose to do this by examining five different moral points
of view on homosexuality. Four of these distinct perspectives are
heterosexist; one is not. Although not a comprehensive or even a
particularly balanced spectrum of opinion, these perspectives reflect
some of the common ways in which people think about homosexuality in our culture.

We realize that we are shifting our attention at this point from
heterosexism to homosexuality. This is a necessary shift because (1)
how persons view homosexuality shapes the ways in which they live
out heterosexist biases; and (2) the whole system of heterosexism is
supported by a variety of negative judgments about homosexuality.
Inattention to what causes or lies behind heterosexism will hinder
attempts to dismantle it.

We intend in our description of these moral positions to be fair,
but as our subsequent analysis of heterosexism will make clear, we
are not neutral in regard to them. We understand this to be
inescapable and note that all others who come to such deliberations
are equally (though obviously not identically) biased. To avoid
manipulation we delineate our key premises for public scrutiny and
outline five basic positions about the morality of homosexuality. We
introduce our typology of these positions on homosexuality by
reviewing a basic distinction.

ORIENTATION AND BEHAVIOR

A person's *sexual identity* consists of a number of components. It
includes that individual's biological sex (various chromosomal, hor-
monal, and anatomical factors), his or her gender identification
(sense of being male or female), the person's social sex role (the cultural definition of being male and female), and the person's sexual
orientation.[4] Broadly speaking *sexual orientation* includes (1) arousal

patterns (including fantasy), (2) affective preferences, and (3) behavior (patterns of physical contact with others).[5] Of the three aspects of orientation, behavior can be separated out insofar as it is voluntaristic. One cannot choose not to be aroused by or to "feel" drawn to others. Such an electric charge simply happens. One can, however, choose whether to nurture or repress and how and when to act on these impulses and feelings.

Recognizing the distinction between orientation in its first two aspects and behavior shapes moral arguments. For example, it would be wrong to blame or praise people for conditions over which they have no personal control.[6] It would be morally inappropriate to hold individuals responsible or to ascribe to them blame or merit for what they experience as erotically attractive in adolescence and beyond. This includes people who are attracted sexually to children or close relatives. The issue is whether and how people act in response to their erotic attractions.

It is important to take note of this distinction between sexual orientation and behavior for at least two reasons.[7] First, all who debate this issue agree that people to some degree can change and therefore be held responsible for their sexual behavior and public sexual lifestyles. Nevertheless many do not believe that an individual's sexual orientation can be significantly altered.[8] Second, it is possible to engage in sexual behavior and to have a public sexual lifestyle that is inconsistent with one's basic sexual orientation.

Orientation and Change

Many researchers now believe that the basic or constitutional sexual orientation of most individuals has been determined by the age of 4 or before.[9] A review of the literature regarding the etiology of homosexuality reveals that no compelling and coherent explanation of its origins is available to us at the present. We do know which hypotheses have failed to account for it. For example, the traditional Freudian theory that homosexuality is a result of arrested or abnormal psychosexual development resulted in over sixty different specific hypotheses. Many of these theories—that homosexuality stems from cold father-son relationships, from the impact of hostile domineering mothers on fragile egos, or from a sexually traumatic childhood experience like incest or exposure to pornography—have been clearly disproven.[10]

Considerable debate remains about whether a person's sexual orientation is psychosocially, biologically (for example, from stress

related hormones released during pregnancy), or genetically determined.[11] Whatever combination of causes lies behind a person's sexual orientation, it is for each one personally a "given" in one's life
beginning early in childhood. One discovers one's orientation
rather than chooses it, as the following brief vignette dramatizes.

> I first remember being "turned on" while watching the Academy
> Award presentation of the Oscars on TV. That naked little statue
> gave me such strong feelings that I searched for it in all the movie
> ads in the newspapers for months after that. All of my friends were
> fascinated with the ladies' underwear ads in the J.C. Penney cata-
> logue, but these did nothing for me! Back then male models were
> never used. I was very young, and it seems silly, but that is the kind
> of thing that first awakens one's sense of sexual identity.

Although significant variations exist in the reasons given for the
causes of sexual orientation, two basic approaches have characterized the research and writing on sexuality in the past four decades:
one is biological; the other is social. These are embraced by a
broader, though parallel, set of terms: nature and history. Both
approaches conclude that individuals are either heterosexual or
homosexual. Those who ascribe biological-natural origins to sexual
orientation view it as an actual innate essence. Those who ascribe
sexual orientation to largely social-historical origins view it as constructed over time.

The conviction that only heterosexuality is normative emerged
from the debate about what constitutes "natural" in human sexuality. The most frequent charge leveled at same-sex behavior historically has been that it violates nature. Heterosexuality (even when the
term was not used) was assumed to be the natural form of sexuality.
The biological-natural arguments have provided the justification for
centering sexual authority, value, and power in heterosexuality. A
key assumption has been that what is natural is good and right.
Since heterosexuality is statistically dominant, a corollary assumption holds that it is obviously natural, and alone good and right.

Much recent scholarship on the origins of homosexuality has
called into question through the use of historical analysis these more
traditional arguments about what is natural.[12] Sexuality in the historical perspective is an enormously diverse set of historical constructs,
not an immutable given in creation. Homosexuality varies tremendously in this view. The biological-natural versus social-historical distinction continues to fuel current conversations about homosexuality.

Where one settles on the question of origins obviously affects what factors one subsequently recognizes as morally relevant. Even if future research reveals that a person's sexual orientation is at least in part a social construction, it does not automatically follow that we as a culture should not allow or encourage the construction of a homosexual identity. Such a prohibition rests on the premise that there is something wrong with being homosexual in orientation, and that is precisely the question under examination.[13]

Many therapists do not believe that an individual's sexual orientation can be changed once it is established, not even through the so-called reparation therapy of ex-gay groups. Although Masters and Johnson believe in theory that under the right conditions even a totally or decisively gay person might be able to alter his or her sexual orientation, they offer no scientific evidence in support of that conclusion.[14] In fact, the only documented "successes" at such alteration have been through behavioral modification programs using aversion therapies, including electric shock. These homosexual persons have been conditioned for a time against attraction to their own sex. Such programs have had no documented success at reorienting homosexuals; that is, at fostering in them an attraction to persons of the other sex.

The question of the origins of homosexuality has come under broader examination only in the past two decades. Until recently the parameters of and participants in the debate have been constrained by the "disease model" of homosexuality. As long as a homosexual orientation was considered medically abnormal or dysfunctional in a clinical sense, genuine exploration of it was truncated.

The American Psychiatric Association removed homosexuality from its list of mental illnesses in 1973.[15] Studies demonstrated that gay men and lesbians were no more or less likely to be socially dysfunctional or emotionally disturbed or to engage in violent, exploitative, or sexually abusive behaviors (such as pederasty) than were heterosexual people. This judgment has received global confirmation. The new edition of the World Health Organization's (WHO) *International Classification of Diseases* does not list homosexuality as a disease. All thirty-seven member nations from the Americas agreed to delete homosexuality from this WHO index.

Behavior and Change

The distinction between orientation and behavior is significant for a second reason. A person can both have a public sexual lifestyle and engage in sexual behaviors inconsistent with their basic sexual orientation.[16] For example, someone with a basically heterosexual orientation can engage in homosexual behaviors. Sexual behavior in prison populations gives evidence of this as does the exploitation of gay people by heterosexual people seeking the thrill of variation or the comfort of having some kind of sexual intimacy.

We see the converse of this inconsistency among homosexual people. Statistically we know that somewhere between 4 and 13 percent, many would say roughly 10 percent, of all males and females in our culture are primarily homosexual in orientation. The vast majority of these 28 million or more U.S. citizens closet themselves behind the facade of heterosexual identities and marriages for decades if not their entire lifetime. Their public sexual identity and their sexual orientation are at odds.

For this reason an individual's sexual orientation cannot be defined on behavioral grounds alone. Some heterosexual people are circumstantially homosexual, usually for short periods of time in our culture. Similarly, some gay people are circumstantially heterosexual, typically in our culture for much longer as they often closet themselves in long-term heterosexual marriages. Clearly, affectional or imaginative responsiveness are more central than genital behavior to the identification of an individual's sexual orientation. Thus a woman who is predominantly and persistently attracted to other women may be lesbian even if she has never engaged in genital contact with another woman.[17]

These examples represent some very important but frequently neglected moral problems. The human capacity to behave sexually in a manner inconsistent with one's basic sexual orientation and to establish a public sexual lifestyle incongruent with that orientation provide the background against which the moral significance of sexual authenticity becomes clear (see chapter 7 for a more detailed discussion).

Many supposedly value-free researchers, especially those who represent the essentialist (biological-natural) approach to sexuality, treat homosexuality as a naturally occurring departure from heterosexuality. They seek to explain and defend why such alternatives exist. This situation illustrates how social scientists who pride themselves on objectivity beg the question of homosexuality. The very terms *departure* and *alternative* presuppose that heterosexuality is normative. Heterocentrism has dictated both the content and structure of the debate in ways that make it impossible for us to see homosexuality as anything other than an aberration (even if it is called a *naturally occurring* aberration).

To overcome this problem we must be willing to shift radically the terms of the debate. The only way not to prejudge homosexuality is to regard as normative the fact that human beings are sexual beings. Why we are sexual, and how in any given time and place we ought to live sexually are the appropriate foci of moral debate. This does not mean that we must abandon the terms *heterosexual* and *homosexual*. We need a variety of words to converse about our same-sex and different-sex attractions and behaviors. We must avoid the unexamined assumption that has accompanied the use of these terms—the assumption of the normative character of heterosexuality. This premise has imprisoned inquiry and thwarted dialogue with the gay community. It has proven costly on a personal level as well.

> My best friend from the fifth through the eleventh grades and I are now middle-aged men. As boys, Joe and I were inseparable. Long past the time it was considered "socially acceptable," he and I walked around holding hands. We hiked, read, studied, and vacationed together. In high school we often double dated.
>
> Between the eleventh and twelfth grades our families moved apart. After high school graduation we went to different colleges. We kept in touch for a year or two but then the letters from my friend stopped. Finally I stopped writing too. We didn't get together again for two years.
>
> When we finally did see one another two years later as a result of his mother's death, he was cold. Our conversation was cerebral. He spoke of this or that action as being "valid" or "invalid." He had grown disaffected with the church to which we had both been devoted. He questioned my very sanity in pursuing the ministry. I left his mother's funeral knowing that but not understanding why I had lost my best friend.
>
> It never even occurred to me why he might be distancing himself. Some twenty years later my old friend finally "came out" to me. Since that time we have begun to reconnect with one another. Looking back, it is clear to me that he must have been struggling with his sexual identity and feeling besieged. I didn't understand anything except that I had been shut out of his life. The time we lost can never be recovered. I will always regret that.

FIVE MORAL POSITIONS REGARDING HOMOSEXUALITY

We intend here to give flesh to the concept of heterosexism by introducing the reader to four of its many faces in our culture and to a fifth, nonheterocentric position. We will describe the major components of each point of view and briefly relate them to an analogous "problem." These analogies serve as the primary principle of classification around which we have organized our typology.[18] By clearly 'typing' these positions we hope to make them readily accessible to people new to the broad parameters of the debate.

The use of analogies in moral argument is of mixed value. All analogies are inadequate because they inevitably fail at certain junctures to illumine their terms. People risk using them in the wager that they will shed light on more than they obscure. We hope our use of analogies here will clarify rather than distort the perspectives we wish to describe and evaluate.

Each of the descriptions that follows begins with a heading that characterizes the main tenet of the position and identifies the basic judgment proponents of the position make about just, loving, and faithful homosexual behavior. We describe each position from the perspective of a person within it. The value judgments are those made by advocates of the type under consideration. Obviously not all the factors in each position would be held unequivocally by every person who locates his or her primary stance there. Some generalization is necessary to provide sufficient breadth for comparison of the positions. These positions are summarized in Table 1.1.

Position 1: Homosexual orientations are unnatural; just, loving, and faithful homosexual behavior is evil

Advocates of this position view homosexual orientation as a learned sexual response, acquired through a series of choices both unfortunate and immoral.[19] In the spectrum of our five-part typology they present the most negative and critical judgments on homosexuality. Some of them argue that it is erroneous to describe it as an attraction to persons of the same sex.[20] They describe the dynamic behind homosexuality as hatred of the opposite sex. From this point of view, for example, all lesbians are "men haters."

The repugnance that people who hold this position feel about homosexual activity is perhaps akin to how people in our culture feel about cannibalism. They can label as evil only what they believe is so contrary to "right and natural" behavior. Advocates of this position frequently view homosexual desires as temptations similar to the sexual temptation to fornicate or commit adultery. Thus we use the term *immorality* to name this analogy in the typology. Unlike the other four positions which are characterized by a specific, nonsexual moral analogy, no satisfactory, single analogy has emerged that highlights the significant elements of this position.

Table 1.1   Analogies for Moral Positions on Homosexuality

	P_1: Immorality	P_2: Alcoholism	P_3: Blindness	P_4: Color Blindness	P_5: Left-handedness
Theological Axiom	A paradigmatic sign of the brokenness of the world	A greater sign of the brokenness of the world	A lesser sign of the brokenness of the world	Not quite the fullness of God's original blessing	Part of God's original blessing
Anthropological Axiom	Evil	Disease	Defect	Imperfection	Variation
Personal Culpability	Lots	Little	None	None	None and irrelevant
Primary Moral Judgment	Just, loving, and faithful homosexual unions are evil; sexual reorientation required	Just, loving, and faithful homosexual unions are more evil than lifelong and total abstinence	Just, loving, and faithful homosexual unions are less evil than lifelong and total abstinence	Just, loving, and faithful homosexual unions and lifelong and total abstinence both fall short	Just, loving, and faithful homosexual unions are good
Derivative Moral Rules	No Blessing of unions; no ordaining of any gay person	No blessing of unions; ordain only closeted gay people committed to lifelong and total sexual abstinence	May or may not bless unions; may or may not ordain chaste, closeted gay people	Bless unions privately; ordain chaste, closeted gay people	Publicly bless unions; ordain chaste, uncloseted gay people

According to this position homosexual orientation is a paradigmatic expression of original sin, or concupiscence, for which individuals can be held responsible. Whereas lust merely disorders heterosexual behavior, lust expresses both the disorientation of homosexual passions and the disorder of homosexual behavior. Adherents of this position view homosexuality as a perversion of the natural order of sexuality on one or both of two different grounds. First, some argue that homosexuality is immoral because it does not lead to procreation. God made human sexuality to serve the species through reproduction. Second, some argue that sex serves not primarily or even essentially for reproduction, but for human completion through gender complementarity. For example, proponents of this view believe that a man can become genuinely human only when he has a sexual relationship with a woman, and vice versa. Homosexual relationships pervert the natural order on both counts. They are completely unnatural.

Proponents of this position argue that gay people ought to change their sexual orientation and engage in heterosexual behavior. Abstinence may be permissible during the initial stages of their transformation, but just, loving, and faithful heterosexual marriages provide the only setting for holiness and moral health. Obviously, the Church ought not ordain persons who are homosexual in orientation, whether sexually abstinent or not, nor allow them to serve as lay professionals in the Church. Likewise the Church ought not bless homosexual unions, even if just, loving, and faithful. The Church should oppose any civil legislation that permits or supports any gay or lesbian lifestyle. Heterosexism is a fully justified system of discrimination from this point of view.

Position 2: Homosexual orientations are diseased; just, loving, and faithful homosexual behavior is not justified

Advocates of this position view a homosexual orientation as a disease analogous to alcoholism.[21] They perceive alcoholism as a consequence of the Fall and consider it incurable. It has a tremendous impact on the individual, his or her interpersonal relationships, and on society as a whole. Sobriety constitutes the only healthy moral response to it. Similarly, advocates of this position understand homosexuality as incurable and destructive. Thus sexual abstinence provides the only reasonable response to it. Analogously one can be at best a recovering homosexual similar to the sober alcoholic.[22] Even though sexual abstinence may be difficult (perhaps even impossible) and emotionally costly to practice, it is far less destructive of others and society than sexual lifestyles characterized even by just, faithful, and loving homosexual unions.[23]

We must be clear about what the demand of lifelong sexual abstinence means. The Church appropriately expects all Christians to practice the virtue of chastity. Chastity means that Christians should abstain from any and all reprobate sexual conduct. Thus we expect married as well as single persons to be chaste, although they restrain themselves in quite different ways. For example, the wife who proves chaste refrains from entering into an adulterous relationship. The single man who refrains from sexual behaviors expressive of more intimacy than his dating relationships warrant demonstrates chastity. All who make the concerns of justice integral to their sexual lifestyles practice chastity. The characteristics of justice, love, and fidelity mark chaste sexual practices.

We usually associate chastity with single people because they must abstain from a broader range of sexual activity than people who are married. However, for heterosexual single people chastity is not identical to the requirement of total sexual abstinence. We permit, if not encourage, dating and a modest degree of sexual activity among heterosexual single people. Although some may view them as immature or incomplete, they do not view them as diseased simply because they are single.

We expect homosexual persons whom we require to be abstinent not to be sexually active in even chaste ways. In this respect a demand for lifelong sexual abstinence is tantamount to a calling to perpetual celibacy.[24] Yet the differences between abstinence and celibacy are significant. We understand the call to celibacy as above and beyond the call of most humans. We tie it to a special vocation in service of the Church. We tie abstinence to the belief that homosexual persons are wounded or diseased. From this point of view, homosexuals ought to adopt sexually abstinent lifestyles and communities should support their abstinence. It is ironic that Protestant advocates of this position are arguing for sexual abstinence for such a large class of people. Martin Luther above all was sensitive to the extensive costs of such an expectation.[25]

Since advocates of this position believe no cure exists for the underlying condition and that no one is able to choose this sexual orientation apart from a physiological predisposition, they attach little to no moral blame to being homosexual in orientation.[26] Homosexuality is a disorder, not primarily a sin.[27] They would claim that people make choices in response to but not in regard to their sexual orientation. The analogy with alcoholism is clear: it is a sin only when one does not take up the struggle to control it.

Proponents of this view would also claim that gay people committed to sexual abstinence lead morally exemplary lives when by their commitment to sexual abstinence they bear witness to the morally normative nature of heterosexuality. The ordination of such gay people and the installation of sexually abstinent homosexual lay professionals is acceptable. Prayers for reorientation are affirmed because "all things are possible with God," but like St. Paul (2 Cor 12:9), advocates of this view recognize that not all wounds are healed in this life. In reality, however, openly homosexual persons would not readily be called to serve or be welcome in many parishes, even if they were sexually abstinent.[28] Advocates of this position really demand that homosexual persons called to ordained or lay professional ministry remain closeted as well as abstinent. Similarly, an alcoholic person who "falls off the wagon" would not readily be called to serve as an ordained minister.

According to this stance, opposition to homosexuality as a lifestyle constitutes neither an unjustifiable nor a futile prejudice. Any activities that promote gay lifestyles as legitimate are morally unacceptable. However, advocates of this position would condemn all violent efforts to restrain or punish gay men and lesbians. As with alcoholic people, the task of others is to love and care for them in order to keep them on the right path (sobriety for the alcoholic person, abstinence for the gay person).

Position 3: Homosexual orientations are defective; some just, loving, and faithful homosexual behavior may be permissible

People who hold this position view homosexuality as analogous to a defect like congenital blindness.[29] Such a handicap represents a serious sign of the travail of creation. Like blindness, one does not choose a homosexual orientation for oneself nor wish for it in another. One simply suffers it as a result of the brokenness of the world.

Unlike persons who suffer from alcoholism, those born blind are not held accountable in any way for their condition. They do not contribute to it. Analogously, advocates of this position do not hold gay people responsible for their sexual orientation. Just like someone suffering from alcoholism, however, a blind person must find ways to cope with this fact of life. No coping strategies available to the blind person remove blindness although some can minimize its effects. For the gay person lifelong sexual abstinence is viewed here, unlike Position 2, as a cost-ineffective coping mechanism.

According to advocates of this position, the costs of lifelong sexual abstinence are too high. Abstinence denies a person the chance to cope constructively with their "handicap." Just, loving, and faithful homosexual unions at least honor the effort to cope with one's homosexual identity where lifelong sexual abstinence does not. If the argument of Position 2 hinged on the claim that the cure did less harm than the disease, the argument here hinges on the claim that the cure (abstinence) is no real cure at all. It is analogous to the blind person being denied the right to live out his or her blindness by developing ways to accept rather than deny it.

Despite this accommodation, neither lifelong sexual abstinence nor just, loving, and faithful homosexual unions are seen as good. Both are compromised sexual lifestyles, although the latter is judged less evil than the former because it is healthier as a coping strategy. It is legitimate not to bless or encourage either way of life. Yet clearly some compromise with brokenness is pastorally permissible if not necessitated.[30] Thus some proponents of this position would bless just, loving, and faithful gay unions, others would not. They may or may not participate in the ordination of chaste (but not necessarily sexually abstinent), closeted gay people who are qualified in all other respects for such a leadership role. Again the decision hinges on how one evaluates the importance of engaging in sexual behavior that is consistent with one's orientation.

Position 4: Homosexual orientations are imperfect; just, loving, and faithful homosexual behavior is justified

Advocates of this position view a homosexual orientation as an imperfection analogous to color blindness.[31] It constitutes a minor manifestation of the fallenness of the world. Proponents of this view have suggested a variety of causes for this imperfection, such as traumatic injury or arrested development. Being gay represents something wrong or inferior, just as being color blind is less than good from this point of view. It is not ideal. If it were possible to cure the condition in a reasonable fashion, communities would be morally obligated to make this treatment available and gay persons would be morally obligated to avail themselves of the treatment.

According to proponents of this view, however, the fact of the matter is that no cure exists for this condition. People discover themselves to be color sighted or color blind. People discover themselves to be gay. One cannot hold gay people culpable for being gay; it is simply part of the fabric out of which they must shape their lives. Although homosexual orientations cannot be accepted as a normative ideal, gay men and lesbians act in accordance with their particular nature when they adopt a homosexual lifestyle. People who are color blind can choose only between seeing the world in color deficient ways or closing their eyes. Obviously, they live in accord with the way they can see. Generally we justify imperfect behaviors when they represent the best available course of action in particular circumstances. Analogously, in response to their sexual orientation, gay people must choose between the repression or the imperfect (that is, homosexual) expression of their sexuality. The choice is self-evident: color blind people choose to see rather than close their eyes; gay people act on their sexual identity rather than deny its existence.

Proponents of this view reject lifelong sexual abstinence as an expectation appropriate to gay individuals. They do so for several reasons. First, they see it as an unrealistic expectation, and clearly one should not counsel the unreasonable. Although few would question the significance of sexual intimacy to human life, sexual repression is not life threatening. People can live without orgasms. So why do proponents of this position believe that sexual repression is unrealistic, psychologically destructive, and practically impossible for people to embody? Their answer is quite clear: apart from a special gift from the Spirit, those attempting lifelong sexual abstinence find that it necessitates extreme isolation. Orgasms do not represent all of human sexuality. As Daniel Maguire notes, "erotic desire is deeply interwoven into the human desire and need for closeness and for trusting relationships."[32] To be sexually abstinent without the gift of the Spirit calling them to it, gay people must bring this isolation upon themselves. They must avoid "particular friendships," especially with persons of the same sex but even with persons of the other sex.[33]

Only those who have received celibacy as a special charism from the Spirit can genuinely embody it without engendering crippling isolation. Even though they were great advocates of virginal and celibate lifestyles, the leaders of the early Church recognized that such continence could not be commanded, but only recommended. It was a voluntary not an obligatory lifestyle. Although we may exhort, we cannot demand lifelong sexual abstinence of all gay people. To do so is no more realistic than advising all heterosexual people to refrain from taking an active sexual interest in persons of the other sex.

Color blind people fall short of the normatively human way of seeing, but asking them to close their eyes—analogous to asking the gay person to abstain from sexual activity—makes no sense. Such a demand is unrealistic and would result in the poor stewardship of the visual gifts they do have. It would smack of ingratitude. Analogously, gay people are seen as falling short of the normatively human way of sexually relating, but demanding lifelong sexual abstinence would result in poor stewardship of the gifts for sexual intimacy they do have.

Advocates of this position believe that persons living a life of sexual abstinence apart from the gift of celibacy cannot bear witness to or take delight in the gracious goodness of their sexuality. Because they also believe that God calls people to an appropriate fulfilling of their sexual identity, abstinent gay and lesbian Christians cannot model sexual responsibility for the community. Without the gift of celibacy, total sexual restraint becomes purely negative; that is, it does not give purpose to or shed light on the meaning of human sexuality.

In contrast, when marked by justice, love, and fidelity homosexual unions display far more authentic virtue than those neurotic lives warped by frequently futile efforts to remain continent. Advocates of this position view celibacy as a rare and exceptional gift of the Spirit, not routinely given to gay people. Probably most just, faithful, and loving homosexual unions are justifiable. All, however, remain morally less than ideal.

Advocates of this position would encourage and privately bless homosexual unions. Such unions, even though morally permissible, should not receive official civil (public) or ecclesial sanction. Logically, these same persons conclude that because remarriage following divorce is less than perfect, the Church should not officially bless it even though it is now judged both morally commendable and civilly permissible. Most argue that a small, private blessing of homosexual unions is a commendable compromise.

Advocates of this position would usually encourage the ordination of a closeted homosexual person involved in a just, loving, and faithful homosexual union. Debate hinges on to what extent the clergy and professional ministers model only morally normative sexual conduct. If a church ordains (and retains on the clergy roster) persons who are divorced and remarried, consistency requires that it view as eligible for professional ministry those in the less than ideal but morally justifiable lifestyle of a just, loving, and faithful gay or lesbian relationship. In both marriage and ordination the Church's best response is maintaining some kind of distinction between that which it privately blesses and publicly celebrates.

Although one can theoretically justify heterocentric ideals one cannot defend the system of civil discrimination sustained by hetero-

sexism as legitimate. It does more harm than good. Thus proponents of this position view all, even nonviolent, forms of opposition
to homosexuality as imprudent, even if technically justifiable. They
advocate that human rights legislation include gays and lesbians.

*Position 5: Homosexual orientations are natural; just, loving, and faith-
ful homosexual behavior is good*

This is our own position.[34] We state this for two reasons. First, one
best avoids manipulation by placing one's own value convictions in
the light of day insofar as possible. Second, one cannot describe
other perspectives from a value-free or nonperspectival point of
view. Such a claim to objectivity amounts to epistemological nonsense. Thus one cannot view any of the preceding descriptions as
neutral. By specifying our convictions on this matter we hope to
alert readers to the damage our biases may have done to the other
points of view.

This fifth position on homosexuality is not heterosexist, and it
provides a contrast with the heterosexist dimensions of the other
points of view. Advocates of this position view homosexual orientation as a natural variation in the created order analogous to lefthand-
edness.[35] Undoubtedly sexuality is far more central to the mystery of
our personhood than is being right- or left-handed. Additionally,
most people are not so tightly wired sexually as this analogy implies.
Most people can be described more accurately as ambidextrous
rather than absolutely right- or left-handed.[36] The comparison to left-
handedness, however, despite its obvious shortcomings, proves fruitful for illuminating the systemic quality of heterosexism because we
clearly arrange our world in favor of righthanded people. We only
recently stopped advocating efforts to reorient people. We have
gravely distorted our understanding of left-handedness by false
myths for centuries.

According to proponents of this position both homosexual and
heterosexual orientation participate in the goodness intrinsic to all of
God's creation. Just as there is nothing wrong with or inferior about
being lefthanded, there is nothing wrong with being gay from this
point of view.[37] Gayness constitutes a manifestation of God's original
blessing and one ought to claim it as a gracious gift from God. Just as
we do not encourage heterosexual people to tamper with their God-
given sexual orientation, so adherents of this position would not
encourage gay people to change their orientation, even if such alteration were possible. Such activity desecrates the sexual diversity that
constitutes part of the Creator's original blessed design.

Although still prevalent in our culture, negative judgments about and attitudes toward homosexuality arise from misinformation, prejudice, and superstition. Such traditions regarding gay men and lesbians have no more validity than earlier falsehoods and practices surrounding left-handedness. For example, people once believed that all the children born from marriages between royalty and commoners would be left-handed. Sometimes people linked left-handedness with witchcraft and amputated the offending limb.[38]

According to proponents of this final position in our typology, homosexual orientations are fully natural. Gay men and lesbians act naturally when they engage in homosexual conduct. It is unnatural and immoral for gay people to engage in heterosexual behavior or to repress the proper expression and exercise of their God-given homosexual drives (unless they have received from God the gift of celibacy). One should evaluate and govern homosexual behavior in accord with the same norms, such as justice, love, and fidelity, used to evaluate and govern heterosexual behavior.

Many people find it difficult to accept the logical implications of this position. Yet those who see the need for comparable norms press the Church for change on the basis of the demands of justice. Within an equal justice framework civil and ecclesial communities act unjustly and with discrimination when they do not call forth and support-bless the faithful expression of loving homosexual unions. Similarly churches act unjustly and discriminate when they do not install persons authentically called to ordained or professional ministry simply because of their homosexual orientation or their participation in loving and faithful homosexual unions. From this perspective churches perpetuate and authorize heterosexism a system of discrimination that cannot be justified.

CONCLUSION

As the preceding descriptions make evident, no single viewpoint on homosexuality constitutes heterosexism. It has many faces and is frequently associated with and reinforced by homophobia. Definitions and a review of related outlooks can demarcate the landscape, but we need to put a human face on this reality. What does it mean for a person to be heterosexist?

As far as I knew I had never met a homosexual person. I had heard about them, read and talked about them, but had never actually been in the presence of one. So I thought. Naive or not, the situation changed when I left my hometown in Pennsylvania to work for a summer in Sacramento, California.

My wife and I drove to San Francisco one Saturday to see the sights. We decided to walk wherever our inclinations led us after a brief visit in Chinatown. At one point we found ourselves in the midst of a gay neighborhood. How did I know? Because all my stereotypes suddenly became flesh and blood: men dressed as women; women and men in leather and chains; effeminate actions, lisps, public fondling by men with men, women with women; the words *queer, fag, dyke, straight* bandied about by people in doorways. I never felt that we were in any particular danger, but as we walked on through and out of the area I shook my head in dismay.

A few days later I was back in Sacramento meeting with colleagues. I told them of my San Francisco experience. "You should have seen these people!" I exclaimed. "It was incredible." After I finished with the details of the appearances and actions of "these people," one of the men present looked me in the eye. With a mixture of anger and sadness he said, "I had planned to bring some important associates to this meeting who happen to be good friends. I'm sure glad I didn't. They're gay, and it's obvious they wouldn't be welcome here."

I was stunned. I'm not prejudiced! I was simply poking fun at the outrageous scene I had stumbled on to. What was wrong with that?

No one had ever confronted me so directly, so honestly, and so painfully regarding my words and actions, and my unexamined prejudices. "This is just the way things are," I thought to myself, "why is this guy giving me a hard time." The fact that he called them friends is what stung the most. He felt he could not subject his friends to such treatment at my hands. For the first time I began to see the depth of a prejudice I did not even understand.

If one remains unconvinced that American culture is deeply heterosexist, analysis of the use of language about gays, the portrayal of gay and lesbian people in the media, and the legally sanctioned discrimination against gays provides ample evidence that antigay prejudice abounds.

Sufficient study of the treatment of gays in American society has been done to reveal the pervasiveness of this prejudice.[39] The documentation is indisputable. Perhaps the most widespread manifestation of prejudice is the mocking and ridicule of gays and lesbians, as well as the trivialization of their concerns. Discriminatory statutes regarding homosexuality already exist in most states, and proposed changes in civil rights legislation to include protection of homosexual persons usually meet strong resistance. But the physical harm inflicted on gays and lesbians represents the most serious threat of heterosexism. "Gay bashing" is commonplace.

In his now classic text on discrimination, *The Nature of Prejudice*, Gordon Allport noted over thirty-five years ago that the most deep-rooted prejudice in the United States was directed against homosexual people, who, if they could be more easily targeted, would suffer even greater violence.[40] This discrimination is widespread, and it has been present since the early colonial period. "As early as 1656," writes Adrienne Rich, "the New Haven Colony prescribed the death penalty for lesbians."[41]

The fact that we can read and hear more than ever before about the gay community ought to both trouble and encourage us. It should trouble us because even though up to 70 percent of the incidents may go unreported to avoid further victimization, the published accounts reveal the widespread indifference to harassment, stereotyping, discrimination, and violence. It should encourage us because it indicates that emerging public recognition allows us to talk about the prejudice and work to eliminate it.

Heterosexism is not just another "ism," nor one of a long list of trivial injustices identified by small special interest groups. As we suggested at the beginning of this chapter, it is a deeply rooted problem with extensive implications because it is related to the core human experience of being sexual. The fact that we have been so willing to accept heterocentrism uncritically is, arguably, the most significant contributor to this antigay prejudice. Christians have helped to create the climate in which this heterocentric norm has flourished. We proceed now to a brief identification of the various sources of moral wisdom relevant to a critical reassessment of this norm by the Church.

2

Evaluating Heterosexism

"I love the Bible. I have always loved the Bible. No one can tell me that it doesn't tell the truth." I could have said the same words, but they came out of the mouth of a friend of mine. We were at a revival and everybody was talking about the preacher's fire and brimstone sermon about how homosexuals were going to go to hell because the Bible said so. Just a few days earlier I read that the word *homosexual* isn't even in the Bible, at least not in the original languages. I wasn't sure what to think, because my cousin had told us all that he was gay. I always liked him. In fact he was my favorite relative. What did the Bible really say about him? When I began to study all the passages that the preacher was quoting I found lots more than I bargained for. I'm pretty sure some things about homosexuality are condemned there, but I'm not so willing as I used to be to say that I understand exactly what the Bible says about it. Oh, I still love the Bible, and I still think it tells the truth. It's just that I've started to think that maybe I'm missing some of the truth it's trying to tell me.

AN EGALITARIAN STARTING POINT

Arguments about heterosexism are complex and quite heated. Many would contest the way we have defined the problem in this book. By locating the problem in heterosexism rather than in homosexuality and bisexuality we imply that it is heterosexists who must defend their point of view. This premise about who carries the burden of proof will prove decisive in our moral argument. Consequently a brief review of the rationale behind this premise is in order.

We believe that in principle all persons ought to be treated equally because all are made in the image of God. Our dignity and status as children of God provide an unshakable foundation for such respect. That we ought to treat human persons equally does not mean that we ought always to treat them identically. Exceptions to this egalitarian rule of thumb—whether positive or negative, preferential or prejudicial—can and should be made. We routinely respond to people differently in light of how we believe they deserve to be treated. Heroes merit reward; criminals merit incarceration.

We discriminate positively and negatively on the basis of innate factors as well. Any such discrimination, however, whether made on the basis of race, gender, age, ethnicity, physical capacities, or mental abilities, requires justification. Those who would discriminate always bear the burden of proof for their judgments and consequent behaviors. Even when they concede that they must bear this burden, heterosexists conclude that Christian sources of wisdom about sexual matters provide them with ample evidence for their positions.

Some argue that in spite of such evidence the Church was not always heterosexist in its praxis. One could take up these retrieved portions of the tradition and attempt on this foundation to reevaluate and reform its dominant heterosexist bias. This methodological strategy has the obvious merit of at least relativizing the heterosexist viewpoints that have distorted our reading of tradition, but we have chosen not to take this approach. In the second half of this chapter we explore instead how the Bible can function as a basis and norm for the reformation of tradition.

HETEROSEXISM: A NONCREDIBLE TRADITION

It is perfectly reasonable for people who are truly faithful to question radically their tradition; that is, to bring a hermeneutic of suspicion to it. Normally, faithfulness requires that we accept and receive graciously what is passed on to us. People assume that a tradition can be reformed, but they also presume that those who engage in such reformation bear the burden of proof. We will argue that it is no longer reasonable to expect even the faithful to operate with a presumption in favor of retaining a heterosexist bias.

We begin by calling the *credibility* of heterosexism into question.[1] We will use four criteria to assess the credibility of this tradition: (1) its *internal consistency*, (2) its *comprehensiveness* of all the data relevant to it, (3) its *external coherence* with other generally accepted traditions, and (4) its *fruitfulness*, especially but not exclusively in terms of its practical consequences for the community that sustains it. In this chapter we will demonstrate that heterosexist traditions fail to pass the first two of these tests. This suffices to establish the heterosexist elements of the Christian moral tradition as suspect.

To claim a tradition suspect is not equivalent to establishing its invalidity or error. If we succeed in demonstrating that this tradition is not credible, we only shift the burden of proof to those who would retain it. In this particular case we would thereby establish a presumption in favor of abolishing heterosexism. Whether an argument in favor of retaining heterosexism could be developed that overrides this presumption is not yet clear (see chapters 3 and 4).

Consistency

Advocates of heterosexism frequently do not follow the implications of their arguments to a logical conclusion. For example, rationales for heterosexism usually begin with premises about procreativity and gender complementarity as the purpose or primary end of human sexuality.[2] Although it is theoretically possible to be consistent regarding the norms resulting from such rationales, Christians are notoriously unwilling to adopt practices, ecclesial or personal, that embody them consistently.

What are the full implications of the belief that human sexuality ought to be procreative? If homosexuality is wrong to a significant degree because it is nonprocreative, certain other negative conclusions regarding nonprocreative heterosexual intimacy also follow. Officially, Roman Catholics make a case for the significance of procreativity in their sexual ethic more strongly than their Protestant sisters and brothers. Still, even they are not completely consistent in their embodiment of that conviction.[3]

Contemporary Catholic practice, although obviously not legitimately equated with official church teaching, is relevant to an evaluation of official teaching about procreativity. In contrast to the official position of their church, few Roman Catholic spouses in the United States believe that there must be a procreative meaning in each and every act of intercourse. Few behave as if artificial means of exercising responsible parenthood are decisively worse than natural means of birth control. For the vast majority of Catholics, attaching such significance to noninterference with the physical integrity of each and every act of vaginal intercourse does not match their sexual and marital experience. Similarly, few infertile Catholic couples find this line of reasoning compelling enough to prevent them from employing modern reproductive technologies to assist them in procreation, even though these activities separate procreation from vaginal intercourse.

One can argue, of course, that noncompliance with a particular teaching may reflect the pervasiveness and power of sin, or it may reflect a failure on the part of the church to teach or communicate effectively. Lack of consent among the faithful regarding a specific teaching may indicate a problem with the teaching itself. Nevertheless, consistency is not merely a theoretical test. It has practical implications as well. The plausibility of a position is partially tested by its capacity to prove compelling.

Claims about the interdependence of the procreative and unitive ends of sexuality raise some useful questions of consistency with regard to the official position of the Roman Catholic church. For example, if these two meanings are inseparable would not consistency require that Roman Catholics conclude that the unitive significance of a sexual relationship is incomplete or unfulfilled as long as a couple remains childless? Does this not raise questions about whether or not infertility (like impotence) should be an impediment to marriage?[4]

The application of the norm of procreativity raises similar questions for Protestant sexual ethics, despite the fact that Protestants have not argued as strongly that the procreative purpose of sex cannot be separated from the unitive. If procreativity is essential to sexual morality, a childless heterosexual marriage, even as a result of age or infertility, must be viewed as imperfect or less than morally ideal, although it may remain morally justifiable. Logically, there must be a moral presumption against child-free heterosexual marriages as a result of free choice. They must be judged (at least initially) as perversions of this order of creation.[5] Also, because they are nonprocreative forms of sexual expression, masturbation, intercourse during pregnancy, and all forms of oral and anal sex compromise the moral ideal, even when practiced by heterosexual people.[6]

Such were the conclusions of most Christian churches from antiquity up to modern times. They remain the official teaching of some Christian communions.[7] Furthermore the "blue laws" of several states still reflect this moral judgment against all conjugal relations outside the confines of the "missionary position." The moral judgments and practices of most sexually active Christians today, Roman Catholic and Protestant alike, contradict the traditional claim about the centrality of procreativity to sexual morality.

Most who apply this argument to homosexual behavior do so with little credibility in gay and lesbian communities because they are unwilling to apply it to every aspect of their own sexual activity. To be credible a tradition must be free of self-contradiction. Although this is theoretically possible in regard to arguments centered around procreativity, few adherents to them are willing to be consistent in their application of this norm.

Similarly, if homosexuality compromises the procreative ideal because it does not foster human completion through gender complementarity, there must also be something wrong with being single, separated, divorced, widowed, or celibate. According to heterosexist logic "the male and the female know themselves only in relation to each other because they are made for each other."[8] Consistency requires that we view such people as incomplete and unfulfilled human beings, just like gay men and lesbians. Some people do view those who are single, separated, divorced, widowed, or celibate as deficient. Few, however, would be willing to conclude that they lead immoral lifestyles. Yet many heterosexists jump to such a conclusion regarding homosexual people.

Furthermore, according to the framework established by a theory of gender complementarity men should develop only their so-called masculine character traits. Males must leave underdeveloped their so-called feminine side, and vice versa. Such psychic underdevelopment necessitates the codependency that defines many traditional marriages. Individuals who try to develop in themselves both masculine and feminine characteristics pervert God's natural heterosexual plan for humanity according to this view.[9]

Theoretically one could affirm all of the implications just rehearsed. Yet even those who do not find them simply counterintuitive must admit that they are highly debatable and hotly contested propositions today. Furthermore few are willing to live consistently in accord with and in ways that do not contradict these propositions.

Although one can cite some biblical material in support of these implications, many modern commentators would not grant widespread biblical support to either a theory of gender complementarity or to the belief that sexuality was designed essentially for procreative purposes (these issues are addressed in detail in chapter 3). This explains in part why neither concern about procreativity nor concern about gender complementarity weigh decisively in the moral evaluation of most heterosexual relationships. Where then, did these "norms" come from? Can we apply these norms legitimately to homosexual relationships? Certainly not.

Comprehensiveness

We believe that heterosexist theories cannot adequately explain the full range of human sexual experience. They are not sufficiently comprehensive. The adequacy of the explanatory scope of heterosexism depends on the range of experience considered relevant to it. We will show that the comprehensiveness of heterosexism can remain credible only to those willing to continue to dismiss (1) homosexual experiences of love as illusory and (2) female physiology as irrelevant.

All parties to the debate about heterosexism recognize that homosexual experience is not identical to heterosexual experience. Nonheterosexists believe that an adequate account of homosexual experience is basic to a full understanding of human sexuality. That homosexual experience varies and requires interpretation is not a matter of contention.

Like any other kind of human sexual experience it also requires evaluation. Here lies the locus of the debate. Heterosexists presume that *all* homosexual experiences are in one or more ways alienated from "natural" sexual orientation and behavior. From this point of view no homosexual experience could be normatively human or become part of the basis for the reformation of the tradition. In contrast, those who wish to abolish heterosexism presume that at least some homosexual experiences are authentic and can become part of the basis for the reformation of the tradition. Heterosexists dismiss any such claims as delusional. Reformers recognize that some homosexual experiences may be alienating and demand repudiation.

Many of the more liberal heterosexists will concede that the emotional and intellectual ties between gay and lesbian couples may be as powerful and intense as any heterosexual bonds. They sadly conclude that homosexual love always falls short of the normative because it cannot be adequately expressed physically. They derive this conclusion from their view of the physical complementarity of heterosexual anatomy. To put it bluntly, heterosexists argue that anything other than vaginal intercourse merely simulates or imitates the real thing. This argument lies behind many defenses of heterosexism, and remains linked with the perception of what constitutes natural and unnatural behavior.[10]

It strikes many heterosexual people as self-evident that a "two-in-one-flesh" bodily union can be realized in an act of vaginal intercourse. Heterosexual couples are anatomically suited for such activity, at least from the viewpoint of a heterosexual person. What can we reasonably infer from such experiences? Specifically, does it follow that such acts by such couples result in a two-in-one flesh union?

No, such an inference does not follow from these premises and begs the question under consideration. Other sexual activities as well as nonheterosexual couples' sexual relationships could express a two-in-one-flesh union. That such activities may repulse some heterosexual people does not count as compelling evidence to the contrary. If that were the case, consistency would require that we dismiss as invalid the claim that heterosexual coupling can express a two-in-one-flesh union. Why? Because many homosexual persons find even the thought of vaginal intercourse completely repugnant.

To invalidate homosexual claims to authentic experiences of sexual love as delusional on the grounds that gay and lesbian couplings cannot adequately express such love is specious. Such a judgment rests on a heterosexist norm of anatomical correctness, the assumption of which begs the question under debate. Heterosexism does not take adequate account of homosexual experiences of love. Heterosexism does not comprehend homosexual experience given the testimony of gay and lesbian lovers. Heterosexism grows more suspect.

What is said about the natural, bodily link between lovemaking and baby making is a social construction. How people conceive the reality of the link will vary cross-culturally and historically. Conceptions of this link that claim to be bias free frequently acquire a falsely privileged, objective stature by virtue of appearing to be culturally unmarked. Yet most often such objective interpretations foster unchallenged particular interests, usually those of the status quo.

The current debate among Christians about the nature of the connection between sexual love and reproduction reflects the distortive power of such unlabeled, supposedly unbiased conceptions. Without recognizing it Christians have sometimes equated human sexual experience with male sexual experience. We have allowed this partial account of human sexuality to serve to varying degrees in our communions as the sole foundation for our normative account of the link between sexual love and reproduction. Specifically, it is particular to male sexual experience that orgasm and ejaculation are bound together in each and every sexual act. If this account were recognized as biased, and the notion of what constitutes humanly relevant biological data were expanded to include the wisdom of female physiology, then a better, more inclusive, and comprehensive (though no less perspectival) account of this aspect of human embodiment would be forthcoming.

Reflection on female sexual experience reveals the nature of the link between lovemaking and baby making as kaleidoscopic; that is, complex, variable, and irresolute. For example, the clitoris serves no reproductive purpose.[11] For women, the link, if any, between orgasm and ovulation is completely capricious. From the point of view of the wisdom of the female body then, the link between erotic love and procreation is far from indissoluble. When present the link appears to be at best occasional—that is, periodic and seasonal—at worst, completely unpredictable. Any link at all, however fleeting, between a woman's God-given sexual drives and her fecundity occurs only during certain times of her monthly cycle and only during her childbearing years.[12]

Reflection on the physiology of male sexuality in isolation from female sexuality continues to mislead Christians. It directs us to expect that the ends or purposes of sexuality will be uniform; that is, given and ordered universally so that we can require of every sexual relationship, indeed of each and every sexual act, the same identical vocational (procreative) significance. When we introduce women's sexual physiology into the reflective process, the ends of human sexuality appear more pluriform than is otherwise evident. As a consequence, we need not see sexual differences as morally better or worse (though that traditional judgment of variations remains possible), simply different.

The point here is not to advocate a new physicalist reduction of the human person to biological processes, whether male or female. We should not base whatever virtues ought to guide human sexual expression on a body-denying or androcentric vision of human sexuality.

It is at least intelligible (1) to accept as humanly normative the separation of lovemaking and baby making and (2) to associate as equally normative more than one moral meaning with human sexuality. One can do so without adopting dualistic forms of thought and instead develop a structurally pluralistic rather than unitary sexual ethic. Such an ethic would presuppose and maintain the variation inherent in the created order. It would do so without denying what is normatively human about the embodied character of human sexuality and reproduction.

The distinctively Christian affirmation of bodily life may necessitate an appreciation of diversity and difference. To suggest that these are intelligible preliminary conclusions falls far short of justifying them. Still, it begins an important reformation process. An authentically traditional, distinctively Christian sexual ethic does not require dualistic or androcentric frames of reference nor uniformity in its design.

Coherence

Although there is no consensus about the exact causes of either a heterosexual or homosexual orientation, considerable agreement exists among social scientists regarding several characteristics of human sexual orientations. As we demonstrated in the preceding chapter, documented studies indicate that one establishes a sexual orientation very early in childhood probably both by nature and nurture.[13] It is central to an individual's sense of personhood. With the exception of anecdotal accounts, no evidence supports the view that a person's sexual orientation can be changed. People do not make choices about their orientation, though clearly they can make choices in response to it.

One version of heterosexism presumes that people can make choices about that which they find sexually desirable. Consequently, its advocates assign blame to individuals for being homosexual. This position conflicts with scientific findings about the origins and intractability of sexual orientations (see Position 1 in chapter 1). Many who wish to abolish heterosexism believe that these same findings instead prove that all versions of heterosexism are indefensible. Such a conclusion is premature.

The presumption that people have absolute freedom regarding the orientation of their sexual desires is not essential to heterosexism. One can argue plausibly and coherently that homosexuality and bisexuality are a consequence of original sin. According to these versions of heterosexism (see Positions 2, 3, and 4 in chapter 1), homosexuality and bisexuality constitute examples of brokenness and bondage. Various forms of fallenness ensnare all of humanity. According to heterosexism sexual passions, like other innate sinful tendencies, are desires that one cannot eliminate. One can, however, either repress or channel them into justifiable but nonnormative same-sex relationships.

That 10 percent of humanity is so "disoriented" may reflect only the pervasiveness of sin according to these views. The centrality of these sinful passions may reflect only the depth of human depravity. At least three versions of heterosexism (Positions 2, 3, and 4 in chapter 1) cohere with emerging scientific data about the origins and unchangeability of human sexual orientations.

The claim by some heterosexists (see Position 1 in chapter 1) that homosexual and bisexual persons can successfully transform their sexual orientations does not cohere with emerging scientific data. A brief review of the literature indicates that not even one verifiable instance of the sexual reorientation of a decisively gay individual can be offered; that is, of a person who ranks as a 0 or 1 on the Kinsey scale (see chapter 1, note 16). This version of heterosexism, therefore, cannot be judged credible on scientific grounds.

Fruitfulness

In chapter 4 we will examine theoretical and pragmatic consequences of heterosexist and nonheterosexist approaches to sexual
ethics. We can state here in a preliminary fashion that what heterosexism really does protect may not in the final analysis be evaluated
very highly. For example, heterosexism may preserve patterns of
emotional isolation and suicidal desperation among adolescents
who discover that they are gay. It may inhibit the expression of same
sex, especially male-to-male, affection. It may even reinforce certain
forms of sexual violence and promiscuity.

If such negative consequences are indeed the fruit of heterosexism, we must make a judgment regarding their proper interpretation. Some would argue that these negative consequences symbolize
God's righteous wrath against homosexual persons. In such a view
one would respond appropriately to those who suffer them by bearing witness to God's word of both judgment and mercy. One must
call such people to the comforts of confession. In contrast, we and
others interpret these consequences of heterosexism as unjustifiably
destructive and further proof of the illegitimacy of heterosexism.
Their continuing existence presses upon us the urgency of reform.
We will argue in chapter 4 that the real effects of heterosexism are
not those traditionally associated with it (such as the preservation of
the species and the protection of children from pedophilia). This
reassessment of the consequences of heterosexism not only constitutes an argument against it, but also in a preliminary fashion erodes
the credibility of the heterosexist tradition.

We began this chapter with a discussion of the egalitarian principle. We noted that this axiom requires that all who would discriminate bear the burden of proof. Any variation in the treatment of
human beings whether preferential or prejudicial requires justification. We then assessed some of the traditional arguments used to
justify heterosexist forms of discrimination and concluded that they
were noncredible. We significantly challenged the consistency, comprehensiveness, coherence, and fruitfulness of the heterosexist
ethos.[14] Although it is perhaps premature to conclude on this basis
that there is a presumption in favor of abolishing heterosexism, we
can no longer reasonably operate with a presumption in favor of
retaining heterosexism. At a minimum we must now interpret this
tradition through a hermeneutic of suspicion.

A FAITHFUL REFORMATION

We regard it as simply a matter of fact that the Christian moral tradition in this and other matters is historical and has changed over the centuries.[15] Ethicists have always struggled with the question of how, if at all, moral traditions address later and greatly varying cultural situations. One can easily demonstrate that moral theologians have discarded, selected, recombined, ignored, and innovated inherited Christian traditions regarding sexual matters.[16] How and through what language we might best describe such developments is, of course, debated. Obviously not all conceivable developments are necessarily good. Thus the crucial question is on what grounds or by what criteria Christians reform their traditions.

In the case of a tradition like heterosexism, we must test any reform designed to dismantle it. Christian tradition must be not only credible but also in accord with or faithful to the heart of Christianity. Would the abolition of heterosexism be appropriate to the faith? Would it be compatible with what is central to Christianity?

Biblical Fidelity

Christians have been deeply divided about what constitutes orthodoxy and heresy and about who participates in that discernment. The claims to teaching authority of new magisteria, for example, of womanchurch and of the oppressed, often threaten papal, episcopal, and white male theological magisteria. Historical criticism decades ago undermined simplistic claims about the origin of much of the New Testament. Similarly, informed criticism of received tradition undermines simplistic claims about its authority.

Reformations faithful to Christianity have their basis in one or more of at least these three foundations: (1) the teachings of the episcopacy or the office of ministry; (2) selected elements of the tradition itself, especially those about which there is wide ecumenical consensus, like the creeds; and (3) the Bible. We have adopted the Scriptures as the basis for our proposed reformation. We believe broad, ecumenical agreement exists among Christians about the legitimacy in principle of arguments based on the Scriptures. Scripture remains central to Roman Catholic and Protestant Christians alike, and although its significance and exact canonical parameters might vary along denominational lines, much of the Bible is held in common by Christians. Any proposed reformation must be tested by the Scriptures, which for most Christians serve as an indispensable source of moral wisdom for the Christian life.

Whatever consensus-building strengths we can ascribe to such biblical appeals, their supporting arguments have their own complexities. A dialogical relation binds Scripture and tradition. Decades of oral and liturgical traditions gave rise to the Church's Scripture, which in turn gave rise to and continue to nourish the Church's traditions. Thus, biblically based reformations hinge on the adjudication of conflicting interpretations of Scripture. Often the differences among these interpretations have their roots in non-canonical sources of wisdom; that is, in differing traditions. We will return to this fact shortly.

At this juncture we must note that, in its 1986 letter regarding "The Pastoral Care of Homosexual Persons," the Roman Catholic church declared that "the Scriptures are not properly understood when they are interpreted in a way which contradicts the Church's living tradition. To be correct, the interpretation of Scripture must be in substantial accord with that tradition."[17] The terms *living tradition* and *substantial accord* become crucial to the proper understanding of this instruction. The discernment of what is "living" amidst all that is received, and the discernment of what constitutes the "substance" or heart of that tradition emerges from a dialogue between Scripture and tradition. Although profoundly conservative of its tradition, Roman Catholicism is open in principle to calls to reformation that stem from this discernment process and emerge out of the dialogue between Scripture and tradition.

Any proposed reformation of Church teaching regarding human sexuality, including that of abolishing heterosexism, must be biblically faithful. What this means precisely will vary. Normally when one judges a tradition as credible those who stand in it are biased in favor of the tradition as it is received and against its modification. In this sense the maintenance of a tradition is inherently conservative. However, when one seriously questions the credibility of a tradition the bias among the faithful may begin to shift.

On the one hand this shift may be quite dramatic. If a tradition were judged completely unbelievable, the burden of proof would rest on those who would retain it. They would need to find in some additional foundational source, such as the Bible, compelling arguments against the abolition of that tradition because its demonstrated unbelievability would alone suffice to abolish it. Retentionists would need to discern in Scripture the wisdom that would clarify what at first glance was questionable to contemporary Christians.

On the other hand the shift may be more modest in scope. Once the credibility of a tradition has been significantly questioned abolitionists need only demonstrate that additional foundational sources, like Scripture, provide no compelling arguments against the reformation of the tradition. We understand that our preceding analysis justifies only the more modest shift. The evidence we have presented demonstrates the reasonableness of questioning heterosexism; it does not prove it ludicrous. In sum these first two chapters have simply established a foundation for mounting a case against heterosexism.

We intend to begin that task in chapter 3 where we argue that Scripture provides no compelling arguments against the abolition of heterosexism. Prior to making that argument, we explore the nature of the relationship between the Bible and moral decision making. The debate over heterosexism is highly combustible in its own right. Now we are adding to it controversies about how we can best use Scripture in moral arguments. This is the theological equivalent of throwing dynamite into a firestorm. Such a move is dangerous and can become truly explosive. But we must make the move if we expect to contribute usefully to the debate over heterosexism.

Why should the Bible play this decisive role in our arguments? Why make the Bible central to the moral life? Scripture is God's Word. It promises to work in us as God's living, creative power.[18] Believing this marks the faith of the universal Church.[19] Christians believe that God speaks to human beings through Scripture. Scripture has the power to transform those who hear it.[20]

When people wrestle with the Word, they depend on the promise of God in that Word. God will enable us to learn what God wants us to know and do. This is so even though God has given this Word to us over many centuries and through many peoples and cultures whose ways of thinking and whose life situations differ greatly from ours today. Still God promises in ways beyond our imagining to guide and empower us in our own day and also in ages to come.

What does it mean for Scripture to function as such an authority and norm for the moral life?[21] Does it mean that it constitutes the only or exclusive source of moral wisdom for Christians? Absolutely not. One can build a case against scriptural positivism primarily on the basis of the nature of Scripture itself.[22]

Biblical Warrants for Other Sources of Moral Wisdom

Four specific aspects of Scripture invite Christians to utilize other sources of moral wisdom in resolving their moral debates. The *silence* of Scripture regarding some questions and the morally *suspicious* character of its witness at certain junctures invite Christians to place Scripture in conversation with other sources of moral wisdom. So, too, the historical particularity of Scripture necessarily raises questions about its moral *applicability* to contemporary circumstances. Last, the genuine *diversity* within Scripture on some issues orients us toward other sources of wisdom. We turn now to a brief review of these features of the biblical witness.

Silence

Scripture contains no direct witness regarding some very important contemporary moral problems. For example, no texts speak specifically to the questions of genetic manipulation or in vitro fertilization. One can certainly consider general texts on stewardship and sexuality relevant to these issues. The paucity of texts speaking directly about homosexuality should create caution in our assessment of precisely how the Bible evaluates it. The relative silence of Scripture on this issue, in comparison with so many other moral concerns that receive repeated attention, may be the clearest sign that our tradition has blown it out of proportion.

Morally Suspicious or Mistaken Texts

Some texts are not only dispensable now (like Levitical dress codes and dietary regulations), but also quite simply morally suspect, if not wrong. The curses found in the imprecatory psalms, although expressive of authentically human emotions, are morally problematic. Most Christians today would find the projected treatment of innocent noncombatants rehearsed in the following text morally repugnant: "Happy shall they be who take your little ones and dash them against the rock!" (Ps 137:9; cf. Ps 109:1–14). Nevertheless, texts that call on God to work revenge (like the imprecatory psalms and Rom 12:14ff.) can remind us that God controls the ultimate restoration of justice. This theological framework appropriately limits the realm of human responsibility. Still, the formative impact of such prayers on the moral imagination remains morally suspect. Clearly, one should interpret biblical prayers for wars that result in total annihilation in relation to texts that limit warfare or call for nonviolent responses to evil. Many texts that we judge morally mistaken form part of a diverse set of biblical materials on that issue.

Applicability

Texts carry varying degrees of applicability in accord with the similarity of the circumstances between ancient and modern contexts. We may apply biblical wisdom about the possibility of the just use of force only on the most general level, if at all, to questions regarding the use or threatened use of nuclear weapons. The chasm, the qualitative difference, between conventional and nuclear warfare necessitates this restraint.

We may judge some texts completely inapplicable when we can no longer assume the truth of the presumptions that shaped them. In their history of moral reasoning, *The Abuse of Casuistry*, Albert R. Jonsen and Stephen Toulmin provide us with three sample cases of such foundational shifts. For example, after centuries of debate, people finally judged biblical texts prohibiting the charging of interest on loans or usury as irrelevant to economic life.[23] This happened as a result of a paradigm shift with regard to presuppositions about loans and common economic life. This paradigm shift occurred between the eleventh and eighteenth centuries! People began to perceive loans as a form of relief for the poor rather than a form of capital enterprise. Initially, charging interest on loans given to those in distress was considered tantamount to stealing from the poor. Gradually, people concluded that charging reasonable interest on capital ventures was equivalent to getting a just price for one's risk, for the loss of the use of one's capital, and for one's administrative costs. By the eighteenth century people no longer viewed the texts that speak against charging interest as applicable. Why? They could no longer affirm the economic presumptions behind them.

Less significant issues also bear witness to the problem of varying applicability. For example, few churches require women to wear hats during worship (in accordance with 1 Cor 11:5) nor do we insist on using only courts that are established by the church to air our grievances with other Christians (in accordance with 1 Cor 6:1). Why? We do not hold either the gender or the political presumptions that shape these texts.

Changed circumstances do not render such texts meaningless, however. For example, one should still consider how we might transform the overly litigious character of our society by the call of 1 Cor 6:1. Similarly, how we think about social decorum, whether in dress or behavior, affects how we respect one another in community (1 Cor

11:5). We need not return to ancient economic systems to apply or see the relevance of biblical messages about solidarity with the poor.

On the one hand, fidelity to Scripture demands that we take seriously its cultural contexts, attending with care to the ways in which these contexts may differ from our own. This makes the discernment of their relevance more complex. On the other hand, fidelity to Scripture demands that we not cavalierly dismiss it as so bound to particular cultures that it cannot speak to our modern concerns.[24] Yet an inescapable chasm exists between our world and the ancient worlds of the Bible. Lisa Sowle Cahill calls the faithful to search for "a creative way to appropriate the Bible as morally normative . . . while recognizing that the discrepancy of cultural contexts can limit the relevance of specific commands."[25]

Diversity

Ultimately the very diversity of the biblical witness on some moral issues makes it impossible to view Scripture as the exclusive source of moral wisdom for Christians. Our assumption about the overall character of the moral witness of Scripture has changed from an expectation of inner harmony to the assumption of inevitable discord. Christians assumed that the individual parts of Scripture were basically compatible. They believed that the plurality of the moral witness reflected different but essentially complementary perspectives on a common tradition. They also thought it possible ultimately to harmonize the various passages one with another.

In contrast, modern exegetes no longer assume complementarity in the testimony of various biblical communities. Biblical scholars recognize that the scriptural witness on moral as well as theological issues produces truly diverse and various insights often in conflict with one another, if not contradictory. At least on the surface the prospect of canonical diversity seems to outweigh that of canonical coherence. Yet we can affirm God's inspiration of the biblical word precisely because we take seriously the changing contexts to which God speaks. Scripture's diversity thus becomes an access rather than a barrier to our discernment of God's will.

Examining in some detail an example of moral diversity found within the Bible will illustrate our point.[26] We have selected one historical example of a moral issue hotly debated over a century ago. It proved tragically divisive. Many individual congregations and even whole denominations experienced schism over the issue. People engaged in civil disobedience in response to their deeply held convictions. The nation even took up arms. The question of course was slavery. Willard M. Swartley reviews the diverse witness in Scripture on this question.[27]

The Patriarchs seem to accept slavery as divinely sanctioned.[28] The Lord blesses Abraham by multiplying his slaves (Gen 24:35). The angel commands the slave Hagar to return to Sarah her mistress (Gen 16:9). God seems to demand that slavery become a lifelong arrangement even among Hebrews under certain circumstances (Deut 15:16, 17); for example, if a bondman is unwilling to abandon his wife and children (Ex 21:1-6). Yet God's deliverance of Israel from slavery in Egypt shows, once and for all, that God hates and condemns slavery (the Exodus account) and that we should identify with those in bondage and cry out for their freedom.

The New Testament, although critical of its abuses, seems to approve of slavery. Some texts call slaves to hearty obedience and enjoin them repeatedly to subject themselves to masters (Col 3:22-25; 4:1; Tit 2:9-10; 1 Pet 2:18-19). The author of 1 Timothy declares that the call for the submissive obedience of slaves is based on the words of Jesus (1 Tim 6:1-6). Yet when Paul sends the fugitive slave Onesimus back to Philemon, he asks that he be received as a brother (not a servant) in the flesh as well as in the Lord (v. 16). In this letter Paul presses the Christian community to anticipate the eschatological Jubilee when slavery is gone. Given his apocalyptic vision, Paul understandably did not challenge directly the structures of society at other junctures in his writing. He understood, however, that God would transform them and that the Church in its life needed to anticipate that divine transformation (see 1 Cor 7:21ff.).

Christian ethicists have harmonized these mandates by arguing that they are directed to different individuals in the overall economy of the Church or that they apply to different historical situations. On the one hand, nothing in these texts suggests that we should assume one or more of them as morally absolute. Indeed Scripture reveals only one absolute Word of God; that is, the Son, Jesus Christ (Heb 1:1, 2a). On the other hand, nothing in these texts suggests that we should not assume one or more of them both relevant and applicable to us.

Responses to Biblical Diversity

One can respond in many ways to the hermeneutical problems posed by the very nature of Scripture, especially those generated by biblical diversity. We will explore three of the most common responses: (1) to assume substantive canonical integrity; (2) to assume formal canonical integrity; and (3) to assume a canon within the canon. The inadequacy of these responses leads us to recast our questions about the relationship of the Bible to the moral life and to explore in a revision of the third model their proper relationship to noncanonical sources of moral wisdom.

The Assumption of Substantive Canonical Integrity

Some Christians respond to the problem of biblical diversity by claiming its *substantive canonical integrity* despite appearances to the contrary. The hermeneutical process along with the authoritative nature of Scripture demands attention to the canon as a whole and to the full range of biblical testimony on a particular moral issue.

The diversity found in the canon will result in a dialectical process through which various texts will modify and qualify one another. This interaction will yield a coherent substantive perspective on the issue in question. The hermeneutical process requires no other extrabiblical or noncanonical sources of moral wisdom.[29] Occasionally, following this procedure alone will work. For that reason this approach should always be tried first. For example, attention to the canon's witness as a whole clearly establishes a moral presumption in favor of the poor and a moral presumption against the use of violence.

Such presumptions do not solve all significant moral debates. For example, both pacifists and those who believe in the justifiability of some wars hold this biblically based moral presumption against the use of force. However, Scripture does not offer a universally compelling testimony in favor of either the pacifist or just-war position. Furthermore, the specific criteria (just cause, last resort, etc.) used within the just-war tradition to discern, for example, whether the Gulf War was justified, trace their roots to ancient Greek and Roman political thought, not the Bible.

Likewise, standing on the side of the poor does not begin to solve the economic and political debate about what kind of tax and welfare systems would best serve them, or what kind of material lifestyles Christians and their pastors should adopt. Finally, as we established earlier, the diversity of biblical insight is often so great that no single presumption or set of coherent directives results from it (see slavery).

The Assumption of Formal Canonical Integrity

When confronted with biblical diversity, some Christians conclude that they can only argue for its *formal canonical integrity*. Advocates of this response, as in the one above, believe that the hermeneutical process and the authoritative nature of Scripture necessitate attention to the canon as a whole and to the full range of biblical testimony. They conclude, however, that the diversity of Scripture on moral issues makes the search for substantive moral insight on particular moral issues futile. Thus they argue that we should relocate canonical authority from the level of content (substantive moral insight) to a more formal level; for example, to the level of communal structures and interpretative patterns (processes of decision making). One can maintain as normative the Bible's formal polarities (e.g., between priestly and prophetic roles) or the process of theologizing to moral action modeled in the Bible.[30]

We believe that these patterns and structures, albeit important morally, do not provide Christians with sufficient assistance on a substantive level regarding moral problems. Although not completely without merit, neither of these "solutions" resolves the problems dramatically posed by Scripture itself. As James D. G. Dunn argues, the pattern of biblical diversity canonizes the continuing need for reformation of moral teaching.[31] In other words, biblical diversity mandates the task of reform.

The Assumption of a Canon within the Canon

Diversity has led some Christians to construct a *canon within the canon*. Even though they recognize the entire Bible as God's Word, they believe that some texts are privileged. They give such texts more authority than others and use them as a criterion against which to measure other biblical passages. Advocates of this approach trace their strategy back to Jesus himself who is described as privileging what is countercultural, as for example in Mark 10. Jesus establishes God's will as expressed in creation as the criterion against which to evaluate God's command to Moses allowing divorce.[32]

A modern example of this approach can be found in red letter editions of the Bible. Some Christians give the words attributed directly to Jesus special status because the immediate source of the words is infallible. Similarly, some assume countercultural texts as less likely to be distorted by their Sitz im Leben or by particular historical concerns or biases.[33] Furthermore texts that speak of "originating revelatory events" or "foundational events" for the community gain privilege on the grounds that they are either (1) more pristine because of their historical proximity to the events they describe or (2) essential to the community's sense of identity.[34] Advocates of such approaches base the selection of their inner canon on claims about the special nature of the texts they privilege.

Those who sacralize the sayings attributed to Jesus should remember that those very sayings are mediated by human communities and are therefore like any other biblical texts. We do not have access to Jesus' Aramaic words—only to conflicting Greek translations of them. In addition, fully fallible human communities remembered, translated to Greek, preserved, contextualized, canonized, and translated them into English. Similarly, we must recognize that even a countercultural text is conditioned by the culture it criticizes. Finally, the fact that a text dates from close to the time of the occurrence of an event does not in itself guarantee its accuracy. The foundational status of a text is not self-evident. For example, we have considerable consensus that Jesus' crucifixion and resurrection are events foundational to Christian identity, yet some choose to focus on the cross as a key to their identity whereas others emphasize the resurrection and a "theology of glory" as central to their lives.

Choosing privileged texts does not in itself present a problem. As one reads and weighs how various passages relate to each other and function as God's Word one must make such choices. At this point we do not wish to argue with any of the previous reasons for evaluating texts. We simply want to acknowledge the inadequacy of the justifications for such selection. While we would argue that all of Scripture is inspired, no portion of it is historically unconditioned. In this sense no texts can take absolute precedence over others.

Because this is the case, we must ask how we might reframe the question about the relationship between the Bible and Christian ethics. The question is not *whether* an individual or a church body interprets Scripture (from the most fundamentalist to the most liberal), but rather how one does so. Being as honest and open as possible about our concerns, cultural biases, denominational loyalties, and so forth, allows Scripture as God's word to challenge us fully.

Reframing the Question(s)

The diverse nature of Scripture invites us to ask tough questions about the relationship between the Bible and moral decision making. These questions include the following. How can we avoid picking and choosing biblical texts that support moral judgments that we have already made on other grounds?[35] Can we avoid choosing and emphasizing those texts that then conveniently corroborate (or seem to corroborate) our cultural and personal mores? If we cannot avoid being selective in our use of Scripture in moral argument, what ought to govern our selection of texts?

Thus, the nature of the Bible itself, especially the diversity and historical conditioning of its witness, necessitates that all Christians confess their use of noncanonical sources of moral wisdom. To this point we have established only that such noncanonical sources are and must be used in making moral judgments. The honest recognition of these sources leads to additional questions. What role do nonbiblical sources of moral wisdom play in the selection and interpretation process? What does it mean to claim primacy for Scripture among these sources of moral wisdom?

Noncanonical Sources of Moral Wisdom

> I was sitting in an introductory college psychology class when the professor began to explain the research that led to the development of the Kinsey scale. I was fascinated by the possibility that all human beings fell somewhere on a sexual continuum. Such a possibility had never entered my mind. I assumed that because people were either male or female whatever behavior characteristics belonged to each were fixed. I had no sense of how differences in being masculine or feminine fit into the picture.
>
> Some time later I went to an Institute at the Johns Hopkins Medical Center that discussed experiments on the sexual development of animals. It showed how male and female sexual traits could be altered in different ways by interfering medically with sexual development (such as by giving artificial doses of testosterone or estrogen at key points during gestation).
>
> All of this convinced me that I could not "blame" a person for being homosexual because it was some arbitrary, perverted choice they had made. I began to realize that scientific evidence did not allow me to hold on to my prejudices and still have integrity.

We can identify at least four nonbiblical sources of moral wisdom for Christians. *Classic texts* consist of creeds, confessions, liturgies, official church teachings and related theological studies.[36] *Normative accounts of the human* (natural law) make reasonable claims as to what is valuable or what is to be promoted or avoided. The Bible itself affirms in its wisdom literature that the Law was the Word by which God created and ordered the universe. This moral law is built into the very fiber of creation.[37] *Descriptive accounts of the human* can be found in literary, historical, artistic, and scientific interpretations of human experience. Our *personal experiences* are appropriate sources of moral wisdom when filtered by our minds and consciences. Experience also provides a testing ground where the life-enhancing and integrating effects of teachings are assessed. God has promised to direct and enlighten the ongoing interaction among these noncanonical sources and Scripture, especially when we prayerfully have dialogue with one another as sisters and brothers in the name of Christ.

Our earlier discussion of the biblical warrants for other sources of moral wisdom established the need for using nonbiblical sources. A key to understanding how Scripture relates to the moral life today resides in understanding the relationships between and among these various sources of moral wisdom. We believe it is necessary to bring these nonbiblical sources to our deliberations about what should function as a canon within the canon.

Frequently, people use arguments about the diversity, inapplicability, suspicious nature, or silence of the biblical witness on moral matters to establish the need for an interpretative framework for the Bible. The tradition has functioned in this way vis-à-vis Scripture. However, we argued earlier that we can reasonably place portions of the tradition under suspicion. Thus "traditional" heterosexist premises cannot function as our interpretive framework for Scripture, at least not axiomatically.

In such circumstances the faithful must turn to other sources of moral wisdom, external to Scripture and tradition. Such external sources include all that might be grouped under the broad categories of experience and reason, including historical, literary, and scientific accounts both normative and descriptive of the human. These other sources of moral wisdom are in themselves never the final arbiter of what constitutes authority for Christians. Instead, listening to their voices enables the faithful to hear Scripture anew and to test their interpretive traditions in light of that fresh Word. These nontraditional sources of wisdom do not replace or usurp the authority of Scripture.[38] They are conversation partners that open our hearts to God's Word, inviting either the affirmation or reformation of our tradition. We will examine this interplay as it shapes our initial selection of a canon within the canon.

Canon within the Canon: A Revision

Even though we believe that the entire Bible is God's Word, giving special priority to some texts has proven historically inescapable. People give some texts more authority than others in certain periods of history due to prevailing circumstances. These texts then serve as a criterion against which to measure other biblical passages. We believe this process has significant historical and contemporary precedents. Martin Luther (1483–1546), as a result of his historical context and experience, defended many of the insights found in St. Paul's letters over those in the epistle of St. James. Today many scholars would argue that the letter of James corrects distorted appropriations of Pauline emphases.

In contrast, the treatment of texts that address gender questions poses many problems for us. Christian feminists treat passages that call for a discipleship of equals as privileged texts. They believe that we should evaluate nonegalitarian or patriarchal texts about the proper roles and status of women and men in the light of their privileged texts.[39] Conversely, many traditional Christians grant privileged status to nonegalitarian or patriarchal texts about the proper roles and status of women and men. In light of these texts they evaluate other egalitarian texts that call for a discipleship of equals. Contemporary Christians are deeply divided about which set of texts to privilege and about the proper basis for this decision. Usually they base this selection on an experience outside of the text. It originates "in front of" the text. They make the selection of this privileged canon on an extrabiblical or noncanonical basis.

Initially, people make their selection of a canon within the canon on the basis of a norm or conviction they bring to the text. A reformer of the tradition like Luther based his selection on his experience of justification by grace through faith or God's free gift of salvation in Christ. Some abolitionists base their selection on the faith experience of Christian slaves and their struggle for liberation. Feminists base their selection on the experience of womanchurch and the struggle for women's liberation.

This process poses obvious problems. What prevents this selection of privileged texts from being biased or arbitrary?[40] In one sense, circularity of argument is inevitable. So the question becomes "How can we avoid a vicious, arbitrary, or prejudicial circularity of argument?" Some interpreters try to test whether what lies experientially *in front of* the text can also be found historically *behind* the text. Is the selection of a canon within the canon compatible with a historical reconstruction of what lies behind the text?[41] We can never verify historical reconstructions objectively, but we can demonstrate whether they are plausible or not falsifiable. We can judge the truest or most credible of the available alternative theories if they are the most consistent, comprehensive, coherent, and fruitful.

Even such modest claims must remain questionable. Considerable debate continues about whether we can recover any of the historical basis of the canon. On what grounds can we reconstruct the events behind the texts? We have no single word of Scripture that does not embody at the same time the confession and selective memory of the believing community that preserved the text. Claims to more than fragmentary knowledge about what might lie behind these texts are at best speculative.

The circularity of such hermeneutical arguments is inescapable. In moral matters, Scripture is necessary but not sufficient. If we do not wrestle with it in our deliberations, that process cannot claim to be Christian. But its interpretation demands that we grapple with insights from other sources of moral wisdom as well. Inevitably what lies *in front of* the Bible will influence the interpretation of individual texts and decisions about which texts to privilege over others. This process is least arbitrary when we place nonbiblical and biblical sources of moral wisdom in open conversation with each other.

Like all other sources of moral wisdom, the Bible functions in this process in two ways. It has both problem-setting and problem-solving capacities. Biblical narratives, the parables, wisdom, and prophetic literature can all help shape the vision, virtues, and beliefs of the Christian community. We usually greatly underestimate such influence. Yet it provides the means by which we define problems. How we define a problem determines how we resolve it, largely because the definition circumscribes the considerations deemed relevant.

Additionally, the Bible can influence the problem-solving process. Explicitly normative biblical materials are especially relevant here. As we have already discussed, sometimes Scripture establishes initial moral presumptions (e.g., preference for the poor); sometimes it establishes who carries the burden of proof (e.g., those who would use force); sometimes it challenges and transforms noncanonical wisdom, and sometimes it corroborates that wisdom.

Ultimately the relationship among the sources of moral wisdom must be *dialogical*, introducing the possibility of mutual or reciprocal correction. As a community of moral deliberation the Church fosters such dialogue, claiming for itself the promise of God. In such a prayerful context God's Word will not return empty but will accomplish within the Church and our times that which God proposes (Isa 55:10, 11).

CONCLUSION

How does the Bible relate to ethical debates among us about heterosexism? It provides a necessary, indispensable source of moral wisdom for Christians. Apart from the careful and prayerful consideration of its wisdom, a decision to retain or reform traditional teachings on this matter cannot claim to be Christian. The consideration of scriptural testimony is essential to our continued faithfulness. In this sense it has primacy *for Christians* among all other sources of moral wisdom.[42]

The Bible is not in itself, however, a sufficient source of moral wisdom for Christians. The nature of Scripture invites us to reflect on other, nonbiblical sources of moral wisdom. These other sources play key roles in our interpretation of biblical texts and in our selection of what should serve as a canon within the canon. Hence biblical primacy is inescapably dialogical in character.

One cannot restrict moral wisdom to the Bible. However, the Bible enjoys a privileged position among multiple sources of moral wisdom for Christians. It governs what the Church recognizes as wisdom over the ages. Christians profess the Bible as disclosive of what is primordially revealed in Jesus Christ. This faith claim about the revelatory, ultimately salutary character of Scripture provides the basis for its moral authority within the Church. We recognize the Bible as inspired because we experience it as disclosive of God's Word to us in Jesus Christ. Thus our appeal to Scripture does not hinge upon a claim about its absolute moral inerrancy or sufficiency. Rather we appeal to the disclosive or revelatory power of Scripture. Such an appeal is by definition dialogical and relative.[43]

An authentically Christian position on homosexuality must be faithful to the scriptural wisdom about it. That very reliance on God's Word necessitates that we engage in interpretation. The nature of Scripture invites us to consider other sources of moral wisdom in the interpretive process. Some of those other sources of wisdom raised the initial questions about the continuing credibility of heterosexist traditions. Those questions drove us to search for a biblical basis either for retaining or abolishing heterosexism. In brief, this is what biblical scholars call the *hermeneutical circle*. No matter where one jumps on board, prayerful evaluation in the context of a community of moral deliberation seeking to bear witness to God's Word will bear fruit. This is God's promise: "If you *continue* in my word you are truly my disciples, and you will know the truth, and the truth will make you free" (John 8:30; emphasis added).

3

The Bible and Heterosexism

Even though I am out of the closet, I am not very political. I am not sure why I went to the Gay Pride Day march with the pastor of my Metropolitan Community Church.

The crowds along our route were not very friendly. We were walking toward the middle of the column. Those on the outer edges took most of the heat. From our vantage point we could see the curiosity, amusement, support, and animosity of many onlookers, but usually could not hear their comments.

With one exception. I will never forget the placard she carried. It said: "Love the sinner. Hate the sin." She broke through the column and ran smack up to my pastor. With a flushed face she screamed at him: "I hate your sin." Gently, knowing she would not understand his response, he said with genuine sadness: "So do I."

Most gay and lesbian people can tell similar stories. They still experience God's Word primarily as a weapon used against them. Christian heterosexists often recite chapter and verse at them. The Church does not name or claim gay and lesbian people as delightful sons and daughters of God. Instead it condemns them and proclaims them to be at the core of their very being abhorrent to God. Many gay and lesbian Christians experience the frequent rehearsal of the texts we are about to study as quite painful. More than once we have heard them referred to as *Bible bullets.* Such sarcastic terminology does not come from those who have left the Church. It comes from Christians who continue to find their lives sustained by God's Word.

No one can presume that God's Word is always easy to hear. Deep in their hearts, all Christians know that God's Word can and should be difficult and convicting. No one who is party to these deliberations about homosexuality and heterosexism claims to be without sin. God exhibits a "tough" love, not a shallow or sentimental consolation. Those called to hear a difficult Word know that it is ultimately Good News. It is life giving. A comparison may illustrate our point. All animals facing environmental starvation must be tranquilized in order to relocate them. They must all be shot. One can imagine that tranquilizing pellets hit with terrifying force. But we know that in the end these wounds will prove to be life-giving.

Christians, one and all, are shot through the heart by God's Word. The question we will ask is this: "Are the traditional hetero-sexist interpretations of these biblical texts ultimately death dealing or life giving to gay and lesbian Christians?" Can the wounds that accompany their use, like those made by a surgeon, potentially bring health? Or are they like the painful misinterpretations of God's Will referred to in Luke's gospel that frequently resulted in the social ostracism and explicit religious exclusion of those sent by God to reform the community? "Blessed are you when people hate you, and when they exclude you, revile you and defame you on account of the Son of Man. Rejoice in that day and leap for joy, for surely your reward is great in heaven; for that is what their ancestors did to the prophets" (Lk 6:22–23).

A question lies behind the exploration in this chapter: "How can we bear witness to God's unqualified love for all people?" Just because words or actions are critical does not mean they are by defi-nition unloving. Christians have long recognized God's love for humankind as a passionate and faithful but "tough" love. Both law and gospel express this love. Both declarations of judgment and of affirmation give testimony to it.

At their best Christian heterosexists believe that they are called by God to respond to gay and lesbian people with precisely such tough love. At its best their response is not phobic or harsh; they perceive it as prophetic in character. Many heterosexists believe that the kindest, most loving thing for them to do is speak a clear word of judgment about the "fallen" (specifically the disoriented) character of all nonheterosexual orientations. From their perspective, how-ever personally painful this Word may be for some, it constitutes the truth about God's intentions for humankind. This truth, and this truth alone, will set gay and lesbian people free.

We are convinced that only through the prayerful study of God's Word on this matter will the Church find the proper founda-tion for the reform of its heterosexist traditions. Some who wish to argue against heterosexism cite only social scientific data in defense of their claim that homosexual orientations are not abnormal. They believe that all who disagree with them are either dismissing or ignoring recent documented scientific research on sexual orienta-tion. They are correct in that regard only with respect to the most conservative of heterosexists (see Position 1, described in chapter 1). More liberal heterosexists accept much of the recent scientific wisdom regarding homosexuality (see Positions 2, 3, and 4 described in chapter 1).

Many Christians who wish to reform Church teaching find these more liberal heterosexists most frustrating. They do not understand how they can remain heterosexist. They find these liberal versions of heterosexism terribly confusing and confused. Yet there is nothing inherently incoherent in these liberal positions.

All who wish to reform Church teachings must recognize that no scientific evidence about the origins and changeability of sexual orientation will solve the normative question at stake in these deliberations. This evidence *is not relevant* to the question of whether or not this de facto variation is pathological. The mere existence of a phenomenon or its intractability do not make it natural or normatively human. The reform of any moral tradition will rest on a normative base not disconnected, but clearly distinguishable, from these facts. For Christians the Bible forms the cornerstone of that base (see chapter 2). Thus the reform of Church teaching regarding human sexuality must find its roots in Scripture.

In this chapter we will examine two interrelated clusters of biblical texts frequently cited to support heterosexism. People usually interpret the first cluster of passages as mutually corroborative in condemning homosexuality. The second interrelated cluster of texts they interpret as mutually corroborative in supporting heterocentrism. We will argue that neither set of texts constitutes a compelling case for the retention of heterosexism.

All who come to Scripture bring with them an interpretative framework. The interpretative lens through which these texts have traditionally been read is heterosexist. We will argue that their traditional translation, interpretation, and clustering reflects a heterosexist ordering that hinders these passages from speaking. The clustering itself is more a reflection of heterosexism than a consequence of textually based ties; it obscures rather than illumines the passages. Because they have been forced into this framework the texts speak in a limited way. Christians have assumed that they will provide us with the answers to heterosexist questions. Reading them only to get answers to such questions filters out or distorts their authentic meaning.

In the preceding chapter we established that it was reasonable to be suspicious of, and therefore temporarily suspend, traditional heterosexist approaches to Scripture. Sufficient evidence exists to call heterosexism into question as an interpretative framework. Following this trial suspension we must proceed to ask questions of the texts from a nonheterocentric perspective. For example, if we presume that homosexuality is a God-given, good gift of creation, what will these texts say to us? What do these passages teach when we remove our heterocentric lenses and try looking at them with different eyes?

It is crucial for us to clarify the authority or status of this alternative set of interpretative presumptions. Our proposed framework makes use of nontraditional sources of wisdom. Specifically, it employs emerging scientific evidence about human sexuality and incorporates the experience of gay, lesbian, and bisexual Christians. This in no way compromises the primacy of Scripture or other authoritative sources of wisdom. Instead it sparks a dialogue among all these sources enabling Scripture to speak afresh to us about whether traditional views should be reformed. All sources of moral wisdom in some sense reflect human experience. As Margaret Farley points out, "Scripture, tradition and secular disciplines all reflect on experiences, past and present."[1] Reliance on the experience of gay Christians means taking it seriously as a contribution to moral discernment for the whole community. This reliance stands apart from any judgment one might finally render regarding it.

Such serious attention to gay and lesbian experiences, just as to modern scientific evidence, is qualified by the fact that no broad historical base exists for judging either. In other words, because the data is contemporary it has not been as fully tested as other, traditional sources of wisdom. The refiner's fire has not yet separated dross from gold. The obvious point here is that such refining can occur only as Christians open their moral deliberation to the inclusion of such testimony.

The false or mixed consciousness generated by internalized heterosexism also qualifies how one interprets the experience of homosexual Christians. Simply because one is gay does not mean that one has a clear perception of what is important in biblical or traditional sources of wisdom. Gay people are just as capable of self-delusion as anyone else. Not all gay men and lesbians can or will speak authentically of their sexual experience precisely because of the power heterosexism has to distort it.

Ultimately the faithful reader will need to make a conscious, critical choice between traditional heterocentric and nonheterocentric interpretative premises. This decision ought to hinge on which framework best enables the faithful to hear God's Word. We are convinced that a nonheterocentric interpretative framework is more faithful. We hope that "laying our cards on the table" at this point creates an atmosphere of candor and promotes critical analysis. We do not want readers to feel manipulated, but rather invited to serious study of the arguments. We are not trying to get rid of biblical texts that are problematic or challenge our point of view. On the contrary, our biblical position emerges from serious and systematic study of Scripture.

REEVALUATING TRADITIONAL
BIBLICAL INTERPRETATIONS

Historical, literary, and socio-cultural methods of biblical criticism indicate that all portions of Scripture require interpretation. In our opinion two factors prove decisive in this debate. The ancient Hebrew people and St. Paul were (1) deeply offended by same-sex desires and behaviors and (2) had no understanding of the fact that some people might be homosexually (or heterosexually) oriented.[2] We will suggest that the first of these factors must be interpreted in the light of the second and that nonheterosexist interpretations are compatible with (if not more suited to) the overall biblical witness.

TRADITIONAL TEXTS
"AGAINST HOMOSEXUALITY"

Six biblical texts are traditionally brought together in the construction of a biblical case against homosexuality. The story of Sodom and Gomorrah remains perhaps the most prominent both in religious arguments and in the construction of civic legislation against sodomy.[3] Heterosexist interpreters argue that the sin that prompts God's harsh judgment against the people of these two cities is homosexual behavior per se. We will argue that this is a mistaken reading and that the traditional misinterpretation of this story has distorted in significant ways our understanding of the other biblical texts with which it is clustered.

Genesis 19:1–29

The two angels came to Sodom in the evening, and Lot was sitting in the gate of Sodom. When Lot saw them, he rose to meet them, and bowed down with his face to the ground. He said, "Please, my lords, turn aside to your servant's house and spend the night, and wash your feet; then you can rise early and go on your way." They said, "No; we will spend the night in the square." But he urged them strongly; so they turned aside to him and entered his house; and he made them a feast, and baked unleavened bread, and they ate. But before they lay down, the men of the city, the men of Sodom, both young and old, all the people to the last man, surrounded the house; and they called to Lot, "Where are the men who came to you tonight? Bring them out to us, that we may know them." Lot went out of the door to the men, shut the door after him, and said, "I beg you, my brothers, do no act so wickedly. Look, I have two daughters who have not known a man; let me bring them out to you, and do to them as you please; only do nothing to these men, for they have come under the shelter of my roof." But they replied, "Stand back!" And they said, "This fellow came here as an alien, and he would play the judge! Now we will deal worse with you than with them." Then they pressed hard against the man Lot, and came near the door to break it down. But the men inside reached out their hands and brought Lot into the house with them, and shut the door. And they struck with blindness the men who were at the door of the house, both small and great, so that they were unable to find the door.

Then the men said to Lot, "Have you anyone else here? Sons-in-law, sons, daughters, or anyone you have in the city—bring them out of the place. For we are about to destroy this place, because the outcry against its people has become great before the Lord, and the Lord has sent us to destroy it." So Lot went out and said to his sons-in-law, who were to marry his daughters, "Up, get out of this place; for the Lord is about to destroy the city." But he seemed to his sons-in-law to be jesting.

When morning dawned, the angels urged Lot, saying, "Get up, take your wife and your two daughters who are here, or else you will be consumed in the punishment of the city." But he lingered; so the men seized him and his wife and his two daughters by the hand, the Lord being merciful to him, and they brought him out and left him outside the city. When they had brought them outside, they said, "Flee for your life; do not look back or stop anywhere in the Plain, flee to the hills, lest you be consumed." And Lot said to them, "Oh, no, my lords; your servant has found favor with you, and you have shown me great kindness in saving my life; but I cannot flee to the hills, for fear the disaster will overtake me and I die. Look, that city is near enough to flee to, and it is a little one. Let me escape there—is it not a little one?—and my life will be saved!" He said to him, "Very well, I grant you this favor too, and will not overthrow the city of which you have spoken. Hurry, escape there, for I can do nothing until you arrive there." Therefore the city was called Zoar. The sun had risen on the earth when Lot came to Zoar.

Then the Lord rained on Sodom and Gomorrah sulfur and fire from the Lord out of heaven; and he overthrew those cities, and all the Plain, and all the inhabitants of the cities, and what grew on the ground. But Lot's wife, behind him, looked back, and she became a pillar of salt. Abraham went early in the morning to the place where he had stood before the Lord; and he looked down toward Sodom and Gomorrah and toward all the land of the Plain and saw the smoke of the land going up like the smoke of a furnace. So it was that, when God destroyed the cities of the Plain, God remembered Abraham, and sent Lot out of the midst of the overthrow, when he overthrew the cities in which Lot had settled.[4]

About this the text is clear: the men of Sodom threaten the men-angels who visit the resident alien Lot and his family. It is reasonable (though not undebatable) to interpret the threat as the threat of same-sex gang rape. Such a threat reveals the refusal of the men of Sodom to respect Lot's offer of hospitality (which includes sanctuary as well as shelter) to the strangers. The crux of the current interpretative debate is why Sodom and Gomorrah are destroyed by God. We believe that the violent threat of gang rape is what breaks God's patience in the unfolding of this story.

The close parallels between this story and an analogous account of gang rape found in the Book of Judges reinforces our interpretation.

Then at evening there was an old man coming from his work in the field. The man was from the hill country of Ephraim, and he was residing in Gibeah. (The people of the place were Benjaminites.) When the old man looked up, and saw the wayfarer in the open square of the city, he said, "Where are you going and where do you come from?" He answered him, "We are passing from Bethlehem in Judah to the remote parts of the hill country of Ephraim, from which I come. I went to Bethlehem in Judah; and I am going to my home. Nobody has offered to take me in. We your servants have straw and fodder for our donkeys, with bread and wine for me and the woman and the young man along with us. We need nothing more." The old man said, "Peace be to you. I will care for all your wants; only do not spend the night in the square." So he brought him into his house, and fed the donkeys; they washed their feet, and ate and drank.

While they were enjoying themselves, the men of the city, a perverse lot, surrounded the house, and started pounding on the door. They said to the old man, the master of the house, "Bring out

the man who came into your house, so that we may have intercourse with him." And the man, the master of the house, went out
to them and said to them, "No, my brothers, do not act so wickedly.
Since this man is my guest, do not do this vile thing. Here are my
virgin daughter and his concubine; let me bring them out now.
Ravish them and do whatever you want to them; but against this
man do not do such a vile thing." But the men would not listen to
him. So the man seized his concubine, and put her out to them.
They wantonly raped her, and abused her all through the night
until the morning. And as the dawn began to break, they let her go.
As morning appeared, the woman came and fell down at the door
of the man's house where her master was, until it was light.

In the morning her master got up, he opened the doors of the
house, and when he went out to go on his way, there was his concubine lying at the door of the house, with her hands on the
threshold. "Get up," he said to her, "we are going." But there was
no answer. Then he put her on the donkey; and the man set out
for his home. When he had entered his house, he took a knife, and
grasping his concubine he cut her into twelve pieces, limb by limb
and sent her throughout all the territory of Israel. (Judges
19:16–29)

In both stories male visitors are threatened with gang rape.
Though some question whether it is appropriate to impose sexual
connotations on the townsmen's request "to know" Lot's guests, we
believe subsequent events in the plot invite such an interpretation
and reinforce its plausibility. In the story from Judges the narrator
first describes the men of Gibeah as seeking intercourse with the
stranger. Later in the account the visitor reports that the lords of
Gibeah surrounded the house and intended to kill him (Judges
20:5). The violent character of the request is reinforced by his subsequent interpretation of it.

In both stories men are threatened with, but ultimately spared
from, gang rape. In both stories women are offered as surrogate victims. In the Sodom story, Lot's daughters are offered as a substitute
target for the attack to protect the visiting men from violation. In the
Gibeah story the householder offers his virgin daughter and the visitor's concubine as surrogate victims. In the Genesis account, neither
the visitors nor Lot's daughters suffer assault. In the story from
Judges, the householder, the visitor himself, and the householder's
virgin daughter remain safe but the concubine is brutally gang raped.
According to the Levite's account, her rape ended in death (Judges
20:5). In the narrator's version of the assault, neither the moment nor

the agent of her death is specified, leaving open the terrifying specter of her being slaughtered by her own master subsequent to her attack.

In both stories, the cities that prove so inhospitable to the wayfarer are destroyed. Sodom is subjected to direct divine retribution even though no crime takes place. Gibeah is razed by the tribes of Israel on the third day of a battle directed by God. The crux of the matter for our purposes is what can be determined about the reasons for this divine wrath.

Heterosexists conclude that it is the homosexual character of their threat that makes these towns so heinous. We believe such an interpretation actually obscures the true focus of these stories. Though the threat and assaults in both cases are undeniably sexual and same sex in character, their applicability to (1) erotic relationships and (2) homosexual desires is highly questionable.

First, the lust behind rape is not especially sexual. Many rapists never ejaculate during their crime. Rape expresses the desire for power over and to dominate others.[5] Gang rape epitomizes the violent nature of the act. No one would condemn all sexual activity on the basis of a judgment against sexual assault. We do not condemn all heterosexual behavior per se on the basis of the brutal abuse of the Levite's concubine. For the same reasons, it is wrong to jump to the conclusion that all homosexual behavior per se evokes God's wrath on the basis of the assaults threatened in both stories.

Second, the texts themselves speak against a facile equation of same sex and homosexual behavior. In both stories the householder offers the bloodthirsty townsmen women as surrogate victims for their wilding. Neither Lot nor the old man of Gibeah interpreted their threat as rooted in homosexual desire. The men of Gibeah accept the concubine as a substitute, making it crystal clear that their desire is not homosexual. What they want is to humiliate and degrade the traveler. In patriarchal cultures, one belittles men by treating them like women or by demeaning their women (their wives, daughters, concubines.) To this day enemy soldiers are often raped by their male captors, as are their female dependents. Rape is a nearly primordial sign of contempt and subjugation—whether same or different sex.

The men of Sodom reject Lot's cowardly offer of his daughters and turn their desire to defile against the resident alien, Lot himself. The text makes it clear that this same-sex threat does not stem from homosexual desires, but is a furious reaction against Lot's courageous word of judgment spoken on behalf of his guests. That this relative stranger would be so bold only confirms the xenophobia rampant among the men of Sodom. These words threaten degradation; they do not give voice to homosexual desire. To conclude on the basis of this text that all homosexual desire intends or submits to degradation is spurious. Even though God directed the wrathful destruction of Gibeah, we do not conclude on the basis of the criminal gang rape of the concubine that all heterosexual desire intends or submits to degradation. Heterosexism necessitates the denial of what is plain: the significant difference between the desires behind rape and mutually erotic genital activity.

Intrabiblical commentary on the sin of Sodom and Gomorrah suggests that these cities were notorious for a wide variety of reprehensible activities. The texts describe those sins variously as inhospitality (Wis 19:13–14), lack of repentance (Mt 11:20–24), indifference to God (Lk 17:28–29), pride and stinginess (Ezek 16:49–50), adultery and deception (Jer 23:14), or insolent pride and brazen arrogance (Sir 16:8; Isa 3:9).[6] Although our heterosexist tradition has tended to interpret that sin as homosexual behavior, many biblical writers did not.[7]

Two late works of the New Testament (2 Pet 2:4–10 and Jude 6–7) are frequently treated as if they identified the sin of Sodom and Gomorrah as homosexuality. These texts do not support such an interpretation.[8] Only the passage from Jude specifically identifies as sexual the reason for the destruction of Sodom and Gomorrah, and the Greek terms used there are ambiguous.[9]

In any case to interpret *unnatural lust* as equivalent to *all* forms of homosexual desire begs the question at hand. No one argues that homosexual (like heterosexual) people cannot be lustful, promiscuous, or rapists or that heterosexual people cannot experience what are for them unnatural lusts for persons of the same sex or engage in practices like the gang rape of persons of the same sex. The broader issue here is whether something is innately wrong with just, loving, and faithful unions of gay men and lesbian women. The story of Sodom and Gomorrah does not provide scriptural support for such a conclusion.

When one interprets this passage from Genesis without bias, it is evident that heterosexism finds no support in it. The story of Sodom and Gomorrah does not name and condemn homosexual behavior as sin. It does condemn sexual violence, as epitomized in gang rape. The parallels between the stories of Sodom and of Gibeah help to reveal this.[10] When we consider them together, the condemnation of sexual violence is mutually reinforced.

Other dimensions of the story that have been shamelessly

ignored by some traditional interpreters are also highlighted when the stories are compared. For example Lot's own cowardly effort to use his daughters as scapegoats is highlighted and gives an ironic twist to the tale. Heterosexist readings of this text allowed his brutal offer to let his children be gang raped slide into the background. This is so in part because of the connections between heterosexism and sexism (see chapter 4). Interpreting these stories together without a heterosexist bias can prevent the neglect of this pattern of violence against women.

Leviticus 18:22; 20:13

Two other passages from the Old Testament condemn male same-sex behavior itself and thereby appear to support heterosexism. Both are from the Holiness Code as outlined in Leviticus. The first is apodictic in form and identifies male same-sex behavior as self-evidently wrong: "You shall not lie with a male as with a woman; it is an abomination" (Lev 18:22). The second is a casuistic interpretation of the appropriate penalty for such action: "If a man lies with a male as with a woman, both of them have committed an abomination; they shall be put to death; their blood is upon them" (Lev 20:13).

These texts suggest to most interpreters that anal intercourse between males is the specific activity forbidden. Few clues surface as to the precise context for or nature of the male same-sex liaison. Some interpreters have argued that the practice referred to in these texts is actually idolatrous temple prostitution.[11] Much historical evidence can support this interpretation. Clearly ancient Israel wished through its Holiness Code to differentiate Yahweh from the gods worshipped in the fertility cults of its neighbors. Several intrabiblical texts verify the seriousness of this concern among the Hebrew people (Deut 23:17; 1 Kings 14:24; 15:12; 22:46).[12]

Although cult prostitution presents a probable context, nothing in the language of the two passages from Leviticus suggests that this represents the *only* form of male same-sex behavior so condemned. Even when one assumes such a context, three options remain. Male same-sex activity may have been condemned (1) solely because of its association with Canaanite cultic practices or (2) for moral reasons other than this association. The association of an immoral practice with idolaters would serve to discredit them. Some viewed the association as (3) bilaterally contaminating. This certainly fits the case of human sacrifice, which we judge *both* idolatrous *and* immoral.

Male same-sex activity clearly violated the purity code that distinguished ancient Israel from her neighbors. It resulted in cultic defilement. For us the crucial question is this: "Do such rules reflect the inspired conformity of the Holiness Code to the spiritual and moral Will of God, or do such texts meet the purity, economic, or political concerns of the people of Israel, which are culturally particular?" When divorced from its pagan cultic associations, does same-sex behavior continue to warrant condemnation on moral (rather than purity) grounds?

According to the Holiness Code, some forms of incest as well as intercourse between a husband and his menstruating wife violated Hebrew purity concerns and resulted in cultic defilement. The Hebrews judged both of these behaviors abominable and prescribed severe penalties for both. Presumably most Christians today would uphold and even expand the ancient prohibition of incest, and yet most would ignore the condemnation of genital activity between spouses during menstruation. On what grounds do we dispense with the latter but uphold the former prohibition?

The New Testament makes it clear that the purity requirements of the Torah do not bind Gentile converts. Yet the new covenant rarely dispenses with these regulations in a specific way. Paul is unusually explicit when he suggests that married couples should abstain from sexual activity only for prayer (1 Cor 7:5). Most purity concerns are not individually identified and dismissed. In general, what distinguishes Jew from Greek amounts to naught before the impartial grace of God incarnate in Christ. These laws are no longer selected on grounds of purity; communal identity and cultic differentiation have ceased to be primary concerns of selection.[13]

Often, advocates of certain moral judgments will raise their concerns in the context of the purity code in order to use the formative power of the code to reinforce their concerns. For example, moral judgments against child sacrifice (Lev 18:21), bestiality (Lev 18:23), or adultery (Lev 20:10) are reinforced when labeled defiling. On the other hand, the language of morality sometimes is applied to merely ritual concerns. Few would question the purely ceremonial nature of the instructions about clothing (Lev 19:19) or haircuts and beards (Lev 19:27) found in the Holiness Code. Thus to demonstrate that one ought not dispense with a particular portion of the purity code because of its moral import, one must identify independent sources of scriptural support for that concern. Purity agendas cannot influence such other sources of biblical corroboration. In Ezekiel 22 we find a list reminiscent of the Holiness Code (interestingly, same-sex activity is not mentioned). Ezekiel condemns incest and spousal intercourse during menstruation but this condemnation is not sufficiently independent of concerns about community identity and cultic differentiation to help us sort out moral matters from purity concerns. If the reason for their condemnation is only their impurity, such laws in Scripture ought not be upheld.

Some have proposed that we can distinguish truly moral matters from merely purity concerns by attending to the penalties attached to their violation. The hypothesis states that when a severe penalty follows from a violation, the regulation is moral in character. For example, because eating forbidden foods renders one unclean only until evening and having sex with one's spouse during menstruation renders one unclean for just seven days, these are obviously only purity concerns. On the other hand, because adultery, bestiality, incest, and male same-sex activity warrant the death penalty according to Levitical casuistry (Lev 20:10), they are obviously moral matters.

Though perhaps suggestive, this proposed criterion falls short. We would miss at least three moral concerns central to Leviticus if we relied on this technique. The regulations regarding the land as described in the proposals for a sabbatical year and the call for a year of jubilee (Lev 25) are moral concerns central to the code, but violation of them does not lead to severe penalties. The law of retaliation (*lex talionis* Lev 24:20) is also a matter of moral, not ceremonial concern, yet this criterion would not identify it as such. Finally the heart of the moral commandments found in the code—"You shall love your neighbor as yourself" (Lev 19:18b)—does not require any penalty if violated. One cannot distinguish moral concerns from purity matters on the basis of the penalties associated with them.

We propose that moral concerns will be (1) interpreted as such by Scripture itself and (2) based on sound reason. For example, the second Great Commandment is endorsed several times in the New Testament. In contrast the *lex talionis* is explicitly repudiated by Jesus.[14] Without biblical reaffirmation on explicitly moral grounds, one may reasonably label a concern purely ritual.

On the one hand, we ought to prohibit incest today not because it renders those involved defiled, although the power of such a taboo as a step in moral formation remains useful. Rather, we ought to uphold (and expand) biblical prohibitions against incest because it violates the unitive purposes for which sexuality was designed by God. Incest exploits its victims and includes violence; it is not a bond based on mutuality and equality. The Bible establishes that God designed human sexuality for such unitive purposes and that such

unions have as their prerequisite the mutual consent of equal partners (see below on Gen 2:18–25). On the other hand, no corroborative texts independent of purity codes exist to support condemnation of the conjugal act during menstruation. Thus Christians have
rightly ignored this warning as exemplified by St. Paul's remarks in 1
Cor 7:5.

In general, the purity regulations were aimed at fostering communal identity and cultic differentiation. The postexilic priestly
community devised them in a time of threatened social identity. The
Holy People needed to be sharply distinguished from all who were
unclean. There could be no room for ambivalence, ambiguity or gra-
dations. These regulations highlighted contrasts and obscured conti-
nuities. Anything out of its assigned place dirtied up the system and
consequently became an abomination.

What is at stake in the purity regulations governing sexual activities? David M. Gunn has argued that the purity system governing sexuality was designed to regulate and assure male dominion over and
control of men's seed.[15] Use of semen called for regulation because
they thought it carried exclusively the power of propagation, the
means of inheritance, and the power of familial continuity. The system clearly privileges men in regard to the disposition of their seed
and with regard to the ownership of women's genitals (their external
"nakedness"). Men who lie with one another renounce this dominion over women and the privileged control of male seed. According
to Gunn, this is why female same-sex activity is not mentioned—it
does not challenge a system that privileges male dominion over their
seed. It is also why no specific prohibition exists forbidding a father
from having sex with his daughter; it does not challenge male sexual
dominion.

This account of the patriarchal order behind the Levitical purity
rules governing sexual relations is intelligible and makes good sense
of what is missing from the list of taboos. Whether or not we can
consider this reading comprehensive will depend upon the compar-
ative strength of the case made to support the claim that these concerns are moral.

At least three New Testament texts seem to provide the condemnation of male same-sex activity raised in the Holiness Code
with independent (that is, non-purity-related) corroboration. They
are 1 Cor 6:9–11, 1 Tim 1:8–11, and Rom 1:18–32. Thus it appears
that Christians ought *not* dispense with this portion of the Torah.
We believe, however, that genuine moral corroboration for the heterosexist rules found in Leviticus does not exist in the first two of

these passages despite appearances to the contrary. Their meaning is unclear and they have been subject to frequent mistranslations.

1 Corinthians 6: 9–11

Word studies reveal that the two key Greek terms found in 1 Corinthians 6:9–11 are difficult to translate with certainty. Yet frequently they lie at the heart of debates about whether we can justify heterosexism. Neither retentionists nor abolitionists will profit by placing much weight on this text. Because of its ambiguity it will not prove decisive. "Do you not know that wrongdoers will not inherit the kingdom of God? Do not be deceived! Fornicators, idolaters, adulterers, male prostitutes [*malakoi*], sodomites [*arsenokoitai*], thieves, the greedy, drunkards, revilers, robbers—none of these will inherit the kingdom of God. And this is what some of you used to be. But you were washed, you were sanctified, you were justified in the name of the Lord Jesus Christ and in the Spirit of our God." In the 1611 King James Version these two Greek words were translated as "nor effeminate, nor abusers of themselves with mankind." In the 1946–1965 editions of the Revised Standard Version they were jointly translated "homosexuals."[16] In the 1971 edition of the Revised Standard Version they were jointly translated "sexual perverts." The Jerusalem Bible translates *malakoi* as "catamites" or call boys. We believe these more recent translations reflect a backlash generated by contemporary challenges to heterosexism. Careful word studies do not justify such translations.

Malakoi literally means "males who are soft." The word *arsenokoitai* combines "male" and "lying with or sleeping with." About this much there is considerable consensus. Some exegetes have moved from these literal translations to argue that taken together the terms probably refer to the passive recipient of and active partner in sodomy. This constitutes the basis for the heterosexist mistranslations just cited.[17] Yet nothing in the text or context necessitates that the terms be taken together. Therefore, others argue that *malakoi* refers to moral weakness in general, with no specific connection to sodomy. In 1522 Martin Luther translated this term *Weichlinge* or "weaklings." A modern linguist, like John Boswell, could well appreciate this translation. He notes that Philo, a first century contemporary of Paul, applied the term to a man who had remarried his former wife. It commonly designated any male whose behavior was less than respectable.[18]

The meaning of *arsenokoitai* is even more difficult to determine. *Koitai* clearly carries coarse, if not vulgar, coital connotations. For our debate the key issue is whether or not the prefix *arseno* designates as male the subject engaged in sexual intercourse *or* as male the object of this activity. Neither the Greek word itself nor its context resolves the question. This presents the modern exegete with at least four interpretative options.

If the prefix refers to the subject of such activity, then the term could be literally translated a male, "who by insertation takes the 'active' role in intercourse."[19] Paul could be referring to male prostitutes who sell themselves to wealthy women. Or Paul could be referring to male same-sex prostitution. If the term refers to the object of such activity, then the term could be literally translated "males who have sexual intercourse with males." In this case, those designated could include the "insertive" male customer of a "recipient" male prostitute, or the "active" male in a pederastic relationship, which may or may not involve prostitution. It may designate the boy molesters referred to by Martin Luther in his translation of the term as *Knabenschänder*.

The reputation of Corinth in the ancient world only complicates the translation difficulties. Historical studies indicate that this port city (like many of its contemporary counterparts) was well known as a human sexual meat market. Therefore the term may have nothing at all to do with same-sex activity. Then again it may refer only to very common, exploitive forms of same-sex activity such as pederasty or male prostitution. Or by coining this term (rather than using one of the many expressions for pederasty available to him) Paul could have been expressing a judgment against some other particular form of same-sex activity or against such activity in general. We simply do not and cannot know. Neither linguistic nor historical studies can verify which of the translation options is most accurate. Thus the passage cannot provide clear and convincing scriptural corroboration of the traditional claim that the concern raised in the Levitical passages is moral.

It follows from this that the text cannot be used to condemn loving and faithful gay unions as violations of God's Word. Nothing in it or in the context of the passage demands that it be translated as anything other than morally weak men, either men who have sexual intercourse or their partners. Those who translate these words as if they clearly referred to male same-sex activity actually beg the question of whether heterosexism has a sure biblical foundation.

The passage as a whole clearly warns against moral laxity in general, and libertine sexual practices in particular, a most suitable message, given the reputation of Corinth in antiquity. It remains an important word to us as well, given our cultural ethos. However, the text does not speak clearly to the question we pose: "Should we list just, faithful, and loving homosexual unions among activities judged vicious by God?"

1 Timothy 1:8–11

The same Greek term, *arsenokoitai*, appears in the Deutero-Pauline letter of 1 Timothy.[20] The usual translation is "sodomites," but other reasonable translations are possible. Therefore this passage does not provide those seeking corroboration for their "moral" reading of Leviticus with an unambiguous biblical foundation.

> Now we know that the law is good, if one uses it legitimately. This means understanding that the law is laid down not for the innocent but for the lawless and disobedient, for the godless and sinful, for the unholy and profane, for those who kill their father or mother, for murderers, fornicators, sodomites [*arsenokoitai*], slave traders, liars, perjurers, and whatever else is contrary to the sound teaching that conforms to the glorious gospel of the blessed God, which he entrusted to me.

One can reasonably assume that this term refers to male prostitutes or their customers. Such prostitution may have involved different- or same-sex or pederastic activity. Some have suggested as well that the term refers to young male legacy hunters who used same-sex attractions as sexual bait for their prey.[21] In any case, however helpful such word studies may be, they drive us to the conclusion that neither of these texts will prove ultimately decisive in the current moral debate. One overall purpose of this letter was to defend the fledgling church against false moral teachings. That the truth in moral matters requires defense provides the context for the passage we have just considered. Given the heterosexist tradition of interpretation that surrounds it, it is most ironic that the text does not clearly identify same-sex activity per se as subject to the judgment of the law. The text itself calls its interpreters to avoid misleading the community in moral matters. It commends caution and careful discernment, not premature judgments.

Where does this leave us? Clearly, the Hebrew people viewed

male same-sex activity as impure when it was associated with idolatrous temple prostitution and perhaps in general. In either case, the purity requirements of the Torah may be dispensed with by Christians unless they serve some *other* (that is, moral) purpose.

Scripture judges same-sex gang rape as immoral. It condemns male prostitution, whether those solicited are of the same or different sex. We believe it also condemns incest, pederasty, and all other forms of sexual violence, abuse, and exploitation, including the gang rape of women (although the misogyny behind the texts cited earlier weighs against such a conclusion). On the basis of these examples may one jump to the conclusion that Scripture would judge as immoral, not simply impure, all forms of same-sex activity? Such a conclusion rests on the assumption that biblical communities knew of and made negative judgments about just, loving, and faithful same-sex relationships. There is insufficient evidence to warrant drawing such a conclusion.

Romans 1:18–32

This text from Paul's Letter to the Romans reveals that traditional arguments for heterosexism are not just a product of biased translation (1 Cor 6:9–11 and 1 Tim 1:8–11) or poor exegesis (Gen 19:1–29). This passage indicates that Paul believed same-sex desires and activities were dishonorable and unnatural.

> For the wrath of God is revealed from heaven against all ungodliness and wickedness of those who by their wickedness suppress the truth. For what can be known about God is plain to them, because God has shown it to them. Ever since the creation of the world his eternal power and divine nature, invisible though they are, have been understood and seen through the things he has made. So they are without excuse; for though they knew God, they did not honor him as God or give thanks to him, but they became futile in their thinking, and their senseless minds were darkened. Claiming to be wise, they became fools; and they exchanged the glory of the immortal God for images resembling a mortal human being or birds or four footed animals or reptiles.
>
> Therefore God gave them up in the lusts of their hearts to impurity, to the degrading of their bodies among themselves, because they exchanged the truth about God for a lie and worshipped and served the creature rather than the Creator, who is blessed for ever! Amen.

For this reason God gave them up to degrading passions. Their women exchanged natural intercourse for unnatural, and in the same way also the men giving up natural intercourse with women, were consumed with passion for one another. Men committed shameless acts with men and received in their own persons the due penalty for their error.

And since they did not see fit to acknowledge God, God gave them up to a debased mind and to things that should not be done. They were filled with every kind of wickedness, evil, covetousness, malice. Full of envy, murder, strife, deceit, craftiness, they are gossips, slanderers, God-haters, insolent, haughty, boastful, inventors of evil, rebellious toward parents, foolish, faithless, heartless, ruthless. They know God's decree, that those who practice such things deserve to die—yet they not only do them but even applaud others who practice them.

For many Christians this settles the debate. It is one thing to dispense with food and dress codes or other purity regulations from the old covenant. When a moral judgment from either the Old or New Testament reinforces a portion of the Holiness Code it must always be upheld.

What it means to uphold such moral wisdom is not always obvious. The moral judgments of every biblical community have not always been upheld, at least not in a way that did not require their sometimes drastic reinterpretation in various contexts. Christians long ago recognized the need to interpret the meaning of biblical moral norms for their particular context. For example, although it dispensed with many purity regulations, the early Church at the Council of Jerusalem called upon Gentile converts not to eat strangled animals or the blood of meats (Acts 15:19).

Christianity long ago judged that the endorsement of dietary recommendations from the old covenant was historically particular to the primitive church, even though their clear (re)affirmation is found in the New Testament. The New Testament endorsement of a concern does not automatically confirm its underlying moral significance and enduring applicability. Mosaic laws, including the Ten Commandments, and even the moral judgment of a New Testament community (see earlier) should be judged binding for us not only because they are biblical but because they are specifications of God's natural law. Such a conclusion is compatible with Roman Catholic approaches to moral theology and with Reformation-era Lutheranism.[22]

Similarly modern democratic forms of government were resisted for centuries by many Christians, Catholic and Protestant alike. They were resisted on the ground that democratic revolutions violated the divine right of kings to govern, a political order for creation that could be discerned in Scripture. Biblical texts inclined the people of God toward monarchical or, at the very least, hierarchical forms of government. Today we do not view such biblical judgments as morally normative for our context. We do not believe that democracies violate the Creator's intention for our social order.

Paul's moral judgment as expressed in this passage from Romans does morally corroborate and expand to all lesbian and gay desires and activities the Levitical condemnation of same-sex behavior. We do not believe the generic condemnation of same-sex activity found in Romans 1:18–32 can be dispensed with as only a purity concern now irrelevant to Christians.[23] Nor can we narrowly retranslate it on the basis of word studies and other arguments regarding the historical context of the passage. Hence we do not believe its word of judgment is applicable only to particular forms of same-sex behavior.[24] Christians faithful to Scripture must struggle with the question of how to evaluate in light of this text the loving and faithful same-sex unions of constitutionally homosexual persons. How are we to interpret such a judgment in our context today?

Paul thought that there was something dishonorable about both male and female same-sex desires and something unnatural about same-sex behavior. In his judgment, same-sex desires and behaviors violated God's intention for human sexuality. They distort the created order. They are both symptomatic of and caused by sin; that is, by the idolatrous and deliberate rebellion of the Gentiles.

The main point of this passage is not to stigmatize sexual desires or behaviors of any sort, but to condemn idolatry.[25] Although Paul believes that there is something blatantly degrading about all same-sex desires and behaviors, his main point is that these are obviously symptomatic of and caused by idolatry. These same-sex desires and behaviors are for Paul evidence of, not the reason for, God's wrath. They are not behaviors that prompt God's wrath or abandonment. From Paul's point of view, when we distort God we become distorted as a result.

Relying on the assumptions of Hellenistic Judaism, Paul presupposed that all same-sex desires and behaviors among the Gentiles resulted from their insatiable lust for sexual variety, rooted ultimately in their idolatry. He had no concept analogous to the modern notion of a sexual orientation. Like all ancient peoples, although very aware of variation in sexual preferences, Paul had no word for being oriented toward persons of either the same or other sex. As a result, whether one is predisposed to abolishing or retaining hetero-sexism, one must determine on the basis of this scriptural passage how Paul might speak to our contemporary debate about the just, faithful, and loving unions of homosexual persons. The text simply does not speak to this issue.

On the one hand, we can project that Paul might regard our modern data about sexual orientations as sadly corroborative of his thesis about human promiscuity. He might see data regarding the widespread incidence and involuntary, innate character of a homo-sexual orientation as illustrative of his very point about the bondage typical of fallen humanity. On the other hand, he might regard such data as counterevidence that undermines his very presupposition about at least one type of same-sex desire and behavior, specifically about just, faithful, and loving homosexual relations.

Any effort to use this text in the debate about heterosexism requires that its interpreters make a projection about where Paul would stand on this issue. Advocates on both sides of the debate must bridge the gap between first and twentieth century under-standings of variations in sexual orientation. Neither side can be cer-tain of the validity of their proposed applications.

The theological meaning of this text is fairly clear. Paul's moral judgment on same-sex desires and behaviors is also fairly clear. But the meaning and relevance of that moral judgment to our assess-ment of homosexuality is not clear. We must ask: "How ought this text function in contemporary debates among Christians about het-erosexism? What normative relevance does this text have for our moral evaluation of just, loving, and faithful homosexual unions among those so oriented to each other?"

We offer the following interpretation. The heart of Paul's theo-logical anthropology remains authoritative. Although all human sex-ual passions are part of the blessed gifts of creation, they are also all disordered by the Fall. Concupiscence is a reality for both homosex-ual and heterosexual people. Without question some same-sex and some different-sex desires and behaviors bear witness to sin and merit God's wrath.

One can of course logically hold fast to the Pauline vision of God and the world just rehearsed without concluding that *all* same-sex desires and behaviors give testimony to sin and divine wrath. That moral judgment does not necessarily follow. In a radical sense all particular desires and behaviors can be lumped together and be seen as theologically sinful. From a moral point of view, however, it seems quite legitimate to distinguish faithful and loving relationships that are either (1) respectful and responsible or (2) exploitive, abusive, and violent. Such distinctions may be made whether or not the relationships are gay. Nothing in the spectral character of such judgments is incompatible with Paul's overarching anthropology.

Of course, what is logically possible may be theological nonsense on other grounds. Thus we must articulate the reasons for suggesting that Paul might conclude that some nonheterosexual unions can bear witness to grace and God's blessing. Given his ancient world-view Paul did not distinguish between a person's basic sexual orientation and particular variations in that individual's desires or behaviors. Given our modern understanding of sexual orientation, Christians today must project what Paul might conclude about those who are homosexually oriented. All who interpret this passage—whether they agree with us or not—must struggle with the problem of application.

Paul might well conclude that the Fall results in both the sexual disordering of desires and behaviors and in the sexual disorienting of some of us. However, were he a part of our world it is also possible, and we believe more theologically consistent, for Paul to conclude that, although sin has disordered everyone's sexuality, it has disoriented no one's. Paul would more likely reach this latter conclusion for a deeply theological reason.[26]

It expresses better his conviction that people are created good but born broken. Given his emphasis on the universality of God's gracious love, Paul could not abide the conclusion that any individuals at the center or core of their being were created abhorrent to God. Yet this is precisely what it would mean to conclude that a homosexual orientation is a manifestation of God's wrathful abandonment. Heterosexists must conclude that the very existence of such a person is not good.

This conclusion must follow for two reasons. First, an individual's sexual orientation is *central* to his or her personhood. In that sense it is quite different from many diseases and defects, which even if congenital are not constitutive of a person's identity. For example, we do not define people in terms of their diseases or defects. Although the impact of such challenges may be profound and pervasive, we talk, for example, about "people with Down's Syndrome"; we no longer label them mongoloids. People have diseases and defects; they are not those diseases or defects. In contrast people are either gay or straight or bisexual. They do not merely have homosexual or heterosexual desires with relative frequency.

Second, human sexual orientation is *pluriform* in character.

Homosexuality, for example, is not just the absence of heterosexual desires but the presence of desires for the same sex. To be gay is not just to be missing what it takes to be straight. Homosexual people are not "sexually retarded" heterosexual people. Their sexual drives are not diminished. They cannot be aptly described as merely falling short of an exclusively heterosexual mark. They are clearly and simply oriented elsewhere.

This creates a theological problem for heterosexists, who by definition describe homosexuality as a disorientation. Given what we now know about what it means to be gay, it is unclear in what sense heterosexists can describe the sexuality of gay, lesbian, and bisexual people as *created good* (but born broken). They find it easy to describe heterosexuality as created good but born disordered by lust. Heterosexism implies that insofar as homosexual people are disoriented sexually their very existence is not good. Given the centrality of sexuality to human personhood, it is not a giant step to the conclusion that the total existence of such persons is abhorrent to God. Heterosexism teaches that gay men, lesbians, and bisexuals are "sinners in a way that differs from everyone else," as one writer puts it.[27]

This is precisely the conclusion to which gay and lesbian Christians are drawn when the logic of heterosexism interacts with their experience of homosexuality. We presume that St. Paul would listen carefully to the experience of gay and lesbian Christians, just as he was attentive to the concerns of people struggling with questions of sexuality in mixed marriages (between believers and nonbelievers). Had he known what we know today about human sexual orientations, Paul might well argue as follows.

Any sexual orientation, whether heterosexual, homosexual, or somewhere between, is God's gracious gift through which persons can experience God's call of humankind into relationship with one another. It is the medium through which they may taste the joy of such communion. However, all of our particular desires and behaviors are inevitably disordered by sin and fall short of expressing God's original intentions and blessings for us. Desires and behaviors that run counter to one's natural, God-given orientation, whether gay or straight, are vividly expressive of the bondage of concupiscence.

Such an interpretation about the meaning and relevance of Paul's moral judgment for us today coheres with his convictions about the character of God's love for us all. It coheres with the experience many gay and lesbian Christians have of God's grace in their sexual lives. It also coheres with what we know scientifically about human sexuality.[28] Furthermore it is compatible with what little can be discerned about God's intentions from the beginning (as Jesus refers to it in Mt 19:4–6) for human sexuality. We now turn to the passages usually clustered around this topic.

TRADITIONAL TEXTS "FOR HETEROCENTRISM"

The proponents of heterosexism often argue that it is justified because God created human sexuality for procreative purposes.[29] Two passages from Genesis are usually cited in support of that claim. The first is the priestly creation account.

Genesis 1:27–28

"So God created humankind in his image, in the image of God he created them; male and female he created them. God blessed them, and God said to them, 'Be fruitful and multiply, and fill the earth and subdue it; and have dominion over the fish of the sea and over the birds of the air and over every living thing that moves upon the earth.'" In this creation story, human procreation is identified as a blessing and is linked to sexual differentiation.

The passage does not specify the exact nature of the link between sexual differentiation and the blessing of procreation. Nothing in it indicates that human beings were sexually differentiated solely or primarily for procreative purposes. It affirms procreation as a blessing, but does not clearly report it as a command of God. Common speculation making the latter judgment is compatible with this text but fidelity to the passage does not necessitate it. We can speculate that the priestly community would emphasize the link between procreation and sexual differentiation and praise it as a gracious gift from God, in part because of their particular context. During the Exile the very continuation of the people of the Covenant was threatened, and procreation would clearly serve the common good.

Those who wish to make procreation normative for sexuality—that is, an essential or primary purpose—sense the need for additional biblical warrants for their conclusion. Typically they turn to a second text in Genesis, the story of Onan, for such verification. The traditional connecting of these two texts distorts the biblical witness. They are not mutually illuminative. The burden of proof lies with those who would retain heterosexism, but biased misreadings of Scripture will not assist them in meeting this burden of proof.

Genesis 38:1-11

It happened at that time that Judah went down from his brothers and settled near a certain Adullamite whose name was Hirah. There Judah saw the daughter of a certain Canaanite whose name was Shua; he married her and went in to her. She conceived and bore a son; and he named him Er. Again she conceived and bore a son whom she called named Onan. Yet again she bore a son and she named him Shelah. She was in Chezib when she bore him. Judah took a wife for Er his first-born; her name was Tamar. But Er, Judah's first-born, was wicked in the sight of the Lord, and the Lord put him to death. Then Judah said to Onan, "Go in to your brother's wife and perform the duty of a brother-in-law to her; raise up offspring for your brother." But since Onan knew that the offspring would not be his he spilled his semen on the ground whenever he went in to his brother's wife, so that he would not give offspring to his brother. What he did was displeasing in the sight of the Lord, and he put him to death also. Then Judah said to his daughter-in-law Tamar, "Remain a widow in your father's house until my son Shelah grows up"—for he feared that he too would die, like his brothers. So Tamar went to live in her father's house.

The story of Onan has been used by some to defend the notion that procreativity is not just a blessing but a command of God. Such a reading of the text does not withstand careful scrutiny. This story is not about the immorality of coitus interruptus, an ancient and highly ineffective form of contraceptive or nonprocreative sexual activity. Such an interpretation and use of the text seriously violates the biblical witness.

This is a story about how wrong it was in ancient Israel not to facilitate the personal continuity of the deceased through the propagation of offspring. The Hebrew people believed that through heirs the deceased (and their ancestral family) in a sense would live on. Onan's refusal to impregnate Tamar may not only reflect his refusal to fulfill family duties but also his greed. It may have been a refusal to divert property that might otherwise be his inheritance to his brother's widow and heir. Onan's sin is treasonous to his brother's name and property. This text endorses the significance of fulfilling familial responsibilities, but contemporary Christians do not understand these to include a duty to propagate for the sake of personal continuity or for the purpose of creating a great estate, nation or church.

Although clearly claimed as a blessing and linked with sexual differentiation, procreation is not identified in Scripture as essential to or primary for morally normative expressions of human sexuality. No biblical basis exists for such a conclusion. Childlessness is viewed as a curse throughout the Hebrew Scriptures, but for reasons no longer of significance to Christians. In the New Testament the significance of procreation plummets because the promise of God is no longer linked to nation building. Jesus emphasizes the role of women as disciples, not mothers, and Paul focuses on the mutuality and fidelity (rather than the fecundity) of partners.[30] The biblical witness overall clearly affirms procreation as part of God's design yet does not unambiguously identify it as an essential purpose of human sexuality.

A contrasting school of thought in Genesis does make quite explicit the claim that humans were sexually differentiated by God for the sake of companionship and bonding. Heterosexists traditionally interpret this passage as supporting a theory of gender complementarity, as well as a theory about the unitive purpose of sexuality. Once again the meaning of the text has been twisted to conform to preconceived interpretations.

Genesis 2:18–25

> Then the Lord God said, "It is not good that the man should be alone; I will make him a helper as his partner." So out of the ground the Lord God formed every animal of the field and every bird of the air, and brought them to the man to see what he would call them, and whatever the man called every living creature, that was its name. The man gave names to all cattle, and to the birds of the air, and to every animal of the field; but for the man there was not found a helper as his partner. So the Lord God caused a deep sleep to fall upon the man, and he slept; then he took one of his ribs and closed up its place with flesh. And the rib that the Lord God had taken from the man he made into a woman and brought her to the man. Then the man said, "This at last is bone of my bones and flesh of my flesh; this one shall be called Woman for out of man this one was taken." Therefore a man leaves his father and his mother and clings to his wife and they become one flesh. And the man and his wife were both naked, and were not ashamed.

In this Yahwist creation account, human sexuality is described as designed by God for the expression and enhancement of human communion. Sexuality is about love and fidelity. Equality and mutuality should characterize such "one flesh" unions. Only then can we be naked and unashamed. Clearly this passage affirms heterosexual relationships of mutuality and equality. The question is whether or not it reveals the order of creation as exclusively heterosexual. For this to be true the text must reveal that God differentiated the sexes so that they might relationally complement one another. One cannot establish this on the basis of the text.

The passage as a whole overwhelmingly emphasizes the similarities of the human partners not their differences. They can become one flesh because they are alike—"bone of my bones"—not because they are different. They can cleave to one another because they are both human, not because theirs is a heterosexual coupling toward an androgynous wholeness. Such a one flesh union is not possible with other species; they are not fit companions.

The text makes it clear that humans were not made to live in isolation but in relationship. Other animals are unfit sexual mates for humans (cf. Lev 18:23; 20:15f.). Persons of a different sex are suitable partners in light of their differences but not because of them. The text does not speak directly to the question of whether or not persons of the same sex may find in their homosexual unions the companionship and mutuality for which their sexuality was created.

One cannot conclude from these texts that sexual desire was designed for essentially or primarily procreative purposes or for the sake of gender complementarity. Taken together, these three passages from Genesis teach us the following. God has designed human sexuality for human communion. The gift and promise of fidelity serve that love. Children are a blessing associated with heterosexuality. Recognizing this, one must also acknowledge that certain forms of both same- and different-sex behavior are condemned in Scripture (as we discussed earlier).

As Christians we must be faithful to the biblical witness about sexuality. Traditional interpreters of that testimony have concluded that the Bible reveals heterosexual relations as the uniform design of the Creator for genital expressions of love. Such a conclusion is not ruled out by the scriptural witness in a manner that is clear and convincing to all. But we have argued that this uniform conception of the sexual order of creation is not necessitated by the biblical witness. Furthermore, we proposed alternative interpretations of the passages key to the heterosexist tradition. We concluded that they were not only intelligible readings but in significant ways more faithful to the wider theological and literary contexts of these specific texts.

Some Christians charge that those who argue in favor of reforming Church teaching have been too eager to hear the obviously self-interested voices of gay and lesbian Christians and to give too much weight to scientific evidence. As a result they claim abolitionists have turned the scriptural testimony into a weak, nearly inaudible partner in the cacophony that ensues.[31] Our commitment to Scripture as a source of moral wisdom leads us to make the following counter-charge.

Many Christians do not cling to Scripture as their norming authority. They cling to certain heterosexist interpretations of the biblical witness. Those who wish to make a truly faithful case for the retention of present Church teachings regarding homosexuality must open themselves anew to the biblical testimony. They must not let the equally biased and powerful voice of traditional heterosexist interpretations of Scripture silence the biblical witness itself. All parties to the interpretative process must let Scripture speak God's Word afresh in our day to their preconceived, whether traditional or modern, notions. Like Peter, all must respond to God's word: "What God has made clean, you must not call profane" (Acts 10:15b).

That word may result in the preservation of traditional teachings. Or it may, as we have argued in this case, call for their reform. At the very least it is clear that no decisive case for heterosexism (or against homosexuality) can be found in Scripture. It would certainly not be unbiblical to abandon it. It is a position that does not have clear scriptural support.[32]

CONCLUSION

Proponents of a nonheterosexist evaluation of the biblical evidence do not view claims that human sexuality has been ordered by the Creator to serve the species through procreation or to foster human completion through gender complementarity as credible. Advocates of a nonheterosexist approach believe that we must affirm homosexuality as a part of God's original blessing for profoundly theological reasons. Given what we know about the centrality of sexuality to human personhood and about sexual orientation, to contend that homosexuality is an expression of the fallenness of the world entails the conclusion that God is against homosexual people in the very fabric of their existence as human beings. This can only reinforce unbelief among them. Such heterosexist reinforcement, not homosexual behavior, is the real evil in our midst.

4

The Costs of Heterosexism

When I was about 6 years old my father suddenly stopped holding my hand when we went shopping or walking together. I never understood why. At about the same time he stopped tucking me in at night and no longer gave me a good night kiss. I remember thinking that I must have done something wrong to make him stop loving me, but I was afraid to ask.

As a teenager I longed for my father's approval. When I came home from an event at school where I had done particularly well he would always slap me on the shoulder and tell me what a good job I had done. What I really wanted was a hug, maybe even a loving look in the eye. I never got either.

Many, many years later I understood why. I overheard him in a conversation he was having with my cousin, who had a young son: "You shouldn't be showing him affection like that anymore; he's too old for that!" My father proceeded to explain that if he did things like holding his son's hand or giving him a kiss he would "make him gay."

I doubt that my father's withholding affection made me straight instead of gay. Even if it did, the cost was much too high. He and I will never be able to recover the years of lost affection. All I ever wanted was to know that he loved me.

Fear is a primary inhibitor of dialogue about sexual orientation and behavior. Perhaps no other question is more important to ask in discussions of homosexuality and heterosexism than this: "What are we afraid of?" Unless we can be clear about our fears and the threats that give rise to them we will not overcome the barriers that divide men from men, women from women, and men and women from each other.

Heterosexism, like racism and sexism, will not be dismantled easily or quickly. Although we have established that we have good reasons to suspect heterosexist traditions (chapter 2) and determined that no biblical bases warrant retaining them (chapter 3), we must now delineate some of the consequences of our call for a reformation of Christian sexual ethics. One could argue that we should retain heterosexism for reasons other than the ones evaluated in the preceding chapters. For example, the costs associated with its abolition might far outweigh the benefits. So even if one cannot intrinsically justify heterosexism, a concern for the consequences of dismantling it may justify its retention. In this chapter we explore threats, imagined and real, generated by the invitation to treat homosexual and bisexual men and women as our sexual equals. By doing so we also point to the hidden costs of heterosexism. We conclude that none of the fears associated with reform justify heterosexism, while its costs clearly indicate the need to abolish it.

DISCERNING TRUE AND FALSE THREATS

A typical example of the kinds of fears linked with acceptance of homosexuality follows:

> No society, even one with a healthy birthrate, can allow itself to indulge for long in the illusion that homosexual relationships are as valid, normal and natural as heterosexual relationships, or that they are an acceptable alternative to marriage.
>   . . . It would tend to undermine the family structure further . . . so destabilizing society and weakening its ability to renew itself from generation to generation. It would encourage confusion of sexual identity among the young and those vulnerable for psychological and social reasons.[1]

The perceived threats named here, although capable of inducing real fear, cannot withstand careful scrutiny: (1) undermining the family; (2) destabilizing society; (3) weakening procreativity; (4) confusing youth; and (5) preying on the vulnerable. They are imaginary consequences created by an unexamined heterosexist bias.

The professional literature produced by heterosexual as well as gay and lesbian scholars in recent decades has exposed the fallacies in such assertions.[2] It has also provided a wealth of new data that enriches dialogue about these issues (family, youth, procreation, etc.). Unfortunately the perceived threats persist, blocking both Church and society from a broader and fuller vision of human sexuality. They inhibit us from incorporating in Christian theology the good and fruitful insights of the human sciences. Although they are the consequence of heterosexism, these threats simultaneously serve to foster it.

Undermining the Family

The fear that social acceptance or support of gay and lesbian relationships will destroy the family rests on specific assumptions about what constitutes a human family. Most people recognize that such assumptions vary from culture to culture. Within a given culture, however, relatively stable patterns of human relationships enable us to discern how the people within it understand and structure family life.

The traditional definitions of a nuclear family (wife, husband, children) and an extended family (wife, husband, children, brothers, sisters, aunts, uncles, grandparents, etc.), although still used, no longer describe adequately the breadth of contemporary North American cultural experience. Single-parent families, blended families, domestic partners, POSSLQs (the U.S. Census Bureau's acronym for "persons of the opposite sex sharing living quarters"), and multiple-family households indicate the rich variety of family structures that are both prevalent and widely accepted. Traditional versions of the nuclear family, where the father works outside the home and the mother does domestic chores and rears the children, constitute only 7–9 percent of all families currently and did not really emerge until the rise of modern industrial societies.

For many people this variety poses a problem because they believe it threatens the rearing of children, which they define as the primary task of family units. How will the next generation be affected by this bewildering array of family structures? Children need parents, at least a mother and a father—so the argument goes. Only in such an ideal setting can a child be exposed to the traditional models of gender identity necessary for healthy maturation. Recent efforts on the part of the gay community and its advocates to legalize at least some expressions of homosexuality are perceived as threats to this ideal. In his pastoral letter on homosexuality, San Francisco Archbishop John Quinn writes: "A normalization of homosexuality could too easily foster and make more public homosexual behavior with the result of eroding the meaning of family. Both from the religious point of view as well as for the good of society itself, marriage and the family are realities that must be protected."[3] Such statements feed into our culture's deep-seated fears of gay people, at best give birth to legislative proposals like the Family Protection Act, and at worst provoke gay bashing.[4]

What is at stake in this debate? For heterosexists three related issues lie behind the perceived threat to the family that gay and lesbian couples present: (1) the loving relationship of a child-free gay or lesbian couple challenges the notion that only the rearing of children can create a caring, loving, hospitable home; (2) the loving relationship of a gay or lesbian couple if successful in providing parenting challenges the already fragile role of father and mother for heterosexual couples; and (3) the loving relationship of a gay or lesbian couple challenges definitions of adequate parenting.

Evidence from heterosexual relationships helps to answer the first concern. A marriage without children challenges the notion that people can create a hospitable home only when the selfless love required by child rearing schools them in such love. Obviously, some child-free heterosexual couples are selfish and inhospitable. Similarly, child-free gay or lesbian couples can manifest a comparable mix of loving, hospitable households and self-centered, inhospitable ones. Nothing in the same-sex facets of the relationship guarantees success or failure in this regard, just as nothing in the heterosexual facets of male-female couples does. Given the present evidence of child abuse, to presume that the mere presence of children will school people in selfless love is both naive and dangerous.

The second, more subtle concern arises as part of the complex issue of gender roles and the diverse views about them in different ethnic communities. Because we are confused about what it means to be a father or mother in contemporary culture, the addition of gay and lesbian couples to this mix seems to heterosexists to make a bad situation worse. The issue may be whether the present confusion is in fact bad. The experiences gay and lesbian parents provide may clarify rather than confuse the transitional state in which the family finds itself. We suggest that this new witness will challenge the fragility of the traditional, ideal roles of mothering and fathering, yes, but ultimately it will also enrich them.

The third concern of heterosexism is this: "Can two gay men or two lesbian women, committed to one another and to the nurturing of their family, rear children responsibly and healthily?" No evidence (1) suggests that they cannot be responsible, or (2) supports the view that children will become gay or lesbian simply because they have two homosexual men or women as parents. In spite of the lack of consensus regarding the exact causes of homosexuality or heterosexuality, we do know that there appears to be little correlation between the sexual orientations of nurturing parents and their children.

Heterosexual, homosexual, and bisexual men and women are equally capable of being responsible participants in society. No significant data exists to suggest that they cannot all be loving parents and loving members of families.[5] On the other hand, it is equally true that all people are capable of destructive behaviors and unhealthy relationships. The family is not threatened by responsible sexual behavior that expresses authenticity and integrity. Gender identity does not depend on having two parents of different sexes. Gender confusion, whatever its causes or duration, may threaten stereotypical gender roles but does not threaten the development of family.

Even when the nuclear family of one father, one mother, and children constitutes the ideal norm in a culture, people recognize the adequacy and legitimacy of some alternatives. When a spouse dies, for example, many may lament the fact that the surviving spouse has been left alone with all the children. Yet no one questions the validity of the surviving spouse rearing those children. Whether the household consists of all men (a surviving father and sons) or all women (a surviving mother and daughters) or a mixture is irrelevant to the social acceptance of a different, but legitimate alternative for what it now means to be a family. Of course a nagging concern to some people is whether the children will "turn out as good" as they might have if both parents were living. In other words, the "alternativeness" of all this tragic reality simply indicates how it compromises the ideal. The mere fact of this secondary character, therefore, reinforces heterosexist bias about the similarly less than ideal character of same-sex parent families.

The variety of family settings that nurture children and the sometimes unpredictable results—well-adjusted children coming from "broken" homes, incorrigible children coming from stable and loving environments—make us aware of the difficulty raised by the facile assumption that any single pattern suffices for nurturing children. We agree that people must make *informed* judgments about what constitutes healthy or even ideal environments. The heterosexist, however, must defend the bias that says only a man and a woman united as husband and wife can properly rear children. They must also not conclude on the basis of admittedly disturbing data about the negative impact of broken homes on children, that differently constituted families will result in similarly negative consequences for children.

Even if the environment profoundly influences the social construction of one's sexual identity, "becoming gay or lesbian" is a problem only in a heterosexist culture that denies the validity or normalcy of homosexual identity. Only when people view homosexuality as a defect or something that needs to be fixed does one get concerned about a person's gay, lesbian, or bisexual identity. Throughout this book we argue that such a view is unnecessary and unhelpful.

We have the common task, of course, of shaping a society that honors all its members and encourages and nurtures relationships that foster such honoring. When we set ourselves to this task in our personal day-to-day living we build up the community. This is not pious, wishful thinking, but rather the commonsense recognition present in even the simplest observation of how life works.

We find irony in the accusation that accepting or nurturing homosexuality would undermine the family, because heterosexism and homophobia already undermine the family. Many bisexual and homosexual children fail to develop close ties with their parents or siblings because they fear rejection. How can we measure the cost of the pain and alienation that result from parents ostracizing their own children when they find out that they have a gay son or lesbian daughter? How can we measure the cost of marriages between men and women entered into for the sake of protecting one's gay or lesbian identity? Our sons and daughters, our brothers and sisters, our aunts and uncles and cousins become the gay and lesbian outcasts. Heterosexism destroys families.

Destabilizing Society

Practically all political philosophies, except perhaps libertarianism, concede that a society must exercise some control over some of the impulses and inclinations of its individual members for the sake of the common good. If the benefits of such controls outweigh the harms that accompany them, they are usually justified. If homosexual and bisexual relations undermine the values crucial to the welfare of society they might justly be suppressed. In other words, if one could demonstrate that homosexuality destabilizes society (as might be said of chemical dependency), heterosexism would find significant support in this supposed consequence. Although such a charge is frequently made, little substantial evidence is ever mounted to support it.

The charge is rooted in two interrelated fears. First, if pluriform family structures were adopted the larger society would be threatened. This view perceives only one form of the basic family or household unit as adequately providing a foundation for building broader social structures. Second, gender confusion will undermine the capacity of men and women to function. Although many critics are quick to point to contemporary social ills as a consequence of the breakdown of the nuclear, especially traditional, family, there is no compelling evidence to sustain the forging of such links. One can just as easily muster evidence that urbanization, industrialization, capitalism, mass media, or some combination of these have produced the social ills that beset us.

In this view gender roles are often, though not necessarily, restrictive. Only men, for example, should be construction workers. Only women should be nurses. Violating the expected gender roles contributes to an unstable society by rendering people incapable of predictable behaviors. We acknowledge that changing gender roles creates a feeling of instability and that gay and lesbian relations challenge gender stereotypes. All transitions render life momentarily unstable; all social reform movements are in that sense destabilizing. The gradual dismantling of sexism and racism provides ample evidence of this.

It takes time to break down stereotypes and integrate new ways of thinking and acting within a culture, but reformers believe these changes will strengthen social order. Analogously, when a new member enters a family it takes time for the patterns of relationship to change sufficiently to incorporate the person fully. We know the difficulties such integration presents on the small scale of family life in a single household, but we judge the process to be one of growth not decay. When the tasks involve many people and whole societies the complexity seems overwhelming.

Heterosexism, like racism and sexism, creates deep resentments and frustrations that eventually erupt with destructive destabilizing consequences. Even apart from such critical moments of violent outburst, the energy required to keep sexuality inappropriately repressed and render gay and lesbian people invisible tears the fabric of communities. The dishonesty, secretiveness, manipulation, hatred, and ostracism fostered by heterosexism undermine the development of healthy social interaction. Most important, they hinder the ability of people—heterosexuals, bisexuals, and homosexuals alike—to address together the questions of how to develop sexual behaviors that honor and respect each person's sexual identity while contributing to the well-being of the larger society.

One can draw from a variety of intriguing historical examples to make the case that society is stabilized by the full participation of members who are considered a threat at one level, yet are needed at another. In World War II Americans experienced women expanding traditional gender roles to work in positions abandoned by men who had gone to war. "Rosie the Riveter" became a symbol of women's ability to function fully and well in roles that had formerly been assumed to be for men only. Unfortunately, when the war ended and men returned looking for their old jobs, women were again relegated to restricted participation in the workplace.

Such instances in our own history make clear how flexible and productive we can be when we allow ourselves to step outside the prejudices that bind us. Homosexual men and women are already contributors to the stability of society insofar as they are our companions in the workplace, in the arts, in all fields of endeavor. They may be closeted. We may close our eyes to their presence. But they are clearly there as faithful, steady workers and friends. Without them our culture would be diminished and our social structures less stable.

Opening the doors to their closets has the potential to strengthen the commitments and the participation of gay and lesbian people in our culture. The energy presently expended to protect a secret identity would be more usefully and positively invested in using the gifts they, like every heterosexual person, possess. Again, the analogy with racism and sexism is apparent. Some people feel threatened by the possibility that women or people of color will claim a full and equal place in the world. When the blinders of our prejudices are removed, we see instead that the lives of all can be enriched by the unhindered exercise of such freedom (see chapter 7 for a more detailed discussion of issues related to sexual authenticity).

Weakening Procreativity

It is difficult to give any credence to this perceived threat. Heterosexists argue that if the union of gay and lesbian couples is legitimated, heterosexual mating will decrease. To fail to provide heirs and perpetuate the race is to betray the whole social system. In her novel, *The Handmaiden's Tale*, Margaret Atwood rightly surmises that in a strictly patriarchal world homosexuals would be criminals whose insult to their gender roles and the holy purposes of sexual differentiation warrants death.

If people are allowed, even encouraged to fall in love with members of the same sex, no one will want to have children. Such reasoning presumes that childbearing and child rearing are onerous duties.

Additionally it presumes that the heterosexual population would either (1) cease having sexual interest in each other or (2) cease the desire to procreate because same-sex partnerships were nurtured. This assumes that a heterosexual person's orientation can be changed and that interest in procreation is incompatible with same-sex relationships.

We live in a time when the birthrate of almost all nations and ethnic groups is unhealthy, so that our modern problem is overpopulation not the threat of extinction of the species. We need to take seriously such historical and cultural circumstances. If we lived in a time and place where the birthrate was dangerously low, we might indeed have moral grounds for encouraging procreation. Even then it is doubtful that prohibiting homosexual relationships would need to be the means for such encouragement. If the entire population were homosexual in orientation and behavior, nothing would prohibit men and women from producing children through new reproductive technologies. It truly stretches the imagination to the breaking point to propose that the abolition of heterosexism might endanger the survival of the species.

Confusing Youth

Some assume that because homosexual people cannot have children they will recruit children to become homosexual. In addition, children will be confused about whether they are or ought to be heterosexual, homosexual, or bisexual if they are aware of these options through positive role models. We have already discussed the fallacious reasoning regarding sexual orientation that lies behind such views. But there is more to the issue. As one writer put it, "it is inescapable: sanctioning homosexual lifestyles will affect the way the young perceive adult society, and it will have an effect on the kind of people they grow up to be."[6] The irony of this comment is that, taken out of its heterosexist context, it is both accurate and helpful.

Sanctioning homosexual lifestyles will indeed reveal something about adult society. Like sanctioning integration or sanctioning the full participation of women in society, it will reveal that we are capable of recognizing and overcoming prejudices that rob us of much of the richness of life. The young will perceive that their culture need not be heterosexist. They will perceive that responsible sexual behavior is determined by love, justice, and commitment not by prohibition and control.

The effect it will have on the kind of people they grow up to be can be profound indeed. They may be less prejudiced than those who have gone before them. Perhaps they will abandon bigotry. They may grow up to be people who know how to celebrate and not simply tolerate diversity. They may even see more clearly than their parents that sexuality, love, friendship, and marriage are good gifts of God that cannot be reduced to commands.

Because there is no agreed upon etiology for either homosexuality or heterosexuality, we must take seriously this concern about creating confusion in the formation of sexual identity. To take it seriously, however, means acknowledging the inevitable sexual ambiguity that occurs for every adolescent human being. Only in a heterosexist context does it mean hiding from the reality of same-sex affections and from the possibility of a homosexual identity.

Another of the uncounted costs of heterosexism is that gay and lesbian adults are inhibited (and sometimes prohibited) from being healthy role models and counselors for gay youth. Openly gay and lesbian schoolteachers are almost always fired from their jobs. Gays and lesbians are not trusted to lead youth groups or provide support to young people for fear that they will influence the young to become gay.

The loss for Church and society is tragic. Talented, creative people who are gay cannot exercise their gifts to build up the community exactly where the community needs them most. In some respects gay and lesbian people no longer need the Church. It has, after all, continuously condemned and rejected them; and who needs that? The real issue is that the Church truly needs them. Perhaps no one needs them more than youth who are struggling to discover their sexual identity. Healthy sexuality is nourished by honest answers to honest questions about what it means to be sexual human beings.

Preying on the Vulnerable

Children are at the heart of this fear as well. They are among the most vulnerable in any society. The potential abuse of children poses a significant threat in any community. In this case those who would oppose abolishing heterosexism charge that advocacy for the gay community will lead inevitably to a slippery slope on which no case could be made against pedophilia. Some describe reformers as having no way to advocate reform when confronted with the existence of sexual abuse of children. "One wonders how those calling us to be more receptive to homoeroticism would explain the church is not to be inclusive of 'boy love'?"[7] Neither logical nor factual grounds can justify this outrageous claim.

Logically, the affirmation of the goodness of heterosexuality does not entail the approval of *all* forms of heterosexual behavior. Likewise, the affirmation of the goodness of homosexuality does not entail the approval of all forms of homosexual behavior. Experientially, all of the evidence points to the fact that most sexual abuse of children is perpetrated by heterosexual men. Being a gay adult male, just like being a heterosexual adult male, does not mean that one is a pedophile. They are completely separate issues.

To be oriented primarily to a member of the same sex or to a member of the other sex has nothing to do with how one responds to children.[8] "Pederasts (men who are erotically attracted to young boys) are not necessarily exclusively or primarily homosexual. . . . Sometimes they are just as sexually attracted to young girls, and thus might more accurately be termed pedophiliacs (adults who desire children)."[9] Heterosexism does little to protect children. Indeed by mistargeting much of our concern about the dangers of sexual misconduct onto the just, faithful, and loving unions of gay men and lesbians, it leaves our children more vulnerable to all those who would prey on them.

All societies must be concerned for those in their midst who are vulnerable. Clearly children will be numbered among those who are not strong enough to protect themselves. Making homosexuality an open and public reality may help to highlight the concern, but it will not solve the problem. After all, heterosexuality is open and public, yet that fact alone does not protect children from abuse at the hands of heterosexual men and women. What will protect our children is open and healthy understanding and discussion of human sexuality in all its facets.

Sexism

Dismantling heterosexism does pose a real threat to some of the inherited ways in which we have treated matters of sexual ethics and accepted uncritically the biases of a heterocentric culture. We believe that what is threatened in this regard ought to be threatened. We should not shrink from naming evil as evil. For example, challenging heterosexism will include continuing the battle against sexism.

To my knowledge only once in my life was I ever labeled *lesbian*. My undergraduate roommate was dating a law student. They had a rocky, stormy relationship, and she had decided not to see him anymore. Her decision stemmed in part from the pressure he was putting on her to engage in genital activity.

When his phone call came, I was surprised. He asked me to go for a cup of coffee. Once settled in he began to inquire about my affection for and friendship with Kim. He pursued this line of questioning and I finally realized that he thought there was something wrong. To be truthful, I thought he was accusing me of betraying or being disloyal to her. Of course that was not his point. Finally he simply blurted out: "even though you are lesbian, if you really cared for Kimberly, you would let her go." I was absolutely stunned. Speechless, I left and walked back to the dorm.

I was quite settled with my sexual identity. I did indeed love Kim as I had loved no other, but I had no erotic desires for her. I decided to ask Kim what she thought was going on with him. I can still hear her laughing. His line of "reasoning" was clear: women who identify with each other and who are sexually noncompliant with men must be lesbian. Who else would so challenge the male role?

Suzanne Pharr reports that labeling "noncompliant" women *lesbians* is a common ploy in our society.[10] This baiting is designed to keep under control women who are resistant to male dominance. Battered women, she explains, talk frequently about how they are called *lesbians* by those who beat them. She sees this as interconnected with charges made by a constellation of conservative organizations against the National Coalition Against Domestic Violence. These groups accused the coalition of being "prolesbian" and "antifamily."

Such labeling tactics are designed to hold women in line and to isolate and alienate them from one another. Fear of such a designation is one of the several factors that contributes to male domination. This same fear also buries information about alternatives to patriarchal relations. It hides the stories of women who have not collaborated with patriarchy. Lesbians have rejected the dependence on men ascribed to them by patriarchy. Patriarchy demands that history of their independent survival be erased and that lesbians be driven underground.[11]

Lesbians do threaten social orders built on male dominance and control. But the prospect of a man forfeiting his proper place in the pattern most terrifies heterosexists. According to Pharr's analysis, gay men are perceived as breaking rank and therefore endangering the fabric as a whole. Because their refusal to be "men" (as defined by patriarchy) threatens to unravel the whole system, they are attacked with a vengeance.

The sexist slant to heterosexism is not new. Women counted for so little that even their "sexual sins" were not worth attention; hence the lack of concern for lesbianism in history. Rosemary Haughton comments on this phenomenon with a touch of sarcasm: "Moralists (male, of course) were divided on whether sexual relations between women were even possible; they argued learnedly about whether sexual "sin" between women could occur, given that the poor things lacked the essential appendage for intercourse (as they understood it) to take place."[12]

In turn heterosexism reinforces sexism in a variety of ways. Perhaps the most pervasive is in role expectations. Dismantling heterosexism poses a threat to gender stereotyped roles in marriage, family, and society. The following comment by one of the partners in a lesbian marriage highlights the issue: "Treating T.R. and me as 'husband and wife' is not helpful. Those roles are archaic and we reject them completely. We are equal partners of the same sex. We are two people who together are one new thing. We are not the roles of husband and wife and do not wish to be treated as such. When a waitress hands me the check because I'm more butch ('the husband') I hand it to T.R. because she pays the bills and earns the money at the moment." New patterns of partnership developed in same-sex relationships will inevitably influence how heterosexual partners see themselves. Different models for shared responsibility and equality can enhance both. The influence will not be unidirectional.

Our tendency to be rigid in our interpretations of roles will be challenged in general. An interesting example from our media-conscious culture of this tendency to fix our images in one form was the initial reaction to the TV series, "Star Trek: The Next Generation." In interviews and public appearances the new stars were asked repeatedly, "Which one are you? Which of the original show's characters are you?" After the new series had established its own integrity and demonstrated the vitality of its new roles, the questions stopped. The characters were allowed to be themselves.

Our heterosexist success in rendering same-sex couples culturally invisible hinders the ability of gays and lesbians to demonstrate publicly the integrity and vitality of their lives. What are heterosexists afraid will be uncovered? They fear losing the traditional, and therefore controllable, roles of husband and wife. The gender definition of those roles in marriage has already undergone significant revision and many are reluctant to see them challenged further.

The theory of gender complementarity is threatened when we assert that sexual identity can find fulfillment or completion with persons of the same sex just as well as with persons of the other sex. Male-female complementarity, as if two unfinished halves must come together to create a genuine whole, is not the source of the human desire to be in relationship. The fact that two people in relationship are women does not diminish the reality of their being two different women. They can complement each other as well as a man and a woman can.

What is worth preserving in the concept of complementarity is more than the notion of a "fit" based on the *differences* between persons. It is a fit based on common abilities and similarities as well. The abolition of heterosexism challenges understandings like this one expressed by Gilbert Meilaender: "Homosexual acts are forbidden precisely because lover and beloved are, biologically, not sufficiently other. The relation approaches too closely the forbidden love of self."[13] We need not pit love and self-love against each other. To view them as part of each other is especially healthy for women in patriarchal societies in which many women may come to love for self only by identifying with women who love other women.

The subordination and abuse of women provides the clearest example of heterosexism's link with sexism. The most virulent attacks on homosexual men historically have been justified by the argument that those who act like women (that is, the male partner who is "passive") are relegated to the same inferior status that women hold and therefore can be treated (abusively) like women. Such links among power, subordination, domination, and sexuality are strong and complex but not unbreakable. When sexual expression is freed from efforts to control another person it can serve the mutuality of human relationship. Sexual intimacy alone does not create relationships. As a function of the desire for human bonding it is not an end in itself.[14]

In North American culture, however, in both gay and straight communities the objectification of sexual intimacy constantly reinforces seeing and using it as an end in itself. The destructive consequences of this become evident in the near epidemic abuse of women and the spread of sexually transmitted diseases, to name the most obvious. Although heterocentrism and its link with patriarchy are not alone responsible for such dilemmas, we believe that an unreformed heterosexist world-view has not been capable of addressing such concerns. The fundamental reason for this is its inability to take diversity and mutuality seriously.

Because sexism and heterosexism are so intimately linked we cannot dismantle one without attention to dismantling the other. Feminists and gay rights activists have not always been willing to recognize and act on this common concern.[15] It is not helpful to suggest that heterosexism is a mere consequence of sexism or vice versa. Each demands our full attention. Such attention must include exploring, for example, the connections among dualism, hierarchy, individualism, violence, and exploitation. This kind of multifaceted analysis is crucial because the context of the prevailing heterosexist paradigm helps to weave an interlocking web among them. This interweaving strengthens each beyond its power alone to distort human sexuality. The task of reform is formidable and has barely begun.

CHALLENGING CHRISTIAN PREOCCUPATIONS

We seem to fear most in the Church that abolishing heterosexism would result in a moral relativism that would undermine responsible sexual expression. This fear is without historical foundation. There is no empirical evidence to substantiate it. Because same-sex relationships have never been afforded the full range of sexual expression as different-sex relationships, we simply do not know (nor can anyone else) what would happen if the Church taught and practiced a nonheterocentric sexual ethic. We cannot offer a detailed analysis of what does not yet exist. Fear of the unknown is healthy if it does not prove immobilizing. An exploration of uncharted territory ought to be prudent. The questions we are about to pose serve as guides to the exploration we commend.

Raising Questions

Christian teaching has always affirmed that we can discern right from wrong, good doctrine from bad doctrine, constructive behavior from destructive behavior. Christians have indeed wisely taught that we cannot survive in a community where individual desire is the only criterion for appropriate behavior. Even if our actions never impinged on the lives of others this criterion would not be adequate because pursuing individual desire can be self-destructive. The historical wisdom of Christianity claims that certain things in life are sinful and must be clearly named as such.

Support for the judgment that the continuing condemnation of homosexuality is rightly characteristic of Christian teaching is partly, if not primarily, a consequence of biblical interpretation. In chapter 3 we established that there is no biblical basis for continuing to view heterosexism as engendering a faithful expression of Christian life and teaching. Is it possible that sustaining heterosexism in fact engenders the opposite?

Celebrating the legitimacy of homosexuality calls the Church to make some kind of public affirmation of same-sex relating. People fear that celebration, because of its publicly affirming character, moves a community from tolerance or acceptance to encouragement and advocacy. This is a real fear, but in this case it is not connected to any demonstrable threat. Weddings are public celebrations as are ordinations. It is not surprising, therefore, that these two rituals attract attention as people call for both to be open to gays and lesbians with only those preconditions also applicable to heterosexual men and women.

We discuss ordination and marriage in detail in chapters 5 and 6. At this point we simply want to acknowledge that people correctly perceive a connection between public ritual events and the symbolic messages they convey. If we celebrate the marriages of gay and lesbian couples we do symbolize our support for the same-sex relationship that defines them. In particular, we redefine the links between genders and the roles of the partners in the marriage. Traditional ascriptions of gender-based tasks to men and women are obliterated when a person of one sex must assume the role assigned to the other. The question is why this is perceived as threat rather than opportunity for growth and enrichment in Church and society.

Similarly, if we ordain "avowed practicing homosexuals" we acknowledge that their lifestyle can be consistent with Christian tradition and an appropriate model for holiness of life. In part a tension between private and public morality lies behind the reluctance of many to make this move. We may expect the whole community to abide by the ethical norms it establishes, but we acknowledge that in private—"where it doesn't hurt anyone else"—some may not live up to the norm. We expect those in highly visible leadership roles in the community, on the other hand, to exemplify the norms and by doing so to model holiness of life. Why do we perceive that ordaining qualified gay men and lesbians is a threat to rather than an opportunity for modeling holiness?

In each case the public celebration makes visible the lifestyle of the person whose "sin" is thereby made manifest. Churches have tended historically to make such sinners outcasts (through excommunication), particularly with regard to Eucharistic fellowship. Often it is not the specific sexual sins of the gay or lesbian person that are called into question but rather the fact of being a homosexual person. When the Church celebrates the presence of gay and lesbian people in its midst in the same ways in which it celebrates the presence of heterosexual persons it will have taken one step toward embracing the full reality of the human condition. Doing so does not compromise the need to identify sexual sin. Are our moral life and teaching truly threatened by openness to the gay and lesbian people who are already full, though closeted, members of our churches?

Most of our fears are generated by the belief that Christian teaching can accept only a heterocentric norm for understanding human sexuality. If that norm is threatened by any alternative, traditional Christian sexual ethics are threatened. This argument is substantive only if one accepts heterocentrism as an unreformable uniform paradigm for human sexuality. Homosexuality is not an "alternative lifestyle." It is, like heterosexuality, one expression of human sexual vocation.

Describing how and why specific sexual activity constitutes ethical or unethical behavior is one step we can take to dismantle heterosexism's grip on our culture. The Church's opportunity in such an effort is to be appropriately critical of its own role in promulgating a monolithic, heterocentric view of creation. Can the Church embrace such reform without threatening its identity?

One of the strongest psychological inhibitors of change is the fear that the past is thereby rejected. If I change what I have been doing because I learn that it is destructive or unjust, it implies that I am morally culpable, at the least, for not recognizing my error sooner. I must cut myself off from my past. Thus Christians say to themselves: "How can we have been wrong all these years? If we accept homosexuality we will be repudiating our own past."

One establishes reform precisely on the basis of one's inheritance. In this book we invite the Church to review its past in light of the gospel. Many Christians fear that any loosening of heterosexism's grip on sexuality, especially regarding the condemnation of homosexual behavior, threatens the authority of the Bible. This in turn threatens faith and life in the Christian community. As we argued in chapter 3, such fear is based on a biased reading of the few scriptural texts that seem to speak directly to the issue of same-sex activity. When we read these texts without heterocentric lenses, they are freed to teach us rather than being the means by which we justify our prejudices. Dismantling heterosexism does not threaten biblical authority. A real cost of heterosexism in the Church is that it masks how we fail to take the Bible seriously. We close this chapter by exploring how adopting a nonheterosexist paradigm for sexual ethics presents a real threat to the ways in which the Church sustains prejudice through misuse of the Bible.

Interpreting Texts

In a conversation that indicated we were at odds about the meaning of St. Paul's comment in Romans 1 on sexuality, I stated to the other person that we were interpreting Paul's comments and context differently. At this point he became even colder and more stern than he had been and said, "I don't interpret the Bible." His point, of course, was that he took the Bible literally whereas I, as one who interpreted it, was imposing my own meanings on it. Needless to say, the conversation was able to go no further.

Such inability to engage in faithful dialogue is rooted in a biblicism that is both evil and false. It is impossible not to interpret the Bible. Anyone who makes a claim like that of the person in the vignette does so either in arrogance or ignorance. This judgment may sound harsh, but it is absolutely necessary for Christians to make it. The Bible cannot function as the living Word of God and it cannot serve as the source of reform if Christians do not take it seriously. Biblicists like the person in the vignette who claimed not to interpret the Bible, no matter what their denominational affiliation or theological persuasion, do not take Scripture seriously.

Heterosexists would have us believe that they alone take the Bible at its word. They state repeatedly that Scripture clearly condemns homosexuality. To call such misuse of the Bible into the open, which the reform to dismantle heterosexism does, clearly threatens all superficial and legalistic use of the Word of God. People misuse the Bible when they claim that it speaks to issues about which it in fact says nothing. The Bible has very little to say about sex. It has much to say about matters related to human sexuality like faithfulness, justice, mutuality, forgiveness, and love, as well as sin, brokenness, alienation, abuse, and despair.

Heterosexism, along with the biblicism that supports it, muzzles the revolutionary voice of Scripture. It misinterprets or narrowly interprets (usually out of context) the few texts that mention same-sex behavior and, more importantly, ignores the wealth of biblical passages regarding human relationships that can inform a healthy and holistic sexual ethic. A heterocentric approach to the Bible renders monochromatic a potentially rich and deeply colored landscape.

By reducing sexuality to male-female dichotomies, heterosexism creates an idolatrous focus on one part of the whole. Idolatry occurs when anyone or anything is invested with more significance than is fitting. As an interpretive framework, heterosexism is itself idolatry. Perhaps more than anything else, the New Testament witness reveals that Jesus' life, death, and resurrection were a confrontation with idolatry.

In word and deed Jesus repeatedly surprised others with radical reversals. The evidence is so well-known that its impact is sometimes overlooked. When Jesus said that the first will be last and the last first or that people should love their enemies, he stood conventional wisdom on its head. He taught that the kingdom of God is not what one expects, that faith is like a mustard seed, and that children (almost worthless in the social structure of his day) are the model for entering the kingdom of God. His treatment of women, like his treatment of children, invited men of power to look at life differently. And of course his death on a cross—the ultimate human sign of weakness and failure—became the surprising route to strength and victory.

When our own culture demeans children, women, or people of color, such biblical testimony should open us to hear Jesus in our midst calling for the kind of radical reversals he made in his day. Each time we are tempted to jump to a premature conclusion we should be haunted by the image of Jesus asking us to consider the opposite of what we presume to be the case. Such questioning constitutes an important part of ethical decision making. Heterosexist condemnations of same-sex relationships may be like the cultural condemnations Jesus challenged during his ministry.

For example, in the parable of the good Samaritan substitute a gay man or lesbian for the Samaritan and our point about not taking the Bible seriously becomes clear. We are profoundly deceived when we rationalize that such a substitution is illegitimate. This biblical story challenges precisely such a sense of illegitimacy. Heterosexism inhibits us from imaging the substitution; it closes the possibility of our hearing the gospel in our own day.

Traditional interpretations of biblical stories are expanded and sometimes stretched to the point of breaking (as the image of new wine in old wineskins makes so clear) when we open the door to nonheterosexist insights. At one level this is indeed threatening, but at another it is enriching and life giving. Our fear has prevented us from discovering much of the latter with regard to our sexuality. It does not require an anachronistic claim that David and Jonathan, Ruth and Naomi, or even Jesus and the Beloved Disciple were "homosexual" to see that these stories can challenge our biases regarding same-sex friendships.

In a nonheterosexist paradigm no anxiety arises, no concern about anything "hidden" in what we are told about these relationships. Heterosexism demands that we worry about the sexual implications; nonheterosexist readings assume sexuality as a legitimate dimension of the relationship. It does not speculate about whether any specific sexual behaviors were involved because none are prejudged as unloving or illegitimate. In other words, the erotic dimensions of human friendship (as of all human bonding) are freed although not divorced from their genital connections.

To approach this example from the other side, the reason we do not automatically assume that such same-sex relationships were homosexual is also due to heterosexist prejudice. Only because we have determined beforehand that homosexuality is sin are we unwilling even to entertain the possibility that what existed between these people was in any sense erotic. Gay men and lesbians obviously hear these stories quite differently. Heterosexual men and women hear the story of the man and woman in the Song of Songs with the kind of erotic overtones that are present for homosexual men and women in reading about David and Jonathan or Ruth and Naomi. To deny the validity of the latter readings means succumbing to heterosexism's control of the Bible.

This is not a new argument. Others who have experienced oppression make it clear that when they read the Bible it speaks to them in ways that many of the rest of us cannot hear except through their voices. Whether it is the poor in Latin American base communities, women throughout the world, or blacks in North America or South Africa, we are called to recognize the absolute necessity of letting the Bible's living voice speak through living people. This does not mean that we are "reading into the Bible" meanings that are not there. On the contrary, it means freeing the meanings that are there from the bondage of silence that our prejudices impose.

Interpreting Issues

In chapter 3 we examined the few biblical texts and interpretations traditionally used to support heterosexism in all its forms. By taking such an approach we allowed heterosexism to dictate the agenda of the chapter. It restricted our dialogue with Scripture. The previous comments remind us that we must step outside that agenda and allow a wide variety of biblical passages to speak to us anew when we have abandoned the heterosexism that has silenced them. Yet our concern must be still broader. Heterosexist misuse of the Bible is not restricted to the exegesis of specific texts that speak directly or indirectly about sexuality. It includes how we approach a variety of issues that shape our sexual ethics.

Our judgments regarding sexual orientations and behaviors are informed by a broad spectrum of concerns. We will examine three—faith healing, celibacy, and sexual abstinence—as illustrative of the kind of biblically informed dialogue that can be generated outside a heterosexist paradigm.

Faith healing is rooted in the belief that "all things are possible with God." For example, nothing is more certain and intractable in human experience than death. Faith healing could have as its object no greater consequence of the Fall than death. Yet all Christians believe in the resurrection of the dead—the ultimate in faith healing. The healing of defect and disease pale in comparison. Certainly, "repairing" a sexual orientation is far more plausible than the resurrection of the dead.

Advocates of Position 1 (see chapter 1) accuse fellow heterosexists who do not encourage reparation therapy of being people of little faith. They accuse those who accept the givenness of homosexual orientations as not trusting sufficiently in the power of prayer made in the name of Jesus. On the other hand, advocates of Positions 2, 3, and 4 recognize that even persons of great faith and deep prayer will not experience the fullness of the promises of Risen Life. The Eschaton is already and not yet. For them it is not necessary to demand reparation therapies or expect that they can be successful.

The problem with all of these positions is that they bring an a priori assumption that homosexuality needs to be fixed. We would argue that it is impossible to justify on biblical grounds that homosexual feelings or actions are the appropriate object of faith healing. People misuse biblical texts that teach us to pray or assure us of God's power to heal, when they use prayer to manipulate God and avoid appropriate human responsibility. Heterosexism creates and sustains a false need. It saps the energy of prayer and faith from other foci that are its appropriate objects.

Celibacy provides us with another example of this problem. Although there is little biblical testimony regarding celibacy (Mt 19:12 and 1 Cor 7), tradition offers considerable insight on it. Many early Christian writers advocated virginal or celibate lifestyles as morally superior to marriage. These ways of life were recommended to all Christians. But such counsel was lived out only by those with special "religious" vocations. These early Church leaders understood their arguments as exhortative not obligatory. They recognized that such a lifestyle had to be taken up voluntarily; it could not be commanded.

The Church has never taught that it can command a large class of people to practice sexual abstinence. Roman Catholic priests and religious women voluntarily take up this discipline. We presume that their commitment is supported by the gift of celibacy (many Roman Catholics now think this canonical position should be reconsidered). When virginity and celibacy were first commended to gays and lesbians, few Church leaders had any idea of how large a segment of the population was homosexually oriented.

Heterosexism perpetuates the misapplication of an otherwise useful dimension of some vocations, the call to celibacy. In this case it can find neither biblical nor traditional support for the claim that same-sex affections must be subject to it. If we discern the gift of celibacy as rare, can we find any biblical wisdom regarding total and lifelong sexual abstinence? St. Paul was certainly clear that such a lifestyle would be practically impossible for most people when he said that "it is better to marry than to burn" (1 Cor 7:9). Because Paul did not know of human variation in sexual orientation, we must ask how to interpret his remark in reference to gay and lesbian people.

Paul believed that total sexual abstinence was unrealistic and unwise counsel for most people because the result of such a commendation would surely be promiscuity. Therefore, one should marry rather than make or adopt such counsel. This is in light of Paul's expectation that Jesus' second coming would bring the world to an end within his lifetime. Without Paul's expectation that abstinence would be for a brief and therefore manageable time, he might have argued even more strongly against it under any circumstances.

Both those who are inclined to retain and those who want to abolish present Church teachings regarding homosexuality must imaginatively project what Paul might say to the faithful who are gay and lesbian. The meaning of this text for the issue at hand is not self-evident. At least three possible interpretations are imaginable even when it is assumed that Paul would remain heterosexist (which we argued in chapter 3 is not necessarily true).

Paul could be read as recommending to gay and lesbian Christians that they enter into heterosexual marriages rather than attempt total and lifelong sexual abstinence. Although this is perhaps the simplest interpretation to justify textually, such an application does not cohere with what drives the passage in the first place—Paul's keen sense of the moral danger of repressed sexual desire. To state the obvious, heterosexual marriages do not satisfy the erotic desires of homosexual people.

In contrast one could argue that Paul would commend marriage only to heterosexual people. If that were the case he would be saying that total and lifelong sexual abstinence, although unrealistic, is morally better than just, loving, and faithful homosexual unions. The decisive question for him would be which is more harmful—the crippling isolation necessitated by sexual continence (with possibly consequent expression in collateral promiscuous relations) or the destructive impact of the behavioral reinforcement of their homosexual disorientation. Either conclusion must be interpreted in light of Paul's expectation that Jesus' second coming was imminent. His advice regarding marriage and sexual abstinence rested on a presumption that proved to be wrong.

On the one hand, he might construct a case against crippling isolation. If so, it would not be necessary for him to believe that sexual expression is necessary (apart from the gift of celibacy) for psychological normalcy or human fulfillment. But he would need to see erotic desires as interwoven with essential human desires for intimacy and relationships. He would need to see *eros* functioning for most people as a primary avenue to such goods. And finally he would need to view humans as made for such communion with one another and God.

Given these premises Paul could recognize that any proposal that closes off a main access route to such relationships requires an extraordinary justification. He might conclude that the degree of harm accompanying just, loving, and faithful homosexual unions fails to warrant such action. Nothing in Paul's writings contradicts these premises. Still the level of textual support for such a viewpoint is modest.

On the other hand, Paul might argue that gay people live morally exemplary lives when they commit themselves to lifelong and total sexual abstinence. Through such a commitment they could, for the sake of the kingdom, bear witness to the morally normative nature of heterosexuality. He would not perceive sexual abstinence as a purely negative response, based exclusively on a desire to avoid evil rather than grow in goodness. In this way he would counter those who believe that total and lifelong sexual abstinence sheds no light on the ultimate meaning of human sexuality or is poor stewardship of the gifts for sexual intimacy that gay people have. Once again, nothing in Paul's writings contradicts such premises, but the level of textual support for them is modest.

The point we are trying to make with these examples is that Christians must exercise caution in claiming that the Bible is clear in its message regarding human sexuality, particularly homosexuality. Taking the Bible seriously as an authoritative word means living continuously in dialogue with it. It does not serve the Christian community or the world well to misuse Scripture by claiming it for the support of heterosexism.

The real threat in the Church posed by the dismantling of heterosexism is to false biblical security. In honoring the legitimacy of this threat we join our voices with those who struggle similarly to end the misuse of the Word of God that results from the grip of sexism and racism. Heterosexism is, biblically speaking, one among many human expressions of idolatry.

CONCLUSION

It takes considerable energy to sustain hate. Individuals and whole societies pay an enormous cost for prejudice and bigotry. That cost is never limited to those who are directly victimized by the prejudice. Because the costs are often hidden, we have difficulty convincing one another how destructive our prejudices are. Because the prejudices are so pervasive, we also find it difficult to imagine what the world would be like without them.

It will take both a forthright dismissal of the false fears that sustain heterosexism and an imaginative vision of what the world might be like without it in order to create the climate in which the real pillars of heterosexist prejudice can be challenged and dismantled. In this chapter we have only highlighted the most obvious examples of how such foundations can be seen for what they are when the blinders of heterosexism are removed.

The preceding chapters together have invited reflection on the ways in which we are affected in Church and society by an unexamined heterosexism that finds its basis in a heterocentric world-view. We have argued that this world-view and the prejudices that have emerged from it are not the consequence of divine will but rather the result of human sin. If this is true, both Scripture and tradition tell us what must happen. The community can begin to discover what God truly intends only when it is willing to repent. We believe that the time for such repentance is long overdue and that the only real threat reformation will pose is to structures of domination and control that continue to plague both the Church and society.

5

Confronting Heterosexism

> We are the body of Christ and our body is part gay. This is how we find
> ourselves. Denials, apologies, disclaimers follow. But this is who we find
> ourselves to be: we women and men who seek to follow Jesus Christ share a
> body that is part homosexual and part heterosexual.[1]

If the Church wants genuine dialogue concerning homosexuality
such honest recognition must be its starting point. Without recognizing the community as it is we cannot hope to articulate appropriate and gospel-centered norms for its life. It will not help to assert a
priori that the Christian community should not be this way. As we
have done in other chapters, we must emphasize again that such an
approach begs the question. We are talking about ourselves as
Church when we discuss homosexuality. We cannot pretend that the
conversation only concerns others "out there."

Thoughtful and faithful Christians, heterosexual and homosexual alike, are asking the Church to reconsider the reasons for its heterosexist bias. Reconsideration does not mean that we can or even
ought to eliminate all biases. For example, presumptions against
white supremacist positions are consistent with the gospel and we
should not discard them. The issue is whether current biases regarding homosexuality are consistent with the gospel. The lived and living faith of the *whole* Christian community provides the context,
scripturally rooted and historically informed, for addressing this
question. The gay and straight members of the one Body of Christ
must determine together whether and how to undertake reform of
sexual ethics in the Church.

In this chapter we explore how the Church's corporate faith and
life help us to interpret the ethical questions generated by the
debate on sexuality. This includes asking how that faith and life may
be responsible for creating some of the thorniest problems. We
begin with a preliminary explanation of the historical foundations
for engaging in reform. We then move to a description of the Christian community and its life and teaching in order to surface the con-

cerns that people of faith have about sexuality, sin, and grace. This leads us to the call for a paradigm shift in the Church's sexual ethics. With such a shift, we can freely reevaluate traditional prohibitions in the Church's own life. Thus we assess the ordination of gays and lesbians as a test case for how the Church's structures can either inhibit or foster reform.

We conclude that gay and lesbian people belong in society and in the Church, and that the Church must both signal and embody their full acceptance as children of God. For this to happen we must challenge and reform the Church's understanding of and attitude toward gay and lesbian people. Acceptance represents only a step on the road of reform.[2] If human sexuality rightly embraces a wide spectrum of homosexual and heterosexual erotic needs, the real goal is a nonheterosexist ethic that nurtures and celebrates its full, God-given diversity.

FOUNDATIONS FOR REFORM

As we noted in this book's Introduction, we belong to different Christian communions, one Lutheran and the other Roman Catholic. Both church bodies have ways of dealing with scriptural, doctrinal, and ethical issues that result from the uniqueness of their own heritages. We cannot hope to present even a cursory review of what we think is distinctive of our traditions and relevant to our subject. It may be useful, nevertheless, to review how we contextualize objections from within our traditions to any call for reforming teaching on homosexuality.

For all Protestants who trace their roots to the sixteenth century Reformation, the phrase *ecclesia semper reformanda est* (the Church must always be reformed) is an ecclesiological axiom. It provides a theological justification for self-critical analysis of issues that Christians might otherwise choose to ignore. Protestant denominations vary in their explanation of what reformation means in specific instances. It is not an all-embracing axiom. No denomination, for example, suggests that Scripture can be reformed.

We sometimes qualify what traditions we reform by distinguishing Tradition (often referred to as the *deposit of faith*, essential to Christian identity) and traditions (beliefs and customs historically conditioned). We also distinguish between what is of divine mandate (*de iure divino*) and of human invention (*de iure humano*). Roman Catholics share this debate, but Protestants engage it most intensely in reform of doctrine. For Lutherans, faithfulness to a specific confessional witness (the sixteenth-century *Augsburg Confession* and related documents found in the *Book of Concord*) compounds the intensity. A broader philosophical question about the existence of objective, timeless truth that stands outside or above the vicissitudes of history lies behind much of the controversy. Although we cannot engage that debate here, we acknowledge our presumption that the Church's traditions can always be reformed.

To discuss the triune identity of God, for example, reforms our understanding of it, even if inherited doctrinal formulations do not change as a result of the discussion. The very use of new language, insights, or analogies creates a cumulative effect that alters the store of relevant data for all future discussion. Hence at some level doctrine is always developing. In any given time and place one of theology's tasks is to discern the significance of this store of data for contemporary questions of faith.

Although committed to the call to reform the Church, Protestants have not been so clear about the Church's role in reforming society. In that area Catholicism has a more consistent record of reform in the history of its social teachings. Sociologist Gregory Baum points out that a declaration of the 1971 Synod of Bishops marked a significant shift in contemporary Catholic theology. Redemption in Jesus Christ, the bishops argued, included the liberation of people from the oppressive conditions of their social lives.[3]

Again, we cannot trace the history of these commitments to reform nor review the current state of the question about the place of both ecclesial and civil reform. We can, however, affirm that questions of homosexuality cannot be settled by deliberations that do not take into account the stories of those who are directly affected. Gays and lesbians need a full voice in the dialogue if the rest of the community lays claim to any integrity in its moral deliberation. We should not presume to speak for others when they can and should speak for themselves.

The reform perspectives drawn from both Protestant and Roman Catholic teaching provide one basis for pursuing a reevaluation of the positions the Church has taken regarding homosexual men and women. Such historical commitment to reform and liberation calls the Church to engage in dialogue with any person or group that claims it is suffering from oppression. The purpose in doing so is to recognize the symptoms, evaluate the causes, and, as necessary, act to end the oppression.

We state this explicitly even though we cannot develop supportive arguments more fully. Others have done such work. The reason for being so explicit is plain. *Any* call for a new evaluation of traditional teachings regarding homosexuality meets great resistance in the Church. It is often treated as an area of theological reflection that is settled and beyond need of reform.

People lodge the resistance to reform in a deeply held belief that homosexuality is sinful. Obviously many nuances exist in the ways in which people of faith describe this position and its consequences (see the typology in chapter 1). The distinction that a homosexual orientation is not sin, but that any homosexual acts are sin, represents such a nuance. Nevertheless we must challenge the foundational position itself. One cannot accept orientation without also accepting that some actions (not necessarily genital) must flow from it. It does not serve the Church or the gospel well to dismiss such challenges as pro-gay apologetic. Such a charge is especially insidious in undermining not only faithful efforts at ethical reform but also pastoral attempts to deal with gays and lesbians compassionately.

For example, a theological consequence of the position that homosexuality is sin is that any community tolerance (let alone acceptance) of an "active gay lifestyle" would deprive gays and lesbians of the motivation to repent. Tolerance would circumvent their being reminded of the power of grace to transform their lives.[4] Such a view undermines attempts at deliberations open to eventuating in reform. The theological argument behind this perspective maintains that such a discussion or reform would hurt the very people it is supposed to help. Repentance and grace express powerful, foundational aspects of faith. To hint that they may be compromised can deal a death blow to any dialogue about homosexuality. It also results in the alienation and necessitates the invisibility that gays and lesbians associate with the Church.

THE CHURCH AS AN INCLUSIVE-EXCLUSIVE COMMUNITY

Belonging is a foundation for community. We can identify or distinguish one community from another because we can say who is a part of it. This has nothing to do with moral questions of inclusivity and exclusivity. It is a descriptive convention necessary for the sake of differentiation (not discrimination). One belongs to the Christian community by virtue of baptism. The Church as an identifiable group in the world, traditionally referred to as the *visible Church,* includes all the baptized. The Church is a faith community that includes all those committed to this faith. It therefore excludes those not thus committed, those, for example, who choose to be part of other faith communities.[5]

A person can be an integral part of a church's life without being baptized. Most of us would say that such a person belonged to the community, although an unsettled question would remain about why someone so involved refused to be baptized. On the other hand, many baptized people take no active part in the Christian community. The sacramental affirmation of their belonging to the people of God is unassailable theologically because God's faithfulness defines the sacrament not ours. Yet from the perspective of human community we question the nature of such a person's belonging.

In spite of such fluidity at the boundaries, we anchor the historical identification of Christian discipleship in baptism. Because most churches baptize infants, one cannot argue that the unrepented "sin" of homosexuality constitutes a barrier to a person's baptism and consequently to membership in the Christian community. Neither the sexual orientation nor sexual behavior of infants compromises their belonging to the people of God. A consequence of the theological affirmation of infant baptism coupled with the scientific data about the early establishment and irreversibility of sexual orientation is that homosexuality per se is not an impediment to baptism. Indeed, disease, defect, and even sin have not been impediments to baptism. This means that the reparation of a homosexual orientation (including at least some inevitable behavioral expressions of it) ought never be a prerequisite for adult baptism. All who practice infant baptism must reach this conclusion. The fact that the early church required renunciation of numerous behaviors, even occupations, does not compromise this point.

Whether one is heterosexual or homosexual in orientation (see chapter 1), one acts sexually. How one chooses to act results from response to cultural and personal values. Here the various communities to which we belong play their most important role. They are the arena for both learning and expressing sexual identity. The Christian community provides the context for evaluating whether our chosen actions are consistent with the gospel.

One cannot repent of feelings if repentance means turning away from something or changing it. We have little control over tears welling up in our eyes or love filling our hearts. We can, of course, cultivate or repress what is stirred within us spontaneously. The fact that we can discipline feelings leads to vice or virtue. We should expect no one to repent of feelings that are a wellspring for the virtues of love and compassion. The responsibility of the Christian community is to nurture those feelings and actions that together build up such virtues in the community and in the individual and exclude those actions that are destructive to the community or individuals within it. We disagree with those who argue that homosexuality is inherently destructive, cannot be a wellspring of love and compassion, or cannot lead to virtue.

What responsibility does the Church have to those who belong to it? Are Christians to treat Christians any differently from the way they treat other neighbors in the world? In terms of outreach, the answer is clearly no. Being Christian neither limits nor focuses a person's call to love others. The Church is not a sect turned in on itself. The primary mission of the Christian community is to bear witness to Jesus and call people to faith. It embodies this witness in service to the world: feed the hungry, set the prisoner free, shelter the homeless, comfort the sick and dying, all in the name of Jesus Christ.

The Church's treatment of those in its midst who are gay and lesbian will serve as witness to the world about how they should be treated in any context. When we treat gays and lesbians as outsiders, we erase their history and ignore their experience. The fact that so many churchgoers claim never to have met or known a homosexual person provides ample evidence that such outsider status is standard treatment for our gay and lesbian brothers and sisters in Christ.

Initial reform in Church and society must concentrate on creating the openness and visibility that dialogue requires. Gays and lesbians must tell their own stories for the rest of the community to hear what lies at stake. Talking about them (as if we were not also talking about ourselves!) or even telling their stories secondhand makes evident a continuing heterosexist bias; it refuses to acknowledge the existence of those who are "other" and who have the right to their own voice.

People are willing to be open and vulnerable in a safe environment. If we sense that others have already judged us or taken a position on an issue that discounts us, we are reluctant to speak honestly about our experience. We are forced to hide for fear of reprisal, condemnation, or rejection. This vicious circle of silence can be broken only if the Church relinquishes a doctrinaire assertion that homosexuality is sin and creates an environment for gays and lesbians to be seen and heard. Such an environment must include the willingness to think critically about heterocentrism.

We engage in such dialogue when we face squarely the possibility that heterosexism constitutes sin. In preceding chapters we have viewed some of the evidence that might contribute to such a conclusion. We turn our attention to one communal implication that results from risking such a judgment. For example, our current situation becomes analogous to the Church's response to racism. When racism was acknowledged as sin (which occurred over time) it provided legitimation for action, such as, for example, working for integration. When churches divided as a result of such efforts it was a tragic but necessary price to pay. Unity had to be sacrificed when the issue, racism, was clearly named a sin. Lack of progress in integrating churches does not compromise the truth to which the Church points when its public teaching confesses and condemns racism. We are all capable, individually and corporately, of hindering truth's ability to lead us to freedom.

In the case of homosexuality the Church's commitment to inclusivity and liberation invites us to be at odds with our culture's heterosexist oppression and discrimination. Heterosexual and homosexual men and women must be equal partners if we expect to arrive at mutually agreeable ways to live with and for each other. Thus open and full membership in churches becomes crucial to healthy discussion of sexual ethics.

We conclude that the Church must be open to and inclusive of gays and lesbians. Only openness and honesty will enable us to overcome our current impasse. Otherwise gays and lesbians will remain invisible or strangers in our midst and we will continue to hide from the implications of the gospel.

CHRISTIAN LIFE AND CHRISTIAN TEACHING

The Church has the responsibility to distinguish true and false teaching, right and wrong behavior. Where will the Christian community locate its sources for discernment? When the authority of Scripture is in dialogue with reason, tradition, and human experience, the components for genuine discernment exist. If we arbitrarily or categorically abandon or truncate any of these components, we compromise truth.[6] We ought not argue whether one must *begin* with the Bible or *begin* with human experience, because each must be engaged for any discernment to be faithful. We must give each its voice—Bible, reason, tradition (history), and experience—for faith to apprehend the truth, even though for Christians Scripture remains uniquely normative.

Because we focus in this chapter on the Christian community we want to examine the workings of its faith and life to illuminate our topic. How do churches today deal with gays, lesbians, their families and friends, and their concerns, hopes, and fears? What do our community actions say?

> The trouble began when I wrote a letter to the editor about being gay and signed my name. I had intended it to be printed "name withheld by request." The next Sunday in church I was called aside by the president of the congregation and informed that I was no longer welcome. I couldn't believe what I was hearing. I had been a member of this church all my life.
>
> Of course I questioned the decision. I forced an open hearing in our church council and, finally, in a special congregational meeting with the bishop present. But when it was all over the vote was for me to be "removed from the membership roll" of the congregation because my gay identity was in conflict with "the teaching of this church."
>
> At least they didn't say that I was outside the kingdom of God—at least not out loud.

* * *

> My heart was pounding. I couldn't believe that it was going to happen. I was being received into membership in a congregation that knew I was a lesbian. It's not that the path leading to this moment was smooth. Far from it. Lots of talking led the parish to vote that they would be a congregation open to gays and lesbians.
>
> I was the first to join after the decision was made. And the really amazing thing was this: they meant what they said! The worship that morning was a celebration. I *felt* the love and acceptance of the community, and I knew what the love of Christ meant.
>
> I've never felt so free, or so humble. It wasn't a "victory" where I had won. It was *our* decision, our willingness to open instead of close doors. I'm not so naive as to believe there won't be painful times ahead. But now I know that I belong to a church that stands with me, not against me.

One can find such stories repeated everywhere. The treatment this Christian brother and sister each received reveals the confusing and conflicting signals homosexual men and women get from the Church. Although we recognize the need for caution in making a generalization, it seems fair on the basis of the written documents and public debate within the Church today to say that many Christian communities are trying to take a "conservative but compassionate" approach to gay men and lesbians. It represents an understandable middle-of-the-road position in this time of tension.

At either end of the spectrum one can still find extreme positions: uncritical condemnation of homosexuality or uncritical acceptance of it. The uncritical condemnation can be unqualified. It includes orientation and behavior issues. Some in this camp, using a supposed biblical justification, still call for the execution of homosexual people. The uncritical acceptance can also be unqualified. Any sexual behavior is justified if the persons engaged in it agree to it. As in most public debate the fringe positions illustrate the boundaries within which others attempt to discern wisdom.

The moderating trend toward a conservative but compassionate approach reveals that we may be at a reformable moment in Church and society.[7] The conservatism is lodged in retaining past formulations of homosexuality as sinful or contrary to nature. The compassion is generated by Christian commitment to a "hate the sin but love the sinner" ethic. It demands some kind of acceptance of gays and lesbians in spite of the reluctance rooted in the conservative teaching. This creates a tension that can become a source for reform.

A different, unreforming consequence of the conservative but compassionate position results when the Church simply decides to live with ambivalence. It must be functionally neutral. It cannot fully accept gays and lesbians as members of a legitimate sexual minority group, but neither can it arbitrarily demand chastity of them.[8] The unresolvedness of this approach does not make it unacceptable. We can all live with a lack of resolution when we see that a premature or forced solution would be unjust or destructive. From our point of view the problem with the conservative but compassionate approach is its inability to be fully faithful to the gospel. The confusion it creates can prevent the Christian community from moving beyond a situation that is *already* unjust and destructive, not only for gays and lesbians but also for Church and society.

One clear sign of the Church's inability to address the injustices of heterosexism is the existence in almost every denomination of gay and lesbian organizations whose primary purpose is to provide support and visibility in a context that denies both. These groups have quasi-official status at best. In some cases the church body with which their membership is identified does not even acknowledge them.

Groups appropriately form to meet the needs of specific people. The Church has many such groups for youth, women, men, singles, retirees, and so on. But the larger body both sanctions and supports them even as it integrates them in the life of the community. Such sanctioning and support are generally not present for gay and lesbian groups. Some people experienced the larger Church's rejection of gays and lesbians as so complete that only the formation of an independent church body by and for gays and lesbians (although in principle and in fact open to the membership of heterosexual people without discrimination) could afford them the opportunity to worship freely. Thus the Universal Fellowship of Metropolitan Community Churches (MCC) was formed.

Theological ambivalence about the role of judgment or discipline in relation to grace creates this situation. Some of our most destructive actions in the Church occur when we confuse these two. When we condemn those who have done no wrong we misuse judgment. Few people have difficulty agreeing that the misuse of judgment is unjust. When we accept those who will not do right we misuse grace. Yet many argue that unconditional acceptance defines grace and calls us to act graciously in turn. Grace cannot be "misused" in this view. One could never be unjust or destructive by being merciful and accepting. We disagree with this perspective insofar as it minimizes the need to confront sin as sin.

The question for the Church in its present circumstances is not whether to exercise compassion toward gay, lesbian, bisexual, and transgender people. Biblically informed Christians know the call to be compassionate, particularly toward those with whom they feel most disconnected—the stranger, the enemy, the ungodly. Jesus' parables as well as his actions in ministry affirm this. But love includes both compassion and justice. Heterosexism fosters the belief that gay and lesbian people are not worthy of equal treatment under the law. Heterosexism relegates all homosexual people to a place outside the gates of justice. Recognition of their cry for justice allows us to reconsider our judgment. The relationship between justice and sexuality will go unaddressed if we refuse to confront the heteocentric biases that have informed our negative assessments of homosexuality.

An approach that maintains traditional teaching on homosexuality while claiming pastoral sensitivity fails the Church here. It divorces compassion and justice. Being nice serves to let heterosexists off the hook as much as it appears to let homosexual people off the hook. What amazed us time and time again as we read the literature on homosexuality was how consistent and cogent discussion of the issues and the evidence was abruptly abandoned precisely at the point where full acceptance of homosexuality and heterosexuality seemed to be its logical conclusion. Why does the conservative but compassionate approach end in such an impasse? When change seems to be invited on the basis of faithful response to the gospel, what hinders our willingness to embrace it? The paradigm itself, out of which we work, blocks our vision. It organizes the data without seeing its truth. We are seeing all the trees, but we no longer recognize the forest.

Change will not occur in our sexual ethic because we repudiate piece by piece every supposedly objectionable element of the Church's past moral deliberation. We find ourselves at the point historically where sufficient data exist to support many responses to homosexuality. The seemingly obligatory, extensive bibliographies one can find in almost every book published on the subject make this clear. It may be that the wealth of data itself immobilizes us. We do not need additional information but the development of a new paradigm that offers a framework for acting on the information we have. As Lesslie Newbigin has observed: "one alleged new fact, or even a number of new facts, does not suffice to discredit an established paradigm. That can only happen when a new and more compelling paradigm is offered, a vision of reality which commends itself by its beauty, rationality, and comprehensiveness."[9] He goes on to explain that such a vision must be held with "universal intent." That is, it must be offered as public truth subject to communal scrutiny and not simply as private opinion. The Church can offer such a new vision.

A PARADIGM SHIFT IN SEXUAL ETHICS

The reigning Christian paradigm often focuses on sex as sin and especially on homosexuality as the most destructive sexual sin. We should not be surprised that calls for reform in Church teaching continue to meet resistance. Critics label attempts at reopening questions, reassessing biblical data, or challenging discrimination as "progay apologetic" and dismiss them. Without a paradigm shift, piecemeal efforts to change attitudes will do little to break down the walls of heterosexism. A paradigm shift will result only as the Church acknowledges heterosexism, not homosexuality, as sin. Another component of this shift, perhaps the foundational component, is appropriating sexuality as gift. The Church has not yet overcome the pervasive view that sex in all its facets is inextricably bound with evil. The Western Church has not escaped the theological legacy of St. Augustine's sexual ethics.

As the Church undergoes a paradigm shift, and we intend this book as a contribution to that process, it can offer society new foundations for an inclusive sexual ethic. The Church can become a positive contributor both to the content of the public debate about homosexuality and the methods by which we conduct it. To do so it must continue to move beyond internal discussions about historical questions of moral theology. It must also be willing to engage the dialogue between biblical authority and contemporary human experience within this new paradigm. Such dialogue both fosters the shift and comes to express it.

Paradigm shifts do not take place as a matter of fiat. Often in science a discovery dramatically sparks the introduction of a new paradigm, even though its implications take time to unfold.[10] In theology paradigm shifts usually result from a cumulative process. The work of the Second Vatican Council serves as a recent example of a paradigm shift in ecclesiology, where recognition of other ecclesial bodies provided a more expansive view of the Church that generated new ecumenical possibilities.

A paradigm shift provides a new intelligibility framework within which to evaluate traditions and experience. Because it challenges familiar patterns of thinking and acting, it can initially create confusion and provoke retrenchment. The overwhelming sense of the magnitude of change implied by the shift sometimes results in complete rejection. The church's condemnation of Galileo is a classic case of such backlash.

Concerning the subject of sexuality, a more recent event provides us with a helpful example. In the summer of 1991 the Presbyterian Church U.S.A., in its much publicized 203rd General Assembly in Baltimore, Maryland, rejected the report "Keeping Body and Soul Together."[11] We believe the report attempted to develop the positive content of an inclusive sexual ethic within a new paradigm. Many strategic reasons account for the failure of the report to garner broader support among delegates. These included issues of content and method. We are not offering an evaluation of the merit of the report. We are suggesting that one reason for its defeat might have been a lack of consensus about the need for a new paradigm.

In other words, the overwhelming rejection of the report resulted from people responding to its parts on the basis of the old paradigm for sexual ethics in Christianity with which they were familiar. The report seemed to condone, even advocate, the commission of sins that the Church had always rejected—and reasonably so under the operative paradigm—as incompatible with Christian teaching. For those who also equated Christian teaching with Christian life, this resulted in the intolerable bind of believing that the proposed changes in teaching would translate directly into unacceptable changes in lifestyle. In drawing attention to this example we honor the fact that the kinds of changes we advocate are painful, and often occur incrementally. The defeat of the Presbyterian report is not a failure for the Church; it is a gracious gift in our history that has contributed to the process by which God brings life from death.[12]

THE FOCUS OF REFORM

The focus of reform in the Church today emerges from considering the phrase *active gay lifestyle*. What does it mean? How does it compare with an active heterosexual lifestyle? What constitutes an appropriate sexual ethic in either lifestyle? Already we confront problems arising from the terminology. We all know that no one heterosexual lifestyle exists nor a single homosexual lifestyle. Nevertheless the phrase reveals two important concerns.

The word *active* refers to the fact that people cannot simply "be" who they are. Their being involves action. To oversimplify, we both do what we are and are what we do. For this reason the distinction between orientation and behavior, although useful, is limited. What we do in daily interaction with people both of the same sex and the other sex is part of our sexual being. In other words, it is impossible not to be active sexually in life unless one isolates sexuality by restricting it to particular actions. Many people do use the phrase *active gay lifestyle* narrowly to refer to genital sexual expression. This obscures the full reality of our sexuality.

The phrase *lifestyle* communicates the fact that our sexual being affects our whole way of life. The need to interact with each other from day to day as men and women is not altered because one is a homosexual rather than a heterosexual person. But we do make choices about how to interact with each other. The cumulative result of our choices produces the style of our lives. We develop patterns of interaction that embody the values we choose to nourish. Sometimes the choices are unintentional or unclear, and we are not conscious of the style of life they are creating. This is why the wisdom of the Christian community is so important. We can receive a wider vision than we would otherwise have. In the end, however, each human being must accept substantial responsibility for the individual choices that have shaped his or her life.

Given the broad acceptance of the orientation-behavior distinction, the phrase *active gay lifestyle* usually means that the gay or lesbian person engages in some kind of sexual activity with another. People who use the phrase usually have sexual activity in mind. Surely the phrase does not mean that people of the same sex cannot share physical signs of affection or that they cannot be roommates. Where, then, do we draw the line?

Because neither Church nor society fully accepts gay and lesbian marriage, it cannot be the point of contention. In other words, if gay and lesbian marriages were normative, the judgmental import of the phrase *active gay lifestyle* might be directed to premarital or extramarital sexual relationships. The ethic would be the same as for heterosexual marriages.

To have an "active sexual lifestyle" as a heterosexual person means engaging in a wide range of romantic expression. In some cases (in the strictest traditional view *only* in the case of marriage) that culminates in sexual intercourse. Although people clearly vary on what degree of sexual activity is appropriate for those who are not engaged or married, considerable latitude accompanies the process of discovering the mutual pleasures and dangers of sexual communication.

Most people appear to draw the line at genital intercourse, hence our traditional emphasis on the significance of virginity. Traditional views also usually consider mutual masturbation or oral sex between two unmarried people out of bounds because they are genital sexual expression. Even so, these do not cross the line that engaging in genital intercourse does.

We grant that this may be a rather narrow view of sexuality, but it seems fair to suggest that it remains the cultural norm. Thus when an "avowed practicing homosexual" is barred from something, what the word practicing refers to becomes crucial. The historical record confirms that anal intercourse is almost universally the focus of legislative action against homosexual people. Sodomy laws provide all the data one needs to show that this remains the case. A connection between sexism and heterosexism lies at the root of this. Heterosexism assumes that we are talking about male homosexuality. In the traditional view anal intercourse involves one male "pretending" to be a female by substituting the anus for the vagina. Ample documentation exists to show that this apparent gender confusion generates hostility.

One of the most telling pieces of evidence in the historical record concerning homosexuality is the almost universal absence of discussion of lesbianism. No one seems to care what lesbians do with each other in sexual expression. Everyone seems to care about males using males as females. Of course what lesbians *refuse* to do attracts attention (that is, refuse to copulate with a male). Thus lesbians are commonly threatened with rape.

So are we objecting to gay men or lesbian women kissing, hugging, or caressing each other? Are we objecting to their sleeping together, snuggling with each other? Perhaps. But the key objection seems to be genital intercourse. To reduce sexuality to genitalia is problematic at best. It should take little imagination to picture men or women who have been incapacitated genitally still being able to communicate sexually. Yet such reductionism seems always to be at work in discussions of homosexuality. We have tried to show that the primary reasons for this are the biases generated by heterosexism. Nevertheless, one facet of this issue remains.

No other form of sexual interaction (apart from issues of sado-masochism) seems to engender personal health risks in the way that anal intercourse does. This is true whether the penis penetrates a man or a woman. The rectum and colon undergo physical trauma during anal intercourse that no other nonviolent form of sexual expression parallels. This raises serious questions about the exploitative or destructive character of anal intercourse. The fact that the HIV virus is transmitted most readily through the exchange of bodily fluids that can occur when the rectum-colon develops fissures simply highlights the perhaps unique consequences associated with anal intercourse. But anal intercourse is not the issue here.

Anal intercourse only symbolizes the broader content of an active gay male lifestyle that heterosexism opposes. With lesbianism, it is the rejection of supposed male-female complementarity that heterosexists cannot tolerate. In other words, it appears that for most people who are against reform of traditional Church teaching that condemns homosexuality, an active gay lifestyle includes the demonstration of *any* affection that confuses the accepted heterosexual roles of male and females in responding to each other sexually. It does not matter that these roles, even in traditional views, have flexibility and breadth. Heterosexists must face their own changing sexual lives and roles. If they open themselves to mining the riches of their own sexuality they might also overcome the prejudices that narrowly delimit "appropriate" kinds of affection within same-sex relationships.

A SYMBOLIC CASE STUDY: ORDINATION

Nothing has focused the difficulties the Church has with homosexuality as intensely as the question of ordaining gays and lesbians. Many people who adopt the conservative but compassionate approach, thereby supposedly abolishing heterosexism yet without reconstructing a sexual ethic, argue that the public teaching of the Church can change only on the basis of grassroots acceptance of gays and lesbians. Only at some future point, after that general acceptance is widespread, can the Church think about installing gays and lesbians in leadership roles.[13] Although a necessary component of reform, this is too narrow an approach given the destructive context of heterosexism.

The Church has an analogous precedent in the matter of ordaining gays and lesbians. The decision to ordain women says in principle that being a woman and acting as a woman are not impediments in serving as a pastor (priest, minister). This does not mean that being female rather than male has no effect on the role of pastor. On the contrary, the Church's understanding and experience of the role are enriched by the gifts women bring simply by being who they are. The same might be true in the ordination of gays and lesbians.

At least two things modify the analogy between ordaining women and ordaining gays and lesbians. The first is that we already have some experience with homosexual pastors. In spite of the conspiracy of silence surrounding it, the Church has always had homosexual pastors and knows of their ability to function well in that role. The Church did not, obviously, experience closeted women pastors. One can hide sexual orientation and behavior; Yentl aside, one cannot hide biological identity. Thus the Church, or more accurately some portions of it, had to decide to ordain women in order to see what the experience of that reality would create.

This leads to the second distinction.[14] On the basis of Scripture and experience, not ecclesiastical tradition, the churches that decided to ordain women agreed that to do so was not contrary to those witnesses. Thus an emerging consensus provided the foundation for legislative reform of the ecclesiastical tradition. Such an emerging consensus does not yet exist for ordaining gays and lesbians in any denomination except the United Church of Christ (UCC) and the Universal Fellowship of Metropolitan Community Churches (MCC). An ecclesiastical mandate, or at least permission, provided jurisdictional validity and legitimacy for women to be ordained.

Some will object that ordaining women is not the same kind of issue as ordaining sexually active gay and lesbian Christians. The objection grows out of the presumption that even if biological sex (being a woman) and sexual orientation (being gay or lesbian) may be equal "givens" of our created nature, the sexual *behavior* consonant with each is not. In other words, the heterocentric bias here states that women's sexual behavior as women is not in question, but that of homosexual men and women is.[15] We are only making the case that the ecclesiastical similarities outweigh the differences in drawing the analogy.

Significant points of similarity exist between the two: (1) many people still believe that it is contrary to God's will that either women or gays and lesbians should serve as ordained pastors; (2) the marshalling of biblical and theological arguments will not in itself resolve the questions (although such arguments must be made more fully than has been done to date); and (3) Protestant congregations must issue calls to candidates to test the adequacy of the Church's position. That is to say, even though a denomination decides to authorize the ordination of women, they cannot be ordained unless and until a congregation calls them as its pastor. This would also result if a denomination authorized gay and lesbian ordination. The ecclesiastical situation differs insofar as some church bodies made the legislative decision to ordain women before any were actually ordained. Churches have ordained gay and lesbian pastors without similar legislative mandate.

Those denominations that chose to ordain women did so knowing that other Christian communities were in sharp disagreement. They proceeded on the basis of conscience and as matter of strategy to ordain women in spite of the lack of ecumenical consensus. Are congregations or bishops *within* a denomination who make a decision to ordain gays and lesbians on the basis of conscience, informed by Scripture and experience, and as a matter of strategy without broader denominational consensus, in an analogous position?

Specific ecclesiastical actions lead to ecumenically significant ecclesiological conclusions. Those denominations that ordain women are inviting the Christian communities that do not to reconsider their position. They are also saying, if they are committed to sustaining the ordination of women, that the inability or unwillingness of other church bodies to do so will continue to result in Church division. In other words they will sacrifice specific forms of unity for the sake of this issue. If denominations can take such a stance with integrity, can congregations and bishops within a denomination do so?

Here we have a few recent cases to inform our reflection. The ordination of Bill Johnson, by the United Church of Christ (UCC) in 1972, is documented in a video entitled, *A Position of Faith*. It was the first instance in the United States of a mainline Protestant denomination ordaining an openly gay man, and it resulted in the United Church of Christ's acceptance (in theory if not always in practice) of gay and lesbian clergy. Actions in the Episcopal Church have raised different ecclesiological questions. Bishops stand in apostolic succession (although this is disputed by the Roman Catholic church) and have the authority to ordain apart from the consent of other bishops. The ordination of a lesbian in a committed relationship in Washington, D.C., by Bishop Ronald H. Haines in June 1991, led to an unsuccessful attempt to censure him. The ordination of a gay man who later repudiated his initial promises, by Bishop John S. Spong, also called into question whether a bishop should act unilaterally because the House of Bishops has not authorized the ordination of homosexual priests. In the Evangelical Lutheran Church in America, two congregations ordained a gay man and two lesbian women without authorization in January 1990.

The issue of *reception* links all these extraordinary exercises of authority. The particular actions in question can lead to reform only if the larger church willingly receives what has been done. The primary issue for the church in each case becomes how to determine the boundaries of legitimate dissent. We believe that one should not risk or threaten unity simply on the basis of possible improvement; only matters of justice merit ecclesial or civil disobedience. If such dissent is respected, a corollary task is to determine how the dissenting group's alternative vision of the given issue might be incorporated in the larger community's life. We will examine the ELCA example in detail.

THE BOUNDARIES OF DISSENT

The basic facts in this case are straightforward. On Saturday, January 20, 1990, two Evangelical Lutheran Church in America (ELCA) congregations, St. Francis Lutheran Church and First United Lutheran Church in San Francisco, ordained Ruth Frost, Phyllis Zillhart, and Jeff Johnson, each of whom had indicated publicly that they are, respectively, lesbian women and a gay man unwilling to commit themselves to lives of sexual abstinence. The bishop of the synod in which the congregations are located, in accord with the constitutional provisions of his synod and the ELCA, did not approve the ordinations.

The ordinands had successfully completed all of the normal requirements leading to approval for call—enrollment in seminary, synod endorsement, internship, graduation with an M.Div. degree, and certification by an approval committee. Their sexual orientation and behavior were the decisive factors in their being considered ineligible for call and ordination. The California congregations decided that they had a right and responsibility both to call and to ordain these candidates even though such actions contradicted the guidelines of the synod and the ELCA.

At least two significant points of controversy resulted from this. The first was whether sexual activity between persons of the same sex disqualifies a person from service in ordained pastoral ministry. The ELCA has stated that homosexual orientation does not in itself disqualify. Broader ELCA norms drawn from statements of predecessor Lutheran church bodies make it clear that sexual exploitation, promiscuity, or abuse in any form are contrary to the church's understanding of responsible sexual behavior. One can assume that this would be applied to homosexual as well as heterosexual behavior.

A specific consequence of the current ELCA position on homosexual behavior, however, is rejection of just, faithful, and loving homosexual activity. Gay and lesbian candidates for ministry are asked to commit themselves to lifelong sexual abstinence to bear witness to the morally normative nature of heterosexual, monogamous, and faithful marriages. The ELCA is not asking for chastity in this case. Chastity is expected of all single candidates for ministry whether heterosexual or homosexual. Lifelong sexual abstinence is expected only of homosexual candidates.

The second point of controversy resulting from the congregations' unauthorized actions was how to resolve a matter of corporate church discipline. This ecclesiastical issue influences how the debate over the first point of controversy can be conducted. Church discipline in this case brings into sharp focus the tension in Lutheran church polity between congregational authority and the broader unity of the church.

Historical precedents in Lutheranism remain important in theological dialogue among Lutherans today. Martin Luther, in a 1523 letter of advice to a congregation in Leisnig, addressed an issue of ecclesial disobedience regarding ordination. He explained why and under what circumstances this congregation had the right and responsibility to call and ordain its own pastor when the structures of the larger church stood against such action. For the Leisnig congregation, as later for all reformation congregations, calling and ordaining outside the ecclesiastical structures of the day became a necessity. It was a matter of exercising legitimate (from the reformers' point of view) dissent in an effort to make the Christian community a community of genuine theological discourse and gospel proclamation.[16]

In the current ELCA dilemma the issue turns on whether the church can recognize the actions of these congregations as an exercise of legitimate dissent. In other words, can the church consider their deliberations and decisions to call and ordain sexually active gay and lesbian candidates as moral acts of moral people who believe an issue of the gospel is at stake? Many people refuse to grant that the San Francisco congregations acted as people of genuine moral conviction who had come, by way of their interpretation of Scripture and tradition, to *a legitimate* conclusion contrary to the larger church's established position.

The concern about a "slippery slope" emerges here. If we accept this particular case as legitimate dissent, why not others? What prevents segregationists from demanding acceptance, or at least minority status, within the ELCA? Nothing prevents it, nor should anything prevent it as a matter of principle. In such other cases, the precedent established here is the legitimacy of dissent that occurs within acceptable boundaries. Others would need to make their own positive, substantive argument for the coherence of their position with the gospel. If that case could be made, then indeed the larger community might be called to some kind of reform.

We are arguing that Lutherans have biblical, historical, and experiential reasons for making a case for ordaining gay men and lesbians that is both substantive and compelling. Furthermore, the arguments, when tested, prove more consistent with the gospel than those made to defend the prevailing patterns of the church's life with regard to these sexual issues. We doubt that such a case can be mounted by, for example, segregationists. Furthermore, we already have historical experience of their destructiveness in the Church. We do not have such historical experience of what open affirmation of homosexual people might mean for the community.

When people of good will within a single community (in this case, the ELCA) genuinely disagree among themselves, what paths are open for resolution of the conflict? The divisive response has a long history among Protestants. If you disagree, split and form your own ecclesiastical body. More than a few congregations in California informed their bishop that they would withdraw from the ELCA if these ordinations occurred and were allowed to stand unchallenged. Such congregational threats reveal the depth of emotional response to these issues.

Many people are deeply convinced that there is a clear right and wrong with regard to their interpretation of the legitimacy or illegitimacy of gay or lesbian clergy. The question remains whether and how a contrary point of view can find concrete expression in the church as a means of fostering genuine theological reflection concerning it.

The larger church has the continuing responsibility to take seriously any member congregation's call to address an issue in a new way when the old ways have been judged inadequate. One can argue that there was a better way than that chosen by the churches in California. The congregations as well as the candidates could have been more patient. Processes are in place for review of such issues. Furthermore, the time was not right for the ELCA (newly established just two years earlier) to tackle such a controversial and potentially divisive issue.

Perhaps these suggestions merited more consideration. When action has been taken, however, the question becomes what the church will do in response to it. Will it provoke a legalistic reaction or will it evoke careful communitywide moral deliberation, as is the intention of all who engage in civil or ecclesiastical disobedience?

The ruling of the ELCA at the moment is clear enough. Either the calling congregations repudiate their action within five years (or be in conformity with church teaching, which could change in that time), or they have set themselves outside the boundaries of the ELCA. Similarly, if no change occurs in church teaching, the ordinations of the candidates in question will be considered illicit; that is, they will not be recognized by those congregations that remain in the ELCA. The dilemma in such questions of discipline is whether applying the law strictly, as this ruling does, will witness to the gospel and serve justice. If one cannot grant that it may be reasonable or intelligible, if not compelling, to believe that the service of sexually active gay and lesbian people in ordained pastoral ministry conforms with the gospel, then no recourse exists but to exercise strict legal discipline.

It is always difficult to accept reforming action. Martin Luther was not happy with his need to advise congregations to circumvent the church structures of his day. Yet we recognize the right of people at times to take radical steps because the circumstances seem *to them* to demand it. It seemed so to Luther and his friends, for example, but certainly not to his opponents. Luther himself did not adhere strictly to the advice he gave in 1523. He backed away from what we would term a purely congregational polity.

In other words, a congregation is not the whole Church and cannot, in the long run, act unilaterally. What the California congregations have done must be evaluated by the larger Church. Yet the reformation emphasis on the calling authority of a congregation as the primary prerequisite for ordination also means that the ELCA cannot claim, except in a narrow, legal way, that these congregations had no right to do what they did.[17] Lutheran tradition has not supported such an absolute stance on the question of who can call and ordain. Both the Protestant and Roman Catholic communions, indeed the whole Church, must ask whether and how congregations have a share in the teaching office of the Church.

Ordination is a privilege, not a positive right. It is a ritual action of empowerment authorized and carried out by the whole Church. Individuals cannot demand to be ordained purely on the basis of their personal conviction that God has called them. Churches have the right and responsibility to develop standards of expectations for those called to serve in ordained pastoral ministry and to say yes or no to their offer of service in that particular role. The current situation poses a challenge to identify the specific threat to the unity of the Lutheran church created by the extraordinary exercise of this right and responsibility by two congregations.

These ELCA congregations believe that they acted to live out their understanding of the justice evoked by the gospel in these circumstances. They may be wrong. It may indeed be contrary to God's will that sexually active gay and lesbian people should serve the Church as ordained pastors (of course, we do not believe this to be the case). The actions of these two congregations, however, inform the rest of the Church. They believe that the best way to test the tradition is to allow sexually active gay and lesbian clergy to function openly as pastors in a congregation (we already know that there are gay and lesbian clergy).

Whether one opposes or favors the action of St. Francis and First United congregations, there is a "safeguard" in ELCA procedures for calling and ordaining. The power to call a pastor resides in the authority of congregations. If the larger church finally determines that this was an unwise choice, the consequence could be that no other congregations would ever call these pastors. In the end it is only the whole community's commitment that will effect change.

For those who support the action, however, that same safeguard has liabilities. Dependence on a congregational call means that unjust discrimination can be sustained for decades, as has been experienced by people of color and women. It is worth asking in the midst of this discussion whether disciplinary pressure should be brought to bear on congregations that continue to refuse to seriously consider calling women and people of color, because such refusal is contrary to the normative teaching of the ELCA. Thus the claim by gay and lesbian candidates for ordination that this is an issue of justice is bolstered by evidence that the application of normative teaching is discriminatory and inconsistent.

Persons who engage in civil disobedience wish to be as public as possible because they want the very prosecution of their case to provide the public forum for dialogue that is hindered or even absent in other channels (e.g., legislative). They want to use the courtroom as a place to give testimony. As defendants they are sure their voices will be heard. People who engage in ecclesial disobedience are trying to do the same thing—to create a forum for dialogue, a context in which their point of view can be articulated and heard seriously.

We must be concerned about both the judgments rendered in a disciplinary process and the process itself. It is unlikely and probably unwise for the church to allow a judicial proceeding to be legislative. Even if its own policy on the matter is not changed at this point, the ELCA's judicial discipline may in the end signal a refusal to continue dialogue on this issue. How can the church establish a zone of respectable debate that honors divergent action? Is there reasonable doubt about the ELCA's current position? Does such dissent stop progress on controverted issues or create or push the church to a fuller dialogue concerning them?

A variety of disciplinary options are open; for example, visitation and remonstrance by the bishop(s), public censure of the congregations, or their removal from the congregational roster of the ELCA. Will allowing the action to stand as a legitimate course for individual parish dissent without formal condemnation or approval by the ELCA better serve the cause of moral and theological deliberation than punitive action? Will taking punitive action result in the proverbial sigh of relief while ignoring the challenges this issue presents?

A primary ecclesiastical concern forced by this event is how to define the limits of legitimate dissent. Perhaps we might at least grant that, in the confusion and controversy surrounding homosexual orientation and behavior, there is room for significant dissent from what otherwise remains the normative interpretation of the larger Church. The issues have been and remain so controverted that we will not be able to convince one another by argument alone.

We have only begun to address the complex questions emerging from our growing understanding of human sexual identity and the social contexts that shape it. The matter is not closed, as people imply when they claim that Scripture and tradition have answered this once and for all. These are troubling issues. Yet the actions of these congregations can be understood and used as an opportunity to reach a level of engagement in theological and moral discourse that is rarely managed. The Church does itself a disservice when it pretends that problems will go away.

CONCLUSION

The challenge in this chapter has been to look at the internal life of the Church as a community of the gospel. We have argued that reform of the Church's life and teaching regarding sexuality is a faithful response to the gospel in the contemporary world. One frequently hears the opposite: that reform will compromise the Church, sell out to secular values, and encourage sin. On the contrary, we believe that maintaining the status quo, undergirding heterosexism, is what results in these problems.

The Church has lost its voice, its credibility, and its capacity to encourage responsible sexual lifestyles precisely because it has adopted a culture-bound and narrowly conceived "human" view of sexuality. At the very point where it can speak a clear word about the divine will regarding diversity, mutuality, and responsibility—seeing sexuality as a gift to be nurtured and channeled in the service of love rather than suppressed and controlled as a means of power—the Church has repeatedly allowed itself to be silenced by prevailing cultural norms.

The test case of ordination clearly illustrates the problem. It reveals our unwillingness to take the lead both in defining the problem and in describing constructive response to it. Ordaining gay and lesbian pastors is not, of course, a solution to the problem. We might consider it one necessary step among many for the Church to provide a coherent and consistent ethic of moral responsibility in its own life. Without that, the world in which the Church bears its message of grace and salvation in Jesus Christ will rightly judge its witness wanting.

6

Dismantling Heterosexism

I've struggled all my life to stay a member of the church. I think I've lived a good life, and I care about others. I volunteer for as much as I can. I truly believe the Bible's story about God and Jesus. But deep inside I know that I'm a worthless person because the church's view of homosexuality has told me so over and over again. No one knows I'm gay, and I've never had a sexual relationship with anyone. I'm afraid of what God will do to me. There's no way God can love me if my whole being is sinful and corrupt because I'm gay. Really, I just wish I would die.

One of the most troubling consequences of heterosexism in the Church is what it does to the faith of believers. These comments by a gay man reveal the depths to which a person's self-esteem can be pushed by the unrelenting condemnation of the Church. Making a distinction between orientation and behavior is of no help here. Even when homosexual persons manage to be abstinent, the judgment of the Church makes them feel alienated from God. Some heterosexist people believe that this reflects God's righteous response to their sexual disorientation.

We contend that this destructive framework does not necessarily follow from God's Word in Scripture and tradition. It results from our heterocentric world-view. One can construct a sexual ethic that frees the erotic dimension of human life from heterosexist prejudices. The erotic as a gift of God can be a genuine path to the holy. In such a view sexuality is not a barrier to the holy but rather is part of the God-given means by which we are able to relate passionately to one another, to the world, and to God.

We open the chapter with a brief discussion of how the Church might draw on the links between spirituality and sexuality that have always been implicit in faith and theology, yet have been devalued or ignored, to begin the process of dismantling heterosexism. We do so recognizing that we cannot offer here a fully developed sexual ethic. We focus on marriage as a ritual test case for exploring links between Christian spirituality and sexuality. Our review of traditional descriptions of marriage includes pointing out weaknesses in those links as forged by heterosexism. We offer a reassessment of marriage based on a nonheterosexist appropriation of the insights of Scripture and tradition. Our approach suggests that by reframing its own experience the Church can contribute positively to the broader culture in developing an inclusive sexual ethic. It does so most effectively when it also recognizes that the broader culture contributes to the reframing.

TOWARD A THEOLOGY OF SEXUALITY

Modern theology has contributed to the developing traditions of the Church in its recovery of the wholeness inherent in Christian faith and life. History, liturgy, spirituality, doctrinal theology, ethics—so often treated as independent categories in the past—are mined for their interconnectedness. Reformation of Christian understanding of human sexuality will need to draw from the insights of all these disciplines.

Despite this interdisciplinary context and the movement toward more holistic theologies, the divisive influence of heterosexism remains basically unchallenged. Heterosexism undermines Christian life by supporting a dualism that is at odds with its incarnational faith. The fact that we are created male and female does not in itself cause dualism or heterosexism. Rather, sexual differentiation constitutes a primary sign of the diversity intrinsic to creation. Unfortunately, dualism rather than this diversity has informed theologies of sexuality in Christian tradition.[1] Theologians tend to interpret sexual behavior in the context of the Fall, often to the neglect of its foundation in the good of Creation. Augustine's theology provides perhaps the classic illustration of this.[2]

Christian tradition has always affirmed that Creation is good, including our creation as male and female in the image of God. But the Genesis accounts of the Garden of Eden and our expulsion from it have been used as the matrix for interpreting human sexuality. A sense of the brokenness of our sexuality so overshadows the affirmation of it as a created good that it undermines attempts to develop a positive sexual ethic. We have tended to treat all sexual desire as lust in an "after the Fall" theological framework. The knowledge of good and evil, shame in nakedness, pain in procreation, and sin have all played a role in shaping the dualistic frameworks we have used to make sense of our sexuality. An influential formulation of this view is Paul's comment that "it is better to marry than to burn" (1 Cor 7:9), which appears repeatedly in subsequent tradition.

If we engage the task of dismantling heterosexism, a new sexual ethic will demand that we revalue the body as a created good, neither always at odds with nor a prison for the soul and spirit. The energy of our sexual desire is not, in this view, a fundamentally evil inclination to be controlled. It represents the foundational dimension of our incarnate capacity to live passionately in the world.[3]

To say this does not negate the reality of sexual sin. Lust is real. In our brokenness and alienation we can succumb to the destructive power of lust, particularly in a heterosexist framework that reinforces dualism. Sexual desire becomes lust when it is used as a means to control or exploit others for the sake of personal satisfaction. Lust cannot serve as the source for sustaining and nourishing human relationships because lust is not a sustainable or sustaining emotion. It takes but cannot genuinely give and receive. It is a transitory channeling of sexual expression that treats the other solely as object. It has no interest in the mutuality of relationship. When sexuality is defined narrowly as lust we diminish our capacity to relate to creation as sexual people. Lust can also be idolatry, when people play god or give to another the role of god. Like greed, lust is self-serving yet ultimately destructive.

Christian faith offers us the freedom to live passionately in, with, and for the world. World includes the whole of the environment, all of the earth's creatures along with human beings. We are invited to delight in this diversity and to find within it appropriate ways of expressing our passionate desire for relatedness. This is especially true for the joyful gift of human embodiment as expressed in the biblical book Song of Songs. In contrast, heterosexism shortcircuits the energy that human sexuality supplies for our embodied relation to creation. It does so through its systemically prejudicial understanding of sexuality.

If the only proper experience of sexual energy is in male-female coupling, our attention will be focused on controlling it, on keeping it within those bounds. When we acknowledge sexuality as an image of and path to the holy, it will necessarily include creation in its purview. The passionate nature of Jesus' Passion provides perhaps *the* most powerful witness of God's intent that our created nature and the whole world's salvation are forever bound to each other. A heterosexist framework encourages the divorcing of sexuality from our embodied relationship to the world. It encapsulates passion rather than freeing it to be the means by which we relate.

The central issue here is one's understanding of sexuality. We understand it as a broad and inclusive term for the fact of our sexual identities in creation. In other words, we cannot be nonsexual people. This means that we can never escape having our thoughts and actions, our ways of relating to others and to the world, somehow shaped by the basic incarnational reality of our sexual being.

Honoring this reality does not automatically lead to the conclusion that "anything goes" in sexual behavior, although we acknowledge that some people are persuaded that such a case can be made. We also hope it is clear that we are not laying a foundation for defending bestiality with this line of argument. We firmly believe that there are legitimate boundaries for specific sexual expression. A completely unrestrictive view of sexual behavior is not defensible for at least two reasons already discussed: (1) the reality of lust as a manifestation of our alienation and brokenness, and (2) the scriptural witness of Genesis, which argues for a particular partnership between humans different, but not disconnected, from our relationship to the rest of creation.

From the perspective of the Christian faith community, faithful response to and use of our sexual being cannot be reduced to biological instincts. We relate passionately through our bodies to the world and all its creatures. It is impossible not to do so unless our bodies are only incidental rather than central to our being. How we relate can be constructive or destructive. Mutuality is a key for constructive human sexual behavior.[4]

For specific sexual behaviors to be mutual neither partner can be the object of the other. All of creation responds to us in ways that bespeak mutuality. All those who love their pets and feel love in return know the deep truth of such experience. But the scriptural witness from Genesis about fit partnership rooted in our shared humanity seems to us to offer an appropriate criterion for developing constructive boundaries.

One might make the criticism that we are guilty of an anthropologism that, in terms of imposing limits on sexual expression, is analogous to heterosexism's limiting of it. The critic might ask, "why draw the line here rather than somewhere else; why draw the line at all?" We can answer only on the basis of how our faith commitments and the wisdom of the Christian community's experience and reflection on such matters persuade us that unbounded sexual behavior is destructive. One of the boundaries comes from the likeness of our sexuality as human beings. We are indeed made for each other as people (but not simply as male and female).

The task of ethical reflection is to articulate the appropriate and, for Christians, theologically responsible and faithful boundaries that create constructive, genuinely mutual sexual behavior. We have argued that heterosexism constitutes a destructive system of prejudice that inappropriately and unfaithfully restricts sexual expression. Developing and living in a constructive framework—an inclusive sexual ethic—that replaces heterosexism remains the unfinished task of the reform we advocate.

The divisiveness of a heterosexist framework is self-evident in our history of struggling with sexual ethics in the Church. We also manifest divisiveness in our reluctance to entertain the possibility that sexuality can be connected with spirituality, let alone be a primary source of energy for the whole of Christian life. Traditional ways of contrasting *eros* and *logos* in Christian discourse reveal the linguistic signs of this reluctance to honor the body as fully as the mind. Yet the biblical witness abounds with evidence that God intends sexuality as a good and precious gift that through our maleness and femaleness mediates the image of God (Gen 1:27).

Sexuality provides us with the capacity to reach out to others. This reaching out and the expression of our identity are grounded in God's reaching out to us and identifying with us as a person (the Incarnation). The biblical witness that "the Word was made flesh" further reveals that human sexuality images God.

Judaism has been clear that the "God of Abraham, Isaac, and Jacob" is not a sexual being like the gods of other religions. Christianity has accepted this perspective but has the additional challenge of explaining the connection between Jesus' historical identity as a male, sexual being and the reality of God. The Church attempts to do this with its ongoing elaboration of the doctrine of the Trinity and Christology within it. That God both transcends and somehow embraces sexuality as we experience it is perhaps a fundamental illustration of the mystery of the Incarnation.

If we can let go of a male-female dichotomy we can avoid the trap of perceiving God's "sexuality" as some kind of hermaphroditic union. We believe that we cannot, however, deny that God somehow embraces the embodiment of sexuality. The Incarnation affirms that God fully assumed our *humanity*, not just maleness, in Jesus of Nazareth. The traditional theological affirmation that Jesus was like all the rest of humankind except without sin provides an uncompromising affirmation of our sexual being. Being fully human includes the breadth and depth of human sexual identity. Again, if we broadly conceive of sexuality as the energy or power that animates our life and our capacity for passionate relatedness, we can incorporate it into more traditional formulations of trinitarian theology. The community of *persons* that constitutes the Trinity is characterized by mutual love, no matter how one describes that interplay.

We are not *reducing* sexuality to the capacity for pleasurable communion with others. Rather we are naming it as the *source* of our capacity for such pleasure. This does not mean that sexuality has nothing to do with issues deeper than pleasure, like commitment, mutuality, and love. People often level this charge at those who challenge heterosexism's centralization of procreation, complementarity, or power as *the* determinative characteristic of sexuality. Feminist theology has been especially helpful in challenging these distortive preoccupations.

In a discussion of Paul Ricoeur's observation that there have been three major stages in the evolution of understandings of sexuality in relation to religion in the Western Church, James Nelson argues that "there is a growing recognition that sexuality is so involved in the center of a person's life and of his or her powers of creativity that its denial thwarts the deepest possibilities of human fulfillment. Sexual expression still needs ordering and discipline, yes, but that is quite different from the denial of the spiritual power of sexuality itself."[5] To acknowledge sexuality as a source of our capacity for communion with the world and God connects us with the deepest issues of life.

To develop a view of sexuality that is expansive, faithful to biblical witness, responsive to the concerns of Christian tradition, and consistent with revelation, we must challenge the heterocentric paradigm that has shaped the questions we ask and the answers we seek. We must challenge our traditional preoccupations. The central issue becomes our willingness to reconnect the breadth of human sexuality and holiness. Furthermore, only within such a view will we be able to reevaluate the place of homosexuality.

MARRIAGE: A RITUAL TEST CASE

One should not assume that an analysis of marriage and the argument that as an institution it might be open to gays and lesbians arises from a univocal demand from the homosexual community. We address our argument to heterosexual and homosexual readers alike. In fact gays and lesbians may be more antagonistic than heterosexual men and women to the suggestion that they marry.

An example of this is captured in the following comments by a gay couple as they planned a public ceremony to announce their union before family and friends:

> We both knew from the start that we did not want to call our ritual a "wedding." We did not want any association with an institution that was rooted in concepts of property, an institution that had oppressed women for centuries, and that still today can imply stultifying possessiveness and confining gender roles. Ironically, our involuntary position outside the law was an opportunity to stand apart from "marriage"; we took that opportunity with relish.[6]

Compare this with the observations of Richard Mohr on his gay "marriage":

> After a decade together, we feel and to many puzzled others appear more married than the married.
>
> All the more strange and enraging it is then that in the eyes of the law we are necessarily strangers to each other, people who had as well never met. In Illinois, one cannot will one's body. By statute, it goes to next of kin. That which was most one's own—the substrate for personality—which was most one's own for another—that in which and by which one loves and makes love—is, for gays, not one's at all. The lover is barred from the lover's funeral. The compulsory intervention of heterosexuality at death is the final degradation worked by The People on gay people.[7]

If we refuse to hear the pain, frustration, and anger that lie behind these comments we cannot hope to be credible partners in a genuine dialogue about human sexuality. As we stated earlier, such dialogue, characterized by deep and sincere listening, provides only the starting point for reform.

Traditional Views

The Western Church has viewed marriage as a relationship of two persons.[8] The underlying assumption in Church and society historically has been that the persons involved are male and female. Can a marriage exist for two persons of the same sex? If marriage describes an exclusive and permanent loving commitment of two people, we believe that there is no reason in principle for restricting it to heterosexual couples.[9]

The traditional objection to an expansion of our understanding of marriage to include same-sex couples is rooted in an argument imputed to nature and a conclusion derived from it. The argument goes like this. Human beings are by nature dimorphically (either-or) differentiated sexually as males and females. At the biological level creation is structured so that procreation requires heterosexual union. From this some argued that marriage can encompass only such a procreative, heterosexual union.

Even if we accept for the moment that dimorphic sexual differentiation is unambiguous, no intrinsic connection between procreation and marriage can be maintained unless one restricts marriage to procreative unions. Even for Roman Catholics, the most consistent in applying this criterion to marriage, the issue yields more nuances than one might expect.

For example, we do not consider heterosexual couples who marry but remain childless less married than others who procreate. The Roman Catholic view qualifies this by saying that if the choice or intention not to procreate exists from its inception, a marriage is never really constituted (it therefore provides grounds for annulment). Some argue that the childless couple, if consisting of a male and a female, possess at least the potential to be a procreative union.[10] A homosexual couple, however, is necessarily rather than contingently childless. Thus, if one defines marriage by procreation, a same-sex couple cannot be considered married.[11]

We affirm that a biblically rooted view of creation connects procreation and our differentiation as male and female. One cannot state the precise nature of that link in terms of marriage and family. Is this male-female distinction and its association with procreation an essential characteristic of marriage? In traditional theological terms the question is whether the distinction constitutes an ontological truth about marriage. Oliver O'Donovan answers in the affirmative.[12] He articulates a position held by many and representative of a heterocentric view. O'Donovan argues that two aspects of our understanding of marriage must be kept in tension for it to have full meaning, the personal and the biological. Like many others, he maintains that calls for a reinterpretation of marriage often emphasize the personal and neglect the biological. This neglect renders ambiguous at best and empty at worst the meaning of male and female differentiation.

At the core of this position lies the belief that the biological foundations for human sexuality are dimorphic. Dimorphism means that we are either male *or* female and that the sexes are oppositional in design. Proponents of this view understand maleness and femaleness as the gift of creation and as inextricably linked with masculinity and femininity. O'Donovan concedes that some dimensions of identity (the psychological) are dipolar. Dipolarism does not deny that people are basically male or female. Physiologically, hermaphroditism is a rarity. It emphasizes the fact that even though we are born with self-evidently male or female genitalia, we do not define our sexual identities by that alone.

With its capacity to respect a sexual continuum, a dipolar view of sexuality may become a better overall framework for organizing the evidence that continues to emerge as our understanding of human sexuality grows. We do not think the debate between advocates of dimorphic and dipolar views will be easily settled. However, even if it turns out that a dimorphic framework better suits the evidence, heterosexism will find no support in it. In other words, the mere fact of our biological differentiation as males and females does not justify the claim that heterosexual marriage is the only normative sexual lifestyle—not even when one restricts sexuality to genital behavior. Our common sense recognition of the validity of being single precludes such a conclusion as much as our acceptance of homosexuality would.

On the basis of a dimorphic view O'Donovan moves to the conclusion that only marriage between a male and female can fully enable human relationships.[13] The logic of such a position is not self-evident. We believe it results from an unexamined heterocentric bias. The research of sociobiologists has called into question any narrow interpretation of the function of human sexuality that restricts it to a procreative purpose. We agree that we must maintain the connection between the biological realities of reproduction and the interpersonal relationships that make their expression meaningful. The fact that we are male and female does have implications for our social interaction. O'Donovan rightly criticizes advocates of a personalist perspective, which holds that nature is arbitrary and to be regarded as a problem to overcome rather than a gift of the Creator.[14] Our disagreement lies with those who claim that a heterosexual marriage is the *only* way to realize fully the giftedness of our biological life as males and females.

The belief that only male-female marriage can hold the personal and biological in proper tension can become thinly disguised biologism.[15] That is to say, in the end we reduce our capacity to be fully human in marriage to the "biological datum" that we are dimorphically differentiated as males and females: "Sexual status in marriage cannot be determined by purely social criteria, since *the biological opposition of the sexes is essential to it* as an institution."[16] For heterosexists, the biological opposition alone can provide the glue that cements human bonds. Challenging the hegemony of this claim is central to dismantling heterosexism.

We believe that marriage as an institution ought not be based on the oppositional character of dimorphic presuppositions about human sexuality. Neither should it derive its personal, social, or theological meaning from that base. One might mount a credible argument, like O'Donovan's, for the dimorphic structure of sexuality being "the generically given foundation for our individual sexual vocations." But it does not necessarily follow that marriage must be a "permanent *heterosexual* union."[17] One can also logically argue that gay men and lesbians can, through their homosexual relationships, do what heterosexists claim can only be done in opposite sex relationships. That is, they can express their individuality as persons and enjoy their masculinity or femininity fully. The experience of gay men and lesbians attests to this.

According to tradition, permanence and exclusivity form part of the defining theological characteristics of marriage.[18] The Judaeo-Christian witness claims that God's self-revelation is marked by faithfulness and also in some sense by exclusivity (chosen people). This is understood as a covenant in the Hebrew traditions and as an unconditional promise in the New Testament. Christianity's unique witness regarding the divine-human encounter comes from its understanding of grace as God's unconditional love. The crucifixion and resurrection of Jesus affirm that nothing, not even death, will prevent God from keeping the promise to be with us always.

Marriage is the only institution in which human beings make publicly supported commitments of permanence and exclusivity. Lest we be led astray by terminology we should state that *institution* is the key word here. Marriage is both a private and public relationship. It has a unique public character as a socially supported institution or structure for human relating. Among such communal support structures for marriage are inheritance laws, tax benefits, hospital visitation rights, bereavement leave, insurance benefits, property sharing, the blending of financial assets, and extended family. All of these contribute to the sustainability of the relationship (they can also, of course contribute to trapping people in relationships).

Obviously many of us make commitments unconditionally to others without knowing beforehand what the terms of those relationships will be; for example, to parents, children, even close friends. But such unconditional commitments are not necessarily qualified by exclusivity or supported by social, economic, and legal structures in the same way as marriage. Nor do they embrace all aspects of sexual identity as marriage does.

Can same-sex unions embody permanence and exclusivity, including the sexual dimensions of being? We believe they can, but recognize that this is not self-evident in a heterocentric framework. Many continue to see as necessary the link between male-female differentiation (the dimorphic structure of sexuality) and the *ability* to sustain an unconditional, permanent union. Heterosexism demands that male-female opposition with its corresponding implications of complementarity be understood as the only glue that makes human bonds last. If one abandons the dimorphic structure, as in homosexual unions, a prerequisite for sustained commitment is absent.

Heterosexists base the human capacity for unconditional commitment on the biological need of male and female for each other. Whether one elaborates this need in terms of procreation or the belief that persons become whole only in relationship to the opposite sex, the result is the same. Heterosexists believe that only males and females can be truly committed to each other.

To summarize, we do not dispute the claim that male-female sexuality defines an essential part of human sexual vocation or that for heterosexual couples this may be a source of energy for making the most of their committed relationship. We challenge the *scope* of the claim. The challenge can be supported by biblical, theological, and experiential evidence.

The energy necessary for sustained commitment comes from differentiation. Heterosexual couples realize that a certain sexual electricity, magnetism, or attraction is rooted in being differentiated as male and female. Heterosexism denies that the experience of gays and lesbians possesses the same kind of electricity, magnetism, and attraction that occurs between men and women. Yet this sexual energy, not heterosexual energy, drives our human capacity for bonding and provides the physiological basis for it, whether one is heterosexual or homosexual.

Such sexual energy does not suffice to sustain unconditional commitment. In conventional wisdom about heterosexual marriages one explains this in terms of the end of the honeymoon or the fluctuations of romance. Whether this view of romantic love holds true or not, traditional wisdom has recognized that a marriage commitment is a decision, a choice, and an ongoing act of the will. When or if we fall out of love we do not automatically dissolve our marriage. The relationship has deeper and richer resources to sustain it.

An examination of the content and structure of rituals surrounding marriage reveals that in spite of the heterosexist bias of the Christian tradition, permanence and exclusivity are more significant than male-female complementarity or procreation in naming the uniqueness of the marriage relationship. The issue of uniqueness, even in a descriptive approach, can tend toward minimalism or reductionism. Nevertheless, if we are to understand what distinguishes marriage from other relationships we must risk it. A key concern throughout history has been what creates a marriage between two people.

Drawing on the evidence of Roman Catholic canon law, Theodore Mackin notes that mutual consent constitutes the key component in the creation of a marriage.[19] The content of that consent includes the mutual granting of a permanent and exclusive right to one's body, especially regarding sexual acts. Mackin correctly points out that this view does not mean that the object of marital consent is procreation itself. This is more evident in cultures that affirm the decision of a couple to marry rather than prearranging marriage.

Because people usually base a decision to marry on both affection and reasoned choice, they highlight the significance of the mutual commitment. The fact that the vows remain a central focus in marriage rites indicates the importance of this personal promise making in a public context. Furthermore, Christian rites have been almost universally characterized by the unconditionality ("until death parts us") of this commitment and the necessity of mutual consent being made in a public rite. Not procreation alone, nor complementarity, nor our dimorphic biology get to the heart of marriage. All of these are important aspects of some marriages. Central or core to the tradition's teaching about marriage is the mutual, lifelong gifting of our bodies one to the other. A fine example of this is the Anglican marriage vow at the giving of rings: "With my body I thee worship." *Worship* here means endowing with worth, not idol making. Homosexual men and women are as capable as heterosexual men and women of making such a gift and of honoring each other's worth.

The "conservative but compassionate" approach to homosexuality discussed in chapter 5 would deny public Church sanction of same-sex unions, although tacitly (even if not officially) accepting the private blessing of them by some clergy. This pastoral response represents neither a neutral nor reforming stance. Clergy who take this approach must keep these blessings private to be faithful to the tradition as it has been understood. We have been arguing that the tradition does not demand this if one dismantles heterosexism. We also believe that the public Church blessing of same-sex unions does not contradict the heart of the tradition.

One approach to reform asks for the Church to incorporate same-sex unions within the current ritual structures that create supportive and gospel-centered links between heterosexual couples and the community. Another argues for developing a range of blessing rites for different kinds of relationships. Both are valuable and needed in our day. Our primary focus here is on whether traditional marriage rites can speak to both same-sex and different-sex unions.

The Content of Marriage Rites

Scripture does not give us a single or developed view of marriage, nor does it provide much evidence for rites that were used to formalize it.[20] The creation story in the earlier J (Yahwist) narrative (Gen 2:18–25) became the foundation in Judaism for understanding marriage as between a man and woman. As a unique companionship it separates the partnership between them from their relationship with the rest of created life: "This at last is bone of my bone and flesh of my flesh" (v. 23). As we argued earlier, we believe that it is their similarity more than their differences that makes their partnership suitable.

In the later creation narrative the companionship implied by the earlier account expands to include God's blessing of it: "Male and female he created them. God blessed them, and God said to them, 'Be fruitful and multiply'" (Gen 1:27–28). Throughout Judaeo-Christian tradition this passage is used to stress the connection between sexuality and fertility and, as we shall see, informs the content of ritual prayers and blessings.

The patriarchal traditions offer a variety of themes that reveal how marriage was understood and practiced, as for example in the stories of Abraham and Sarah or Jacob, Leah, and Rachel. Fertility is clearly an issue in these relationships. Procreation and marriage are so strongly linked that the woman in each case chooses another woman for her husband in order to provide offspring. Yet this very choosing ironically reveals that the marriage bond itself has an enduring significance beyond the fact of the woman's barrenness (for example, the relationship of Abraham and Sarah is not dissolved when Hagar is chosen).

Later traditions, such as the prophetic witness of Hosea, expand the understanding of marriage through the development of a God-Israel, husband-(adulterous) wife comparison. The emphasis in this comparison is fidelity. In texts such as Jeremiah 31:31–33 the faithfulness of God's covenant relationship with Israel clearly presupposes an analogy with the human covenant of marriage.[21] Similarly, the prophet Malachi states the covenant connection explicitly: "The Lord was a witness between you and the wife of your youth, to whom you have been faithless, though she is your companion and your wife by covenant" (2:14). The book *Song of Songs* provides an extended example of the positive assessment of sexual love in Scripture and of the importance of faithfulness: "Set me as a seal upon your heart, as a seal upon your arm; for love is as strong as death, passion fierce as the grave" (8:6).

In spite of such thematic evidence, we know little about the actual process by which people married and thereby symbolized the acceptance of these themes as constitutive elements of the relationship. Liturgical scholar Kenneth Stevenson summarizes the Old Testament evidence by saying that there are hints of the following ritual elements: agreement to marry at betrothal; a bride-price; a blessing; a veil for the bride, or crowns for both bride and groom; a procession; a feast; and the consummation of the marriage.[22]

The New Testament evidence regarding early Christian practice is also minimal and reflects its roots in Judaism. One finds a few references in the Gospels, as for example the wedding at Cana (Jn 2:1–11), the story of the wedding feast (Mt 22:1–14), the parable of the wise and foolish virgins (Mt 25:1–13), the controversy about divorce with the Sadducees (Mt 22:23–33), Jesus' comments on adultery (Mt 5:27), or the adaptation of the God-Israel marriage imagery to Jesus-Christians (Mt 9:15=Mk 2:19=Lk 5:34). But none of these tell us anything specific about marriage rites, prayers, or blessings.

Paul's comment, "I promised you in marriage to one husband, to present you as a chaste virgin to Christ" (2 Cor 11:2), would have made ritual sense to both Jews and Gentiles in the community at Corinth. We know that betrothal and marriage as a two-stage process was practiced among Jews and Hellenistic Greeks. The well-known comparison of earthly marriage and the relationship between Christ and the Church in Ephesians 5:22–33 reveals one way in which marriage was interpreted by Christians. But again we know little about the connections between practices and theological understanding.

An important point in the Ephesians text is its use of the one flesh imagery of Genesis to explain the relationship between Christ and the Church as nourishing and sustaining (v. 29). Such nourishing occurs "because we are members of his body" (v. 30). This connection makes it clear that we must exercise caution and not interpret the one flesh imagery of Genesis as referring to sexual intercourse alone. Furthermore, the diversity of the biblical references prevents us from reducing Christian interpretation of marriage to the issues of procreation or sexual complementarity.

As with the scriptural witness, the literary evidence of the first three centuries C.E. is also mixed and inconclusive. It consists mostly of passing references. For example,[23] Ignatius of Antioch (c. 35–107 C.E.): "It is right for men and women who marry to be united with the bishop's approval. In that way their marriage will follow God's will and not the promptings of lust" (*To Polycarp*, 5:2). Athenagoras of Athens (c. 177 C.E.): "Having, therefore, the hope of eternal life, we despise the enjoyments of the present, even the pleasures of the soul. According to our laws, each of us thinks of the woman he has married as his wife only for the purpose of bearing children. For as the farmer casts his seed on the soil and awaits the harvest without sowing over it, so we limit the pleasure of intercourse to bearing children" (*A Plea*, 33). In both cases people follow some kind of procedure for marrying, but we do not know its content. We might assume that the reason Athenagoras gives for marrying, procreation, would come to expression in a marriage rite, but we cannot verify it. Early Christian apologists, including Athenagoras, would have found this interpretation congenial for making the case that Christians are just like everyone else. They marry and have children and are thus good citizens. This does not create sufficient grounds for arguing that procreation was the single or even primary focus of the early Christian understanding of marriage.

One cannot, however, minimize the significance of the link between procreation and marriage in Judaeo-Christian tradition. We simply wish to point out that the evidence will also support broader and richer interpretations. A good example comes from Tertullian (c. 160–225 C.E.) in a passage from his treatise "To His Wife":

> How shall we ever be able adequately to describe the happiness of that marriage which the Church arranges, the Sacrifice strengthens, upon which the blessing sets a seal, at which angels are present as witnesses, and to which the Father gives His consent? For not even on earth do children marry properly and legally without their fathers' permission.

How beautiful, then, the marriage of two Christians, two who are one in hope, one in desire, one in the way of life they follow, one in the religion they practice. They are as brother and sister, both servants of the same Master. Nothing divides them, either in flesh or in spirit. They are, in very truth, "two in one flesh"; and where there is but one flesh there so also but one spirit. (2.8.6–9, 35f.)[24]

The opening section of this quotation represents "a catena of technical language which . . . is meant to show that for each of the stages in the pagan Roman marriage procedure, there is a corresponding Christian one."[25] The remainder is a rich appreciation of the breadth of the one flesh image for understanding human relationships. We cannot confine marriage narrowly to sexual expression in procreation. For Tertullian to describe a married couple as brother and sister clearly implies a unity that cannot be limited to procreative sexuality.

Prayers, Blessings, and Vows

A rich and complex liturgical history makes it difficult to summarize the evidence of marriage rites. Our purpose here is quite focused: Do the prayers, blessings, and vows permit the conclusion that procreation is the defining characteristic of marriage as the heterosexist tradition has taught us? If not, do they make clear that it is a necessary secondary characteristic? To answer yes to either question must lead to the conclusion that same-sex marriage is outside the bounds of a historical Christian understanding of marriage.[26] But if we answer no, nothing except the presumption that the participants are a man and a woman keeps us from using these same rites.

Traditional marriage rites included a variety of parts, many of which occurred outside the wedding Mass itself. There were, for example, special prayers of blessing to be said at the home: in the bedroom, over the couple, and of their bodies. Nothing intrinsic to the pre-Mass section of the Roman Catholic rite invalidates questions of assent (such as these from the twelfth century) were they to be asked of same-sex partners: "N., do you want this woman? [response] Do you wish to serve her in the faith of God as your own, in health and infirmity, as a Christian man should serve his wife?" or "Do you really want this woman as your wife, to guard her in health and sickness, as long as she lives, as a good man should keep his

wife, and to join her faithfully with your body, and all your possessions?"[27] Although the language here does not reveal it, such questions would usually be asked of both the man and the woman. The
critical issue of consent, whether it is mutual, implicit, or explicit,
gets expressed differently through the centuries. Stevenson notes
that by the twelfth century "as the canon lawyers exert influence on
marital consent, in particular Peter Lombard and (later) Thomas
Aquinas, the man [sic] and wife have to express their desire to marry
each other *publicly*, and no longer assume it is an implicit aspect of
the rite, or part of a rite of betrothal not under the Church's influence."[28] Nothing in subsequent ritual development necessitates its
restriction to heterosexual couples, except the history of heterocentric praxis.

When one examines the content of the prayers in marriage rites
one finds that most of the references can apply to same-sex as well as
different-sex couples. Clearly, the historical rites reflect the assumption that one man and one woman are the subject of the action. The
language about procreation and raising children presumes a husband and wife. Yet, as we have already noted, same-sex couples could
find such language congenial if we did not adopt a heterosexist bias
about procreation and raising children. Nothing in the prayers precludes expanding their referents in such an inclusive way. More
important, minor editing of the rite to eliminate references to procreation (which is frequently done when a woman is past her childbearing years), reveals that its substantive expression of what
marriage is can apply equally to same-sex or other-sex partners.

When one compares the rich tradition of vow language one sees
that the promises intended, and the Church's blessing of them, refer
to the kind of lifelong giving and receiving that any two people, not
just a man and woman, are capable of if they decide to enter such a
relationship. Consider the following, earliest verifiable example of
an active consent vow (that is, one in which the person made the
vow by saying it, rather than responding with a "yes" or "I do" to
someone else's questions): "I take you as my wife, and I espouse you;
and I commit to you the fidelity of my body, in so far as I bear for
you fidelity and loyalty of my body and my possessions; and I will
keep you in health and sickness and in any condition which it
pleases our Lord that you should have, nor for worse or for better
will I change towards you until the end."[29]

Compare this with the language for the questions of intent to
marry and the vows of the Anglican Prayer Book of 1549, which has
shaped the vocabulary of most subsequent English language rites.

[Questions]: N. Wilt thou haue thys woman to thy wedded wyfe, to lyue together after Gods ordeynaunce in the holy estate of matrymonie? Wylt thou loue her, coumforte her, honor and kepe her, in sickenesse and in health? And forsakyng all other kepe thee onely to her, so long as you both shall lyue? [The question to the woman adds "obey him, and serue him" before "loue, coumforte, honor and kepe."]

[Vows]: I, N., take thee N. to my wedded wife, to haue and to hold from thys day forwarde, for better, for wurse, for richer for poorer, in sickenesse, and in health, to loue and to cherishe, till death vs departe: according to Gods holy ordeinaunce: And therto I plight thee my troth.

[At the giving of the ring]: With this ring I thee wed: This golde and siluer I thee geue: with my body I thee worship: and with al my worldly goodes I thee endow. In the name of the father. . . . [30]

The rich expressions of mutual gift, of marital love, of sharing all possessions, of standing by one another through the best and worst of what might come—indeed all the things we have ideally recognized as the intent of the marriage relationship—assume, yet in their language do not require, that they refer to a man and a woman rather than two women or two men.

An incredible array of what one might call "quaint customs" abound in the marriage rites retrievable from history. Many of these customs continue, such as the giving of tokens (for example, coins symbolizing worldly possessions) and the giving of rings (including the medieval practice of placing the ring briefly on the thumb with the words, "in the name of the Father," then on the index finger with the words, "the Son," and finally the middle finger with the words, "the Holy Spirit," where the ring remains). The flexible ways in which the marriage rite has incorporated such customs over the centuries invites similar adaptations for same-sex unions.

One thing is clear, the flexibility of the tradition itself says that such reinterpretation and expansion of the meaning of the event are not only possible but part of its very history. Yale University historian John Boswell has been investigating examples of extant, but well-hidden, blessing rites for same-sex unions that span most of the history of the Western Church. The fact that such rites have been suppressed says more about changing cultural contexts than about the divine will for human relationships of commitment.

The liturgical evidence is not univocal. We are not saying that one cannot read the evidence and conclude that heterosexual marriage is normative. We are suggesting that such a "normative" reading results from a heterosexist bias rather than from the actual content of the rites and what they intend.

A comparison of the history of ordination rites with marriage rites proves illuminating here. When some Lutherans decided to ordain women in 1970 it resulted in almost no changes in the ordination rite. Why? After all, the preceding history had understood the rite as referring only to men. The point is this: the substance of the rite spoke to the heart of what it means to serve the church as an ordained pastor. The sex of the person referred to was tangential to the main concerns of the rite. For that reason only a few pronoun changes were necessary for the rite to serve equally well to ordain women.

Similarly, the content and structure of the marriage rite speak to its main concerns: the lifelong love and faithfulness of the people marrying and the public promise making of the couple and the community to work together in sustaining the relationship. We should not be surprised that, as was the case with the ordination rite, a change in the referents of the marriage rite (to include same-sex couples) results in little necessary change in its content or structure. Our rituals sometimes speak more truthfully and faithfully than our contexts allow us to perceive. When freed from a heterosexist interpretive framework, the marriage rite can speak eloquently to the commitments of two men, two women, or a man and woman.

The Sacramentality of Marriage

In Roman Catholic tradition marriage is a sacrament (one of seven). Protestant traditions have usually recognized only baptism and Eucharist as sacraments. We will note a few aspects of the historical debate about what defines or constitutes a sacrament. Our central focus, however, will be on how the question of sacramentality influences reflection on the possibility of same-sex marriage. Obviously we must simplify complicated and often subtly nuanced arguments from these traditions to keep our focus. We certainly do not intend the following analysis as a developed history or theology of marriage as a sacrament.[31]

Although the early church writer Tertullian was the first to use the Latin word *sacramentum* to describe Christian rites (c. 200 C.E.), St. Augustine's definition some 200 years later has been operative in the western Church ever since. Augustine described a sacrament as a "visible word": the word of God is linked to a sign and together this word-sign reality is the sacrament. For Christians a sacrament is a sacred sign, a "means of grace," through which one encounters God or by which God's self-giving is experienced. The pagan origins of the word *sacramentum* indicate that it referred to an oath or vow, and St. Augustine drew on this meaning to describe Christian sacraments as sacred seals of commitment. In the case of marriage he argued that the *sacramentum* was the joint commitment of the couple to God (not primarily their commitment to each other).[32]

Roman Catholic theology has linked various descriptive categories to define marriage. In particular the tension between contract and sacrament (covenant), and what serves to fulfill the conditions of each, directly affects the argument about whether and how we can consider same-sex unions as marriages. When the controlling image of marriage is a contract, the question of what constitutes and fulfills the conditions of the contract inevitably become juridical. For example, "the contract is consummated by the first complete exchange of the contractual good—by the first act of complete intercourse after the marital consent."[33] When the image of covenant is emphasized different questions emerge. What makes marriage a living sign of God's covenant love for us? Or, drawing more specifically on the Ephesians 5 imagery that appears in much of the theological and ritual tradition for marriage, how does the relationship of the couple create a sign of Christ's love for the Church and vice versa?

Rather than focusing on particular acts that are necessary to meet the terms of the contract, a covenant model of marriage emphasizes the conduct or way of life that embodies the promises made. In both models, contract and covenant, the traditional stress on permanence and exclusivity comes into play. The role of marital love in this matrix remains ambiguous, but renewed emphasis on marital love (especially in Roman Catholic theology after Vatican II) has challenged how we interpret what two people must do to enter into a marriage and have it survive.

Moving from a purely contractual to a covenantal understanding of marriage (remembering that both aspects are present throughout the tradition), shifts the focus of definition. It allows for a description of the role of love in fulfilling the commitments of marriage. We become concerned not primarily with what consummates the contract but rather what kind of conduct fulfills the marriage's (formerly secondary) end of intimate sharing of marital life and love. Protestants and Roman Catholics face different dilemmas in describing the connections among union, the act of sexual intercourse, and procreation in marriage. These still represent key points of interface in the traditions, but recent theological reflection on marriage has shifted the focus of debate to marital love and covenant. This new focus is potentially even better able to mesh with the reality of same-sex partnerships.

Vatican II's document *Gaudium et spes*, which Mackin correctly identifies as the point at which a shift in marriage interpretation from contract to covenant began, maintains the close connection between the covenant model's "marital love" and fidelity and procreation. The document reads as follows:

> Marriage and conjugal love are by their nature ordained toward the begetting and educating of children. Children are really the supreme gift of marriage and contribute very substantially to the welfare of their parents. . . . Hence, while not making the other purposes of matrimony of less account, the true practice of conjugal love, and the whole meaning of the family life which results from it, have this aim: that the couple be ready with stout hearts to cooperate with the love of the Creator and the Savior, who through them will enlarge and enrich His own family day by day.[34]

The statement that marital (conjugal) love is "by nature ordained toward the begetting and educating of children" reveals the ongoing heterocentric bias of the tradition.

This heterocentric bias has a number of possible justifications. For example, if one removes procreation from the essential characteristics, one might assume that none of the other goods or ends of marriage can be realized. Another way to justify it is to say that procreation is primary, a priority that if missing does not allow integration of the goods and ends of marriage. Thus, denying procreation undermines marriage. A third way perceives the *sacramentum* as uniform rather than pluriform. A heterocentric view refuses to acknowledge that there may be multiple constellations of goods and ends for marriage as a sacrament. Nothing in the rich and compelling descriptions of marriage, love, sacrament, covenant, faithfulness, shared life, and so forth, demands restriction to heterosexual relationships unless one is convinced that the "goods" or "ends" of marriage are in fact uniform and cannot be realized by two human beings of the same sex.

In practice, both among Protestant and Roman Catholic Christians, the link between sexual intercourse and procreation has long been broken—*Humanae Vitae* notwithstanding. Even if that specific link were maintained, we recognize that love and sexual intimacy involve more than genital intercourse. We cannot lodge the essential characteristics of marriage in the latter, even though we should not minimize the importance of childbearing and child rearing in the context of marital love.

We have been exploring the evidence of Roman Catholic tradition. The sixteenth century witness of the Protestant Reformation in Lutheran confessional documents reveals concerns similar to those we have been discussing:

> The union of man and woman is by natural right. Natural right is really divine right, because it is an ordinance divinely stamped on nature. Since only an extraordinary act of God can change this right, the right to contract marriage necessarily remains. For the natural desire of one sex for the other is an ordinance of God, and therefore it is a right; otherwise why would both sexes have been created? As we said, we are not talking about sinful lust but about the desire which is called "natural love," which lust did not remove from nature but only inflamed. Now it needs a remedy even more, and marriage is necessary for a remedy as well as for procreation.[35]

One can see here the continuing legacy of St. Augustine. In spite of the Protestant rejection of arguments for marriage as a sacrament, the concerns raised by the debate about what constitutes marriage are not dissimilar. In other places the Lutheran documents discuss the love and faithfulness that mark the union of two people in marriage. The contractual framework that overshadowed the sacramental from the fifth to twentieth centuries in interpreting marriage provided the context for the sixteenth century reformers just as for the Roman Catholic jurists. Yet the broader concerns about marital love and faithfulness as defining characteristics that serve the couple, the community, and God are clearly present.[36]

Where does such evidence finally lead us? The new Code of Canon Law stipulates the requirements for a "definition" of marriage in a variety of places, such as Canon 1055.1: "The matrimonial covenant, by which a man and a woman establish between themselves a partnership of the whole of life, is by its nature ordered toward the good of the spouses and the procreation and education of offspring; this covenant between baptized persons has been raised by Christ the Lord to the dignity of a sacrament."[37] Protestant theology would find little argument here (only with the identification of marriage *as* a sacrament). The significance and scope of the proviso concerning procreation and the nurture of children, upon which the restriction of the covenant to a man and a woman rests remains a key issue.[38] Can same-sex couples accomplish these ends? We have argued that they can and, more importantly, that the broader context of marriage as a loving, faithful union within which these particular ends should be realized is most certainly within the reach of same-sex couples.

If sacramentality offers a useful model for understanding marriage as a sign and seal of the rule of God in our lives and of our attempt to honor its self-giving and unconditionality, it can embrace both same-sex and different-sex unions. Yet there is more to the issue than simply affirming that it is historically defensible for such an embrace to occur. What is the content of this theology for people struggling in our day to make sense of longterm relationships?

In his reflections on marital love, Theodore Mackin has suggested that the basis of human sin is the fear of loss of self.[39] Such fear can make us self-protective or self-negating, careless, and reckless. Any relationship that calls us out of self-centeredness and invites us to be vulnerable and appropriately self-giving involves risking our selves. Marriage makes this invitation emotionally and physically in unique ways because of the trust its commitment presumes. In sexual lovemaking human beings are not talking about the love and trust that exists between them. They are doing what love and trust are, recognizing that the effort to give and accept sexually can damage as well as heal if the trust is broken or betrayed.

When we develop such an intimate partnership we trust that the mutual vulnerability means that we have no intention to harm each other. In marriage this expectation includes the harm of abandonment. The one we marry promises especially not to harm us by someday leaving us. Obviously people often fail to keep this marriage promise. But that does not negate the power of its intent nor the joyous depth of love created when people do manage to keep it until death parts them.

When we bring our passion into the open with another person it intensifies the relationship. The possibility for creating both sorrow and joy is also intensified. Even as we enjoy the power of mutual love we know that it will someday end. Death will succeed in parting us. Here Mackin reminds us that for Christians the fundamental work of life is to defeat the threats posed by death, and if "at heart sinfulness is the incipient victory in men and women of the fear that death gets the last word—then there is a place in sexual pleasure for pleasure in life's victory over death."[40]

The incarnational foundation of Christian belief has profound impact at this point. The embodied love that we express in sexual relating produces the joy of a shared bond that defeats "the death that comes in loneliness, in abandonment and worthlessness, in final despair."[41] The sacramental dimensions of Christian faith constantly call people to honor the bodily reality of love, both God's love for us and our love for each other. In marriage that sacramental bond informs faith even as it is formed by it.

REASSESSING MARRIAGE

Theologically, one can view marriage, whether between male and female or between people of the same sex, as an ideal part of the created order. It is also possible to view the necessity for formal covenants of marriage as a response to human brokenness, as the need to make commitments that we would otherwise not maintain freely. The latter view may help to make sense of Jesus' teaching that "in heaven they neither marry nor are given in marriage" (Mt 22:30). In other words, formal covenants as a hedge against abuse will not be necessary then, but are so in this life.

Either view can be held with credibility and theological integrity. Neither is essential to the argument that one can invest same-sex unions with the traditional significance ascribed to heterosexual marriages. In contrast, one can also argue that same-sex unions require their own interpretive framework and ritual structures. The point of such an approach would be to signal the differences between same-sex and other-sex unions rather than the similarities. All things considered, it seems more helpful to us to work toward ritual recognition of the similarities. Both in the provisional rites produced during the past few decades by gay and lesbian couples for the blessing of their unions and in the explanations given for entering such partnerships of commitment, similarities to heterosexual marriage far outweigh the differences. Yet why not work toward independent rites for same-sex relationships?

One problem with developing a new category of religiously blessed unions is that they are isolated from a broader support network. It is not sufficient to affirm a relationship via symbolization and celebration if no attendant or consequential structures are in place to honor and nurture it. It is the equivalent of stepping across the threshold into a vacuum. It is a door to nowhere. In other words, we cannot create ritual *structures* in the same ways that we can create ritual *moments*. Without broader social, economic, and legal support, "blessed unions" are relegated to inferior, secondary, or subordinate status.

The difficulties a lesbian couple face when one or both bear children or adopt a child are an example of this subordinate status. Neither partner has any legal status given the present delineation of one mother and one father constituting a child's parents. In most states power of attorney is limited, adoption laws vary, and guardianship is variously interpreted. Insufficient language for designating the "parents" of a child means that one of the partners (in this example, the one who is not the biological mother of the child) will have no recourse when denied access (in hospital visitation, for example) to her son or daughter by "marriage." The current cultural climate hinders recognition of gay and lesbian unions.

On the other hand, ritual structures must begin somewhere. If the Church were to honor the worth and status of same-sex unions via public recognition in a rite of blessing, it could serve as the catalyst for generating the growth of support structures in the larger society. This would require a tremendous investment of time and energy by the whole culture. Simply drafting legislation to define the "rights and privileges" of homosexual unions, not to mention judicial wrangling to clarify the law, seems unnecessary when such deliberation has been done for heterosexual marriage. Fine tuning present laws to incorporate the nuances or unique situations created by same-sex couples seems to us a wiser investment of everyone's energy.

A nonheterosexist appropriation of the insights of Scripture and tradition regarding marital love, the permanence and exclusivity of marriage, and the role of friendship in all human bonding affords us ample substance to occupy our best efforts at mutually describing and clarifying sexual ethics for all people. This focus on marriage does, of course, beg one question: What is the role of sexuality for people who are single? The reform of the heterosexist paradigm that we are advocating will surely reshape that question as well. It, however, is the subject of another book.

CONCLUSION

We have not been without our own restrictive assumptions in the preceding discussion of homosexual and heterosexual marriage. The discussion did not take into account the conundrums faced by bisexual people nor the perplexing case of transgender marriage.

Some believe that questions about permanent unions for bisexual people can be addressed within discussions of homosexual-hetero-sexual marriage. The premise behind this states that if marriage is desired by a bisexual person it will be limited to either the same- or other-sex choice of partner. Once the choice has been made, some clarity emerges about the sexual role the bisexual person will have. With either choice the norms for the chosen relationship—same-sex or other-sex union—would then be applied. Their attraction to others outside the union is no different from that of other marriages, except that the "temptation" may be of either sex.

The matter is less clear with transsexuality.[42] For Christians the case of transsexualism presses the issue of how the evidence of the social sciences and modern medicine should influence theology. Some traditionalists would argue that there neither is nor should be any influence. Such an ahistorical approach is indefensible in our day. The everchanging knowledge we accumulate as human beings does not pose an automatic threat to faith.

To honor the knowledge and wisdom we are given over time does not mean that we are reduced to reliance on it as our primary guide for action. It should no longer be necessary to make a case for the primacy of Scripture *and* an ongoing dialogue with experience. The continuing doctrinaire dismissal of new points of view in the Church's moral deliberation by some Christians demands, however, that we at least remind one another that such a case has been made.

We have already seen how the useful but limited distinction between orientation and behavior in homosexuality was brought to the surface by work in the social sciences. When taken seriously this and other evidence invites us to a fuller and richer, although at times more confusing, assessment of our sexuality. We suggest that the dialogue now possible for theology (not unlike the new dialogue between science and religion) can lead to a healthier, more enjoyable, and more ethically responsible appropriation of God's gift of sexuality as well.

We have also been arguing that the Church can now make faithful response. The time for study and reflection never ends, but at some point we must say that sufficient data exist for faithful action. With homosexuality we have been walking across the terrain for centuries, and we have mapped it in a variety of ways. We suggest that the time has come to redraw the map yet again, mindful that we do so to be faithful to the gospel, not to escape it. Ample evidence within traditional prayers, blessings, and vows demonstrates that marriage as both a sociological and spiritual estate (institution) can embrace different-sex and same-sex unions. Nothing, apart from a narrow and heterosexist reading of the ritual evidence about procreation and complementarity, restricts marriage to heterosexual unions.

7

Moving Beyond Heterosexism

My sexual orientation has always been towards men. As a child I was never in conflict about my attraction towards men, but I knew better than to share this information with anyone. Throughout college and after I kept my life "balanced" by dating women in the light and men in the dark. I felt like a hypocrite. Talk about denial. It took me marrying one of these women to finally realize what being gay really meant. For the first time in my life I truly accepted the fact about my sexual orientation.

Our focus on heterosexism has obscured several important ethical questions, like the ones raised by this opening vignette: sexual authenticity, closeting and denial, and marital deception. This obscuring occurs because heterosexism constitutes the traditional moral framework within which all problems in sexual ethics have been identified and defined and the framework within which all lines of moral argument have been processed. It is not simply the conclusion of one line of moral argument among others or one of many possible points of view on human sexuality. We turn in this final chapter to exploring and renaming moral dimensions of our sexual lives *outside* of the heterosexist paradigm. This invites remapping the ethical terrain.

In such a process problems that were previously neglected, if not altogether unrecognized, suddenly come to the forefront. Questions about legal and moral obligations toward the nongay spouses of homosexual and bisexual divorcees, fitting goals regarding parental custody and domestic partnership legislation, canonical legislation prohibiting (without ecclesial dispensation) gay-straight marriages, and sadomasochism, pornography, prostitution, and domestic violence in the gay as well as the straight community all cry out for attention. Other issues once thought central to the field, such as what causes sexual orientation and whether we can change it, correspondingly recede into the background. In any case abandoning heterosexism as a normative framework for sexual ethics shatters many of our preconceived notions about what is important morally speaking.

Our preceding analysis led us to call for a paradigm shift in sexual ethics. In this chapter we identify and briefly explore only two of the dimensions of our sexual lives that surface and command our ethical attention as a result of this shift: authenticity and fidelity. Even when shaken as a normative framework, heterosexism retains ideological power in our culture to shape familial, political, and economic realities. Heterosexism will continue to create problems in sexual ethics even though we no longer give it the power to name them. Indeed, to challenge its power heterosexism must be clearly and repeatedly named a sin. It is an unjustifiable pattern of discrimination against gay, lesbian, and bisexual people.

Before proceeding to a delineation of the issues, we should ask how two heterosexual people can presume to write about sexual authenticity and sexual fidelity for gay and lesbian people. On the one hand, the arguments given in any situation that calls for one to speak on behalf of or be an advocate for another answer this question. For example, as Caucasians we cannot pretend to be African-Americans, but we can claim—especially if we have a history of relationship that supports it—to speak competently about, although not out of, their experience. Furthermore, the purpose of such speaking is to raise questions, share experiences, and clarify issues rather than to offer definitive answers.

We want to acknowledge and honor the fact that we do not belong to the gay community. We will always, to some degree, be outsiders to its culture. Through this book, however, we invite both heterosexual and gay people to make the borders of their respective communities more permeable. We suggest that gay people need to assess their refusal to grant easy access to the gay community. We understand the danger involved in this request. It is unwise to create easy access for heterosexists bent on irrational persecution of gay people. Yet by joining with heterosexual people not driven by such homophobia, the gay community can help all safely to engage in the kind of dialogue necessary for reform.

Public heterosexual support demands particular acts of solidarity. Heterosexual men and women must be willing not only to acknowledge that gay men and lesbian women are complete, healthy human beings, but also take stands against prejudices that discriminate against them. As with racism and sexism, the reformation of entrenched patterns of oppression will require solidarity among those in the oppressing group who recognize the need for change. There is no painless way to dismantle heterosexism.

SEXUAL AUTHENTICITY

Sexual authenticity arises from the integration of our sexual identity and public identity. Such authenticity is not a given or fixed reality, but rather an ongoing process of discernment and learned response. Our sexual identity (see chapter 1) is malleable to some degree. This malleability can produce ambiguity in situations that create the possibility for sexual behaviors that are new to us or are at the edge of our sexual boundaries. For example, when one gives and receives a kiss or hug in a developing relationship, it may be more than a friendly greeting but not yet a signal of the desire for fuller sexual intimacy. How one communicates authentically is neither simple nor unambiguous.

Heterosexism confuses rather than clarifies situations of moral discernment for all people about what is sexually authentic. It confuses by mislabeling our conduct as either not sexual at all or as oriented toward male-female genital intimacy. Much of the time neither label may be appropriate. On the surface these labels seem to produce clarity rather than confusion—the more narrowly one can proscribe meaning the more defined, manageable, or controllable that meaning ought to be. Yet the opposite is true for our sexual communication. Such labeling obscures the authentic meaning of many sexual signals and leads to their misinterpretation.

One cannot reduce a kiss, hug, touch, look in the eye, gesture, or posture to a single meaning. By painting all sexual communication with a single brushstroke, heterosexism blocks the mutual discernment of how one's sexuality impinges on all relationships. In other words, heterosexism restricts sexuality to potentially romantic overtures that will lead to male-female coupling. When we do not expect such coupling, for example because one of the persons is married or simply expresses reluctance for the relationship to develop in that direction, little or no "sexuality" can be admitted or conceded in the relationship. This unwillingness to recognize, name, and appropriately manage the sexual signals we give increases the danger of harassment.

The use of power or authority to gain sexual access to another constitutes one form of sexual harassment. About this we have some clarity. Another form of sexual harassment is the use of one's sexuality to gain power over or control of another. About seduction and its dangers we are deeply confused, in part because we have been conditioned into dishonesty about the sexual realities that inevitably shape all our relationships. We fear signaling the wrong message because we cannot be open and honest about our sexual attractions and fears. Heterosexism obscures the fact that there are sexual connections between us—whether same- or other-sex directed—not aimed toward genital intimacy. One cannot risk admitting this because no room exists for these meanings within the heterosexist framework.

With its bias that one ought not relate sexually to members of the same sex, heterosexism allows us to perceive as sexual only those behaviors directed toward the other sex. When we define "opposite-sex" relationships as the only appropriate outlets for sexual energy, they are forced to bear more weight than necessary. If we free people to honor the sexual dimensions of their same-sex relationships, at least some of this distortive context is removed. We invest too much in sexuality on the one hand (male-female affections), and too little on the other (same-sex affections).

Dismantling heterosexism can lead to a richer, more authentic, and more appropriately diffused expression of our sexual energy. Our sexuality openly becomes part of all that we are rather than a narrowly channeled means to produce male-female procreative or complementary coupling. Heterosexism attempts to control human sexuality by recognizing as sexual only behaviors directed toward male-female genital couplings.

One cannot guarantee that a nonheterosexist sexual ethic would result in easier or less ambiguous decision making. We are simply suggesting that it would be a more honest context for living out human sexual vocations and respecting sexual boundaries. Integrity and authenticity become necessary partners in this ongoing task.

For the most part heterosexual people simply take the authenticity of their sexual identity for granted. We usually assume a coherence between their internal needs and desires, external behaviors, and overall sexual lifestyle. Comparatively little blocks their becoming self-conscious of their authentic sexual feelings to begin with and much reinforces their integral (if not always responsible) expression of these attractions.[1] Overall, we invite heterosexual adolescents in our culture to an awareness of, mature openness about, and even celebration of their burgeoning sexuality.

We do not provide such support and encouragement for teenagers who are gay, lesbian, or bisexual. At best we encourage them to make announcements about their sexual identity that are not consistent with their sexual orientations or activities. At worst we invite them to confess and repent of their sexual needs and desires. Because one can be open about only that which is acceptable, a heterosexist environment forces them to reject what is authentic. So they create for their sexual selves "closets" in which to hide from themselves and others.

We will say more about the size and price of such closets. For now we want to state explicitly that (1) such hideouts provide little real protection for their individual inhabitants, and (2) sexual inauthenticity does not benefit the homosexual community. Ever since the 1969 police raid on Stonewall, a gay disco in Greenwich Village, and the subsequent riots, it has been clear that what is hidden will remain forever unacceptable. Coming out en masse will not guarantee social acceptance, but it provides the only road toward that destination.

The facts about closets are plain. They make good hiding places. They also isolate us. Children know well the quick cover closets offer in a game of hide and seek. Kids also know how vulnerable to discovery they are once ensconced in a closet. Finally, children know well the terror of being trapped or locked in a closet. Heterosexism remains a powerful force in our society. It is not a game. In reality gay people are forced to choose between hiding from or exposing themselves to a hostile world. What does "closeting" entail?

Closets range in size and hence may be more or less suffocating. Some are so small that no whole person can live in them. In such cases the persons may have concealed from their conscious selves the truth about their sexual orientation. Such persons have so internalized the messages of contempt spread by heterosexism that their very survival may depend on maintaining this self-deception. Others can be truthful with themselves, but are shamed by heterosexism into keeping silent about who they really are. They can crouch in their closets, but have no room for others. Still others have walk-in size closets. They shroud their sexual orientations and preferences in a public identity acceptable to our heterosexist world. Only a chosen few—usually other gay people or trusted friends—know their secret.

Those in the latter group have some measure of self-acceptance but spend much energy sustaining and bolstering their cover. The temptation to follow heterosexist scripts and adopt heterosexist roles (enter into courtship or marriage with a heterosexual person) to protect themselves sometimes becomes overwhelming.[2] They live constantly with the threat and fear of discovery. They are frustrated and demeaned by their inability to celebrate openly who they are and whom they really love.

Anyone who does not believe that fully humanizing sexual love demands communal celebration need only listen carefully to those whose loves are closeted. Gay people are not unique in this respect. Heterosexual people know something of this reality. All those who are "kept" for sexual purposes—whether gay or straight—speak quite eloquently of the corrosive power of concealment. Not only is the one hidden away humiliated by the process, but the love relationship itself suffers from an agonizing suffocation. The secret slowly erodes other friendships as well. Concealment inevitably becomes deception when appropriate expectations of honesty among those with whom one is intimate go unmet. Although essentially personal, human sexuality cannot be fully private. What is most personal always has communal implications, affecting many facets of one's relationships with others.

Important similarities of experience exist among those who closet some portion of their sexual life and those forced to closet all of it. One can perceive crucial differences as well, especially in some of the distinctions between gay and straight forms of closeting. The moral judgment one makes about the closeted relationship represents one such difference. However painful and destructive for those involved, most people would argue that "illicit" sexual activities should be kept secret. That which is judged immoral in the community must be hidden from it. For example, we usually closet adulterous affairs. We recognize a world of difference between confession and repentance (even when communal) and the public display of adulterous affections or openly "living in sin." We make the distinction because openness about the latter would signal some measure of moral acceptability.

This means that when we evaluate any sexual behavior we cannot assess it only in terms of its consequences for the individuals involved or for the quality of their relationship. We must also assess its effects on the community as a whole. Is such behavior edifying? Does it corrode our communal sense of the value, significance, and fragility of sexual love relationships?[3] We do not generally commend those who flaunt activity deemed illicit by most for their courageous integrity or their lack of personal hypocrisy. Instead, we usually see them as contributing to the moral confusion of the young or sexually immature among us. They create a scandal harmful to our life together. Their exhibitionism adds communal irresponsibility to their "original" sexual sin.

Two judgments are crucial to these deliberations about sexual closets and the coming out process. First, we must determine whether revealing one's sexual identity or keeping it concealed is *personally* legitimate. Second, we must give care to the correlative question of whether the revelation or concealment is communally edifying. Within a heterosexist paradigm, people see the uncloseting of the gay community as both individually illegitimate and communally unedifying. When outside of this framework the coming out of gay, lesbian, and bisexual people requires dramatic reinterpretation.

Coming out is at least a threefold process. The first phase is a matter of self-recognition and acceptance. It involves saying to one's self: "I am gay (or lesbian or bisexual) and I am glad." Many homosexual people report that they knew from early childhood that they were different. One can see this only with hindsight. In a heterosexist world one acquires the vocabulary to name and hence recognize this sexual difference only by internalizing to some degree an aversion to it. Within a heterosexist framework all who are different are queer and learn early on that they need to be straightened out.

The responses of gay children to these negative messages vary. One is a self-hate so strong it results in suicide.[4] Another strategy is sexual amnesia. Survival requires that this particular truth about themselves be blocked out, even though it damages their overall psychic health. Only much later, sometimes long past their physical adolescence, are gay people strong enough to allow this memory to surface. Another coping mechanism is sexual anesthesia. Survival requires that one shut down all sexual feelings. It is more tolerable to be numb than gay, to feel nothing sexual than to desire another of the same sex. A delayed awareness of one's authentic self may render one's lifestyle suddenly ungenuine and hypocritical. Frequently, the primary moral task for gay people coming out in a heterosexist world is the complex reweaving of their life's relations.

Ultimately the obligation to be sexually authentic creates a spiritual crisis. William Carroll reports that when gay, lesbian, and bisexual young people struggle with their sexual identity in a heterosexist religious environment, they frequently experience God as a sadistic, unloving Father. He writes vividly about his experience of this pattern: "God abhorred me because I was homosexual, did not accept or welcome me in his house as I was and told me through the Apostle Paul that I deserved to die. It's hard to bond with such a father."[5] Bonding with such a god would constitute a form of spiritual masochism. Survival necessitates for many that they leave behind this threatening god. Only some of them have come to see that they turned away from a heterosexist idol, not from God.

After they have identified themselves, gay people may come out to others. Often this second phase begins with a few other people and then spreads to an intimate circle of friends or family members.

This stage of sexual identity development is complex and multifaceted.[6] It expresses the caution that gay people must use in the face of frequent rejection and the sometimes violent reaction that accompanies their revelation.

Since the Stonewall riots, a fully public or third stage in the coming out process has developed in North American society. Participation in gay pride marches or cruising in highly theatrical drag costumes represent one facet of this stage. They are designed to make an ostentatious display of gay, lesbian, and bisexual identity. Such pageantry, like kiss-ins, provides opportunity for homosexual people to revel in who they are and whom they love. The point of gay men who are otherwise not cross-dressers wearing beehive wigs and women's negligees is to do such revelling with humor or for satiric effect. No doubt for some exhibitionism lies behind such behavior. But for most these festivals are public because only by being public can they generate community.

Genuine celebrations cannot be kept private. A party is inescapably public in character, rooted in the desire of the human heart to shout one's love for self and others from the rooftops. Love seeks to be declared out loud before God and the world. Gay, lesbian, and bisexual people must proclaim "We exist!" in a world that aims to erase them.

One crucial factor that distinguishes homosexual people from other oppressed groups is their ability to hide their minority status. Passing as straight has long been a coping strategy among gay people. We need to question how this tactic, necessitated by heterosexism, might be reevaluated. Is it a lie or a secret? Is it always justifiable? In what sense, if any, do gay people have an obligation to come out of their closets? Can they ever be blamed for failing to do so? Is such sexual inauthenticity scandalous?

A sexual closet may be like a lie or a secret. What is at stake in this designation is no small matter. Unlike a lie, keeping a secret carries no moral presumption against it. Secrets are morally neutral, even though potentially either vicious or virtuous in their consequences. In contrast, although lying may be justifiable it always remains ambiguous and morally tragic. People are obliged in a nonabsolute fashion to bear witness to the truth and avoid lying.

Overall, we believe closets and the efforts at passing as straight that frequently accompany them are more like lies. In "Women and Honor: Some Notes on Lying," Adrienne Rich makes it clear that both by her silence and through her words a lesbian may lie about her sexual identity.[7] In a perfect world the concealment of one's sexual identity or vocation would not be judged morally neutral. Whether united or single, gay or straight, candor about and the integration of the major outlines of one's sexual lifestyle would be matters of both personal honor and communal edification.

Much harm results from deceptions about one's sexual identity. Those who keep silent hurt themselves. In "The Closet Syndrome," Stuart Byron poignantly observes: "Every time one refrains from an act of public affection with a lover where a straight couple would not—in the park, on the movie line—one dies a little."[8] Adrienne Rich also notes that a refusal to celebrate a love or grieve its loss publicly erodes one's sense of self: "We deny the importance of an event, or a person, and thus deprive ourselves of a part of our lives."[9] Sexual inauthenticity is no little white lie.

What appeared initially as a prudent practice of discretion slides easily into a habit of lying, especially when one fears conflict or the loss of control. Oppressed people often acquire a nasty habit: they come to value their cages. People can enjoy at some level the freedom from vulnerability and pain that secrecy offers. But such a survival strategy adopted in response to a contemptuous, hostile public can become ingrained in a person. Of this effect of "discretion" Timothy F. Lull writes: "There is a potentially devastating effect on the character of a person who acts in a different way privately than publicly over a long period."[10]

In addition, close friends "feel a little crazy," as Rich puts it, when they have been lied to.[11] Closets harm the deceived as well as the deceiver. Although we do not want to downplay the real hurt felt by those deceived, we must always applaud the courage of the one who comes out. We must also recognize a shared responsibility for the false presumption that "all the world is straight." In a heterosexist world gay people meet this myth with understandable ambivalence. At some points they welcome the safety it brings: "Thank God they think I'm straight." At other points they find its offense outraging: "How dare they presume I'd be interested in them."

Although we are not convinced by it, one can make a reasonable case that keeping one's sexual identity closeted from the general public, especially if this secret is not accompanied by the adoption of heterosexual dating patterns and the like, is not intrinsically destructive. It may simply be a secret and, all things being equal, morally neutral. Sometimes it may simply be better to hide than to expose, to conceal than to share. Others have no more right to know this than to force individuals to remain private or to make heterosexuality compulsory.

Much personal sexual information—say about one's fantasies, fetishes, and even the particularities of one's sexual history—may (or may not) appropriately be kept secret. Such secrets may be legitimately concealed from the general public, most of one's friends, and possibly even from one's lover. To be sexually authentic is not to unrestrainedly tell all. There is no inherent contradiction between sexual modesty and sexual authenticity. While it demands communal celebration, sexual love remains intimate. Its expression ought to be interpersonal. Authenticity demands that what is disclosed about one's sexual lifestyle reasonably match one's sexual behaviors and orientation. Authenticity is a notion appropriately associated with integrity.

But when the context shifts from deceiving John Q. Public to a more intimate circle, closets become more certainly like lies. Rich writes about the expectations for personal authenticity and honesty shared by friends: "I also have faith that you are telling me the things it is important that I should know; that you do not conceal facts from me in an effort to spare me, or yourself pain. Or at the very least, that you will say, 'there are things I am not telling you.'"[12] We do not wish to add guilt about the furtiveness of many gay lives to those who already feel trapped in their closets. Whether it is designated a secret or a lie, remaining closeted *may be* justifiable under the commonplace conditions of our heterosexist world. Even if such concealment, say from one's best friend, is not objectively legitimate, an individual's personal culpability for not breaking such silence may be virtually nil. Our point is not to add to anyone's sense of guilt or shame, but rather to make a moral case for coming out. Lives that are sexually inauthentic do bear the burden of proof.

What are the bases for this obligation to come out? First, people have at first glance (prima facie) an obligation to be truthful to themselves and others. We sustain veracity by habits of personal honesty and integrity. Second, nothing is intrinsically wrong with being gay, lesbian, or bisexual. Therefore coming out is not like openly living in sin. It will not prove harmful to the community. Third, although coming out may generate confusion for heterosexists and make it increasingly difficult for them to closet themselves and others, this does not warrant even hesitation. Heterosexists may be blinded by their prejudice, but they are not weak. The very strength of heterosexists—whether they are gay or straight—that makes coming out so dangerous should not prevent us from requiring everyone to claim the truth about their sexual identity and behaviors.

Like all duties, the obligation to come out is contextual. Decisions to remain closeted may be justified by the weight of other moral concerns. For example, a decision to come out may be responsibly delayed because the obligation to avoid harming oneself or others overrides it in certain circumstances. In general we would argue that the duty to come out is weakest in relation to the general public and most stringent in relation to oneself.

Finally, even if a particular decision not to come out is legitimate for the individuals involved, as noted earlier, concern for the weak among us may dictate a heroic decision to the contrary. Every time we shut a closet door, we harm the wider community. This is especially, but not exclusively, true for the gay community and the young within it. We all need to encounter gay, lesbian, and bisexual people who are authentic in and celebrate their sexual identities. Those who are closeted deprive others of the gift of knowing and learning from them.

We are not merely appealing here for heterosexists to stop forcing silence on the gay and bisexual community nor exhorting members of these communities to be more open. In our opinion the four reasons reviewed earlier constitute sufficient warrant for concluding that people have a prima facie moral duty to come out of the closet. Because coming out is not the only obligation impinging on gay men and lesbians, discerning the proper course of action in individual cases remains a difficult moral task. This is especially true for seminarians, theologians, and clergy, who are torn between their obligation to be sexually authentic and their call to serve the Church.

For example, many options exist for gay, lesbian, and bisexual Lutheran (ELCA) candidates for ministry. They may remain tightly closeted and commit themselves to total and lifelong sexual abstinence. They may commit themselves to total and lifelong sexual abstinence but come out of their closet, in which case they would technically be eligible for ordination, yet unlikely ever to be ordained.[13] They may remain closeted and decide to be sexually chaste and discreet, but not abstinent.[14] They may choose to remain closeted and seek to bolster their cover through the courtship of or marriage to a heterosexual person. They may change their denominational affiliation and seek to serve in churches that might more fully welcome them (such as the UCC or MCC). Finally they may abandon their call to professional ministry altogether. We may find it easy to decide which of these options is wrong. But because more than one may be justifiable, we have the difficult task of discerning the role of each in the overall process of reforming the Church. This requires willingness to engage in difficult personal moral discernment.

We must name two additional issues in this brief review of moral issues related to sexual authenticity: "closet keeping" and "outing" by those who know the truth about the closeted gay person. Closet keeping (or closet breaking) entails holding to or violating an explicit promise of confidentiality. Outing entails the violation of an at least implicit request that we treat the knowledge of an individual's sexual identity as confidential. Some in the gay community argue that membership in that community implicitly includes the promise to keep people's closets. Others resent the privilege attained by those who pass as straight and may refuse to protect it. This is especially true when the privilege can be protected only through disassociation from all that is gay or lesbian. The vignette that follows shows how these issues touch the ordinary fabric of daily life.

> One summer, not too long ago, I was asked by a coworker to join her softball team. Having nowhere else to play ball that year, I readily accepted. I knew the team consisted of mostly lesbians and a couple of straight women. I had been an open lesbian, working in the political arena for some years and was glad for the opportunity to meet these women and spend some purely recreational time with them.
>
> One week we had a practice session at a city park across the street from my sister and brother-in-law's house. They and their three children came to watch. After practice my partner and I walked across the park with my sister's family to have dinner with them. About halfway across the park my partner took my hand as we walked.
>
> I was benched through the next game without explanation, even though no one else on the team had practiced my position. I asked the coach why, and she only replied that she thought it was better that way. After the game, the team sat together for a team meeting, where they told me they wanted me to quit the team. They said that I was too "open" and that association with me would jeopardize their closets. I was forced off the team and told not to explain why to my family and friends because they didn't want any "gossip" about there being lesbians on the team.

Much is at stake morally in such situations, especially among members of the gay community. Our point is to name them as significant moral questions related to sexual authenticity. These are moral issues that we can recognize and fruitfully explore only in an ethical framework that takes the problem of sexual authenticity seriously. This will not happen until we move beyond heterosexist paradigms.

Liberation is usually a communal phenomenon; few people can liberate themselves. We may be unrealistic and unfair when we expect individual gay, lesbian, and bisexual people to "free themselves." Often those muzzled by heterosexism experience the invitation or demand to come out as terrifying. They have been struggling for years with who they are in silent agony. They are exhausted and the risks associated with coming out loom too large. To them heterosexism has sent powerful messages of rejection and contempt. It has created a world that does not really want to hear their story. We have argued that although heterosexism renders gay people mute, they are obliged to learn to speak.

Heterosexism also breeds people who are deaf. The power of this deafness frustrates efforts, both forceful and fledgling, by gay men and women to speak. In our call for the reformation of and a paradigm shift in sexual ethics we believe that all those who are deaf to the gay community are obliged to begin listening. Nelle Morton wrote in the early stages of the women's movement that women must learn how "to hear each other into speech." Like sexism, heterosexism presents a similar communal task. All people in our culture—all parents, siblings, spouses, children, mentors, and friends, gay and straight alike—must learn how to facilitate the coming out process. We must commend for their courage all those who broach the subject (however tentatively). We should celebrate each such conversation as part of God's healing activity in the world.[15] We should assure all who come out that they will be increasingly respected for their candor, praised for their courage, and celebrated!

Every time an individual comes out, he or she wrestles with the threat of abandonment. After coming out, only some gay people lose their jobs, are disinherited by their families, or experience personal rejection. For most, the process of coming out, though always stressful, brings greater integration into the workplace and deeper ties to families and friends. Nevertheless, even though coming out may not always be as costly as assumed, the risks of disaffection associated with it are constant. The vignette that follows displays the checkered quality of most coming out processes.

> Once I accepted my sexual orientation I began to tell my friends one by one that I was gay. I needed to be in an honest relationship with them. Everyone that I told accepted me. By trusting them our

relationships were strengthened. I began to hope that the same thing might happen with my family.

I thought to myself if my parents died, they would never really know who I am. I chose to tell my sister first. Her response to me was damning. She quickly told my parents "for me." My whole family rejected me and said that I could either choose them or being a ho-mo-sex-u-al.

In my struggle to not be forced back into the closet and to not lose my parents I wrote them a letter to try to explain to them who I was and why I wanted them to celebrate with me.

My parents were unmoved. I was called extremely ugly names. I could no longer handle seeing them in so much pain. I repented to them and told them I was sorry that I was gay and I would never act on it or ever think about it again. The subject has never been brought up again and my relationship between my family is "just like it was" before I came out of the closet. Of course I am still gay. I just am gay without my family's recognition or acceptance of it.

We will see the full scope of God's hand in the coming out process only outside of the heterosexist interpretive framework. God beckons gay, lesbian, and bisexual people to come out of their tomb and out of their shroud. Their conversion comes as they accept themselves as they were created. "The greatest sin in my life, the point of my greatest alienation from God," writes William Carroll, "was trying to be something I was not and could not be."[16] Like Lazarus they are called by God to come out.

This call is part of God's passionate response to all forms of human alienation, including sexual self-alienation and alienation from others. Carroll experienced this divine blessing: "But it is only since beginning to emerge from the closet a few months ago that I have begun to feel that I have been as wrong about God not loving me as I have been wrong about not loving myself."[17] God enables family and friends to cry out like Mary and Martha for this divine help.

Christians have known since the beginning that their corporate and individual purpose for living is to give glory to God; the glory of God is creation come fully alive. Homosexual persons have received from God a gracious gift in their sexuality. As stewards of their bodies they have a sacred trust—to celebrate and use this gift for the glory of God. They honor this trust and their Creator when they come out. For the goodness of their bodies and passions to give and receive pleasure and comfort and to build intimacy, they are to give thanks and praise God. This "longing and embodied passion for communion" that comes from our sexuality demands celebration.[18] Each coming out, like every other blossoming in the world, adds to God's glory.

SEXUAL FIDELITY

In "An Ethic for Same-Sex Relations," Margaret A. Farley argues that we must leave behind the fundamental question about "whether or not homosexuality offers one of the possible ways for Christians to live out the sexual dimension of their lives."[19] It, like questions about what causes homosexuality, grow out of the heterosexist paradigm for doing sexual ethics.[20] The time has come to ask new, previously unexamined, questions. For example, it is time to explore together questions like these: For what purpose do homosexual and bisexual people exist? In light of that purpose what norms ought to govern their sexual relations?

The tradition has spoken eloquently, if not compellingly, of these concerns in regard to heterosexual people. It has not explored them in conversation with the gay community. What we discern in this new exploration may result in the reformation of traditional views about the purpose of and norms for heterosexual relations. It would be premature at this stage in our reflection to deny or affirm such a possibility, yet clearly we want all to be open to it. The work of attending to the experience of gay, lesbian, and bisexual people and adding that to our store of knowledge about human sexual experience has just begun.

When confronted with the fact of sexual diversity, one may either focus on what differentiates or what connects people. Farley attends to that which all sexual persons hold in common. She argues that what ought to govern same-sex relations is basically the same as what ought to govern different-sex relations. Justice and the cluster of norms "particular to the intimacy of sexual relations" make up human sexual ethics.[21] She would include within this cluster respect for persons, forgiveness, patience, hope, devotion to the common good, and faithfulness.

In contrast, Mary E. Hunt attends to that which distinguishes homosexual from heterosexual relations. In "Lovingly Lesbian: Toward a Feminist Theology of Friendship," Hunt delineates what she thinks ought to govern sexual friendships.[22] She does not include fidelity in her list. In her reflection on lesbian experience, characteristics like honesty, mutuality, and flexibility appeared much more significant.

Male homosexual relations have not as a rule been marked by fidelity. Neither sexual exclusivity (understood as monogamy) nor permanence (understood as stability) characterize homosexual love, especially among men. This is corroborated by Bell and Weinberg's sociological study of the sexual lifestyles of gay men and lesbians in the San Francisco Bay area. Their statistics about the number of sexual liaisons some gay men have had reveal the depth and pervasiveness of the pattern.[23]

Not surprising within a heterosexist paradigm, one of the main issues facing homosexuals is promiscuity. Gay and lesbian people are constantly accused of promoting sexual promiscuity. Popular media portrayals of one night stands and meetings in bars, bathhouses, alleyways, and restrooms indicate the pervasiveness of this stereotype. It is partly a sexist portrayal because in truth such behavior has been more true of men than women. As has been the case throughout history, little of significance is known or said about lesbian relationships. Statistical evidence substantiates the claim that a higher and significant proportion of homosexual men are extremely promiscuous. When we move beyond heterosexism, two questions emerge as important: On what basis do we define a lifestyle as promiscuous? What lies behind or is the root cause of such behavior?

Consider, for example, that such a lifestyle may be inherent in same-sex relationships. If that hypothesis is true, we would falsify and trivialize the distinctive experience of homosexuality if we were to impose a norm like sexual fidelity on it. Does fidelity make sense only for heterosexual lovers?

Within the gay community some argue that advocating monogamy means adopting a heterosexist model of sexual behavior. They accuse their gay brothers and sisters who argue for committed relationships of selling out to and imitating heterosexual morality. From their perspective such an ethic can be only repressive to them. In this view, gays and lesbians represent a distinct culture that has at least a limited right (limited in terms of its need to coexist with other cultural values) to adopt a distinct sexual ethos.

Although some within the gay community would claim that this represents an alternative normative vision for the heterosexual community as well, most simply argue for consenting gay and lesbian adults to be free to form the kinds of sexual relationships that are authentic for them. Few claim that the choices need to be accepted as the sexual ethic for all people. What constitutes promiscuity is as hotly debated in the gay community as elsewhere. Both gay and straight relationships give evidence of the destructive consequences of specific patterns of unloving behavior. All must face the central issues: What behaviors are constructive? Is there only one right way to form relationships of sexual intimacy and love?

Within the heterosexual community one cannot find a uniform standard of sexual behavior. Nevertheless, it has been reasonably argued that monogamous, committed relationships (usually marriage) provide the proper context for the healthy unfolding of sexual intimacy. At least in terms of straight people's day-to-day experience with friends and lovers, short-term relationships that include genital sexual intimacy seem to create more emotional pain than health for individuals and families. This is not an entirely subjective evaluation because substantial numbers of people seek counseling or therapy as a result of casual sexual encounters. Still, this rationale may prove more relevant to adolescents. It has not proven compelling to emotionally healthy, mutually consenting adults.

In the past, the requirement that sexual relations occur in the context of lifelong partnerships was often justified on the ground that the children born of such unions require stability for their nurturance. Roman Catholics and other mainline Christian denominations as well as modern secular philosophers argued this point.[24] This rationale for fidelity has enjoyed a revival among some mainline Protestants. Although obviously important in some cases, such reasoning does not explain why loving couples who know they will be childless should not engage in premarital sex. It does not explain why married couples might not amicably separate if their children are grown. These couples may be gay or straight, they may be childless as a result of age, infertility, contraceptive rigor, or sexual orientation. Procreative rationales for sexual fidelity are inadequate for the heterosexual as well as the homosexual community.

We believe that a mutual promise of lifelong commitment remains morally important for sexual relations—whether gay, lesbian, bisexual, or straight. Why? Because all human beings must *learn* how to love each other. Such schooling takes time, effort, and patience. The mutual promise and gift of fidelity—of a love that will be steadfast and enduring—bears witness to the patient healing Presence of God in our lives.

Fidelity understood as permanence is a practical requirement necessitated by our need to learn how to love one another. Fidelity understood as exclusivity (monogamy in our culture) is a limit established for practical purposes as well. We can justify this corollary discipline because it is necessary. Exclusivity is necessary because we are finite creatures with real limits that demand our recognition and consent. In "The Body and the Earth," Wendel Berry writes that "the forsaking of all others is a keeping of faith, not just with the chosen one, but with the ones forsaken."[25] We do not judge adultery as wrong only or even primarily because it breaks a specific promise. We do so because everyone is shortchanged in the process. Love for all, including those whom we desire, will keep us out of affairs.

Fidelity remains important because it facilitates love. Our efforts at loving require commitment because, although made for love, we are not born great lovers. We must learn how to love those whom we wake up next to and sometimes feel stuck with. Great loves do not hinge on the maintenance of romantic illusions. Instead they become increasingly intimate and truthful. This is true for all great loves—whether gay or straight. Such loving takes our full attention.

If fidelity is essential to gay love, we can reasonably hypothesize that heterosexism (rather than homosexuality) lies behind the high incidence of gay male promiscuity. What degree of responsibility for promiscuity can be ascribed to heterosexist beliefs both outside of and internalized within the gay community? Heterosexist assumptions surely could contribute significantly to gay promiscuity. When love and fidelity are irrelevant to the morality of one's sexual lifestyle, and covenanted unions receive no social, legal, or ecclesial support, it would be easy to live out, as a sort of self-fulfilling prophecy, the judgments of heterosexism. Summarizing this point of view Paul Jersild writes: "There can be no doubt that the prevalence of promiscuity among gays is encouraged by the public ostracism and the consignment of gay life to a nether world that fashions its own morality of despair and self-hatred."[26] When the only praiseworthy form of sexual discipline is the total denial of one's sexual identity, preferences, or orientation, it would be extremely difficult not to despair and express contempt for both one's self and one's sexual partners through a promiscuity that reduces both the self and others to sexual objects.

Those who do sexual counseling simply take for granted that people who go cruising for anonymous sexual partners, whether they are gay or straight, have low self-esteem. One can easily identify the causes for this among gay people. In a heterosexist world homosexual people must live with the nearly constant disparagement of who they are. Additionally, if they are in a relationship, the pressure to conceal it adds enormous strain. Clandestine promises of commitment are much easier to break.

Many church bodies and their pastoral representatives judge permanent and stable homosexual relationships more harshly than spontaneous acts of homosexual passion. Individuals overwhelmed by lust are judged not so culpable for their sin. People view it as analogous to a "crime of passion." If gay and lesbian people were not forced to live closeted lives, less promiscuity in the gay community might result. In other words, without pressure to hide from a committed relationship for fear of being discovered as gay or lesbian, more homosexual relationships might be monogamous and committed. For these reasons it appears quite reasonable to suggest that the level of promiscuity within the gay community is primarily a product of heterosexism.

Yet this itself is in part a heterosexist conclusion. The heterosexual community has had the freedom to give and receive cultural support for making lifelong committed relationships the context for sexual intimacy. Nevertheless promiscuity still abounds among heterosexual people. Additionally, in spite of the pressure not to form committed partnerships, untold numbers of gay and lesbian couples have done so. Although heterosexism may complicate efforts to form just, faithful, and loving unions, all should remember that sin and grace abound among both gay and straight lovers.

We need an inclusive sexual ethic that provides a context for moral decision making in the contemporary world. Neither heterosexual nor homosexual people who advocate responsible reform argue that no sexual ethic is needed. The charge that people who press for the abolition of heterosexism simply disguise their true goal of an "anything goes" approach to sexual behavior has no substance. The point here is clear and simple: we cannot develop a sexual ethic that honors the holiness of God's gift of sexuality if we ignore the full spectrum of that giftedness. A Christian sexual ethic must incorporate heterosexual, bisexual, and homosexual experience into its dialogue with the tradition and Scripture because that is the reality of the creation God has given us.

The context in which we articulate sexual norms affects how they are interpreted. For this reason dismantling heterosexism requires our full attention. In a heterosexist framework, many gay people hear the advocating of sexual fidelity as prerequisite for learning how to love as yet another punitive word of condemnation that disables them. In a nonheterosexist context, gay, lesbian, and bisexual people might hear the advocacy of such a norm as an empowering invitation to more loving and responsible sexual behavior.

People in the gay community are not helpful when they argue that no one has any business making moral judgments in these matters. Moral judgments will necessarily be made. The issue is whether they are right or wrong. People in the straight community are not helpful when they speak about what ought to govern human sexual behavior in a tone that silences other voices, newly admitted to the conversation. It is premature to reach definitive judgments when the conversation has just begun.

The difficult issue is whether we can make sense of fidelity in our world. John Cobb explains that "it is necessary to demonstrate that (1) fidelity serves love better than other patterns and (2) that such love is achievable only when or is more likely to occur when people are faithful."[27] Although we have not fully addressed these foundational matters, we have started a dialogue on them. We hope our openness to other perspectives on and experiences of these matters proves inviting. Without question, debates about the normative significance of fidelity will dominate the field of sexual ethics when it moves beyond heterosexism.

CONCLUSION

We have tried in this chapter to outline issues created by heterosexism in two ethical categories: sexual authenticity and sexual fidelity. Only from outside of the heterosexist interpretive framework is it possible properly to name and thus begin successfully to exorcise the demons that heterosexism nourishes in each of these areas. Many other important issues will require careful examination following a paradigm shift. We make no claim to be comprehensive in scope or to have provided an in-depth analysis adequate even to these two issues. Our hope is that this work proves suggestive for and inviting of the revisioning which is undoubtedly the future of Christian sexual ethics.

Postscript

Nothing that we have argued in this book belittles heterosexuality. The just, loving, and faithful union of a man and woman who find in each other a mutual complement and who have children together certainly embodies a divine intention for human sexuality. When we recognize and honor this it does not follow that we preclude all other sexual callings; for example, to homosexual or celibate lifestyles. A heterosexual relationship is one of several possible sexual vocations. We have argued against the conclusion that the purpose of this one, admittedly dominant, statistical pattern of sexual relating is applicable to all.

This raises the primary theoretical challenge of whether and how our culture can honor a pluriform rather than uniform understanding of human sexuality. Even when their judgments are not condemnation, all heterosexists refuse to recognize "fundamental pluralism in moral objectivity."[1] They strive instead to discern a uniform standard by which to evaluate, however cautiously, all sexual differences. It is crucial to understand what is at stake ethically in this drive to turn differences in kind into better or worse representatives of a single norm.

An illustration can clarify the issue. One way to challenge illegitimate forms of discrimination based on differences, for example, race or gender, is to advocate a single standard or norm applicable to all. Mary Midgely points out that ever since the Enlightenment people have argued against such discrimination by appealing to some underlying, common standard of reference.[2] Thus women who are denied equal treatment and political privilege on the basis of a hierarchically conceived pattern of differences argued for equality by stating that in spite of the apparent differences they were just like everyone else.

The crucial phrase is "apparent differences." Distinctions rooted in genuine diversity, differences in kind not just degree, are downplayed or ignored for the sake of the equality that one seeks. The experience of dehumanizing discrimination tempts us to continue to assert single norms for all even when reality is pluriform.

Various representatives of such standards could shout past one another, calling each other names ad infinitum, except that some of those shouting have more power. Eventually those with the most power force others into hiding and cloak the ambiguity or short-comings of their own way with the label *normal*.[3] We can avoid the consequences of such power politics only when we dig more deeply into our various natures to discern the value of diversity.

Some moral theologians who refuse to recognize differences in kind fear that doing so will undermine the whole natural law enterprise. As Cahill describes it, the notion of natural law hinges on "the idea that all human beings share certain intrinsic purposes and values, and that these can be discovered by reasonable reflection on human experience itself."[4] Nothing we have argued challenges the notion that we have a "common human nature." Even though our experience and interpretation of it will always be particular, what unites us as human beings has moral significance.

We challenge the assumption that what people have in common may be all that has moral significance. What differentiates us may be just as important. What unites us is not automatically more worthy of privilege than what distinguishes us in our evaluations of natural law and moral life. In his predictions about the future shape of Roman Catholic moral theology, John Mahoney projects a gradual recognition of diversity. He is well aware of the forces working against such a development: "For the most part moral theology has tended to concentrate on elaborating what God wants of all men. Any divergence or deviation from that by individuals has then tended to be treated at best understandingly and sympathetically, in a 'pastoral' manner, as falling short of what is objectively required."[5] The Church is now confronted by a world that recognizes diversity as not only successive (historical) but simultaneous (cultural and natural). Such variation influences judgments about objective as well as subjective morality. Mahoney argues that "what diverse individuals consider God requires of them is in actual fact what God does 'objectively' require of them."[6] If Mahoney is correct, the chains of heterosexism will continue to shackle all of us because we will continue to internalize and justify its demands.

In his observation of the moral significance of human variation, Gerald J. Hughes commented that even Aristotle understood human nature to be "just the kind of thing that can be variously fulfilled."[7] It expresses a simple and straightforward recognition that, although we share some basic needs (or else we would not recognize one another as human beings), there may be some that we do not share.

If no single moral ideal exists, we cannot automatically judge such basic differences inferior or alien. This is not to say that all variations are humanizing. Some expressions of diversity may not be simply incommensurable, but "contradictory opposites" that force negative moral judgments. What we share then becomes the basis for such judgment. What unites us sustains our variation.

The argument we have offered against heterosexism has significant methodological implications for theology and ethics. The failure to value differences regarding human sexual orientation has proven destructive to all of us. To entertain the notion that human sexual orientation is pluriform in character allows us to ponder the moral and theological implications of a biological dictum: the more varied its options, the more successful a given species can be. Our pursuit of standardization shrinks our perception of God's field of play. Perhaps it is time to expand our vision.

Notes

INTRODUCTION

1. John Fortunato, "The Last Committee on Sexuality (Ever)," *Christianity and Crisis* 51, no. 2 (February 18, 1991): 34–35.

2. Dennis M. Dailey, D. S. W., University of Kansas, formulated these definitions and uses them in his workshops on homophobia.

CHAPTER 1: DEFINING *HETEROSEXISM*

1. This vignette, like all the others we use, is a true story. Because some of the vignettes were provided by closeted gay men and lesbians we have decided not to identify any of the sources. This seemed to be the fairest way to honor all the contributors without putting any of them at risk.

2. Over two decades ago lesbian feminists recognized the institutional dimensions of heterosexism and began to describe the coercive nature of this system. The electricity between lesbians must be tremendously empowering, Adrienne Rich argues, if its successful restraint requires physical punishment, economic imperatives, medical "treatment," and extensive covert patterns of heterosexual socialization. See Adrienne Rich, "Compulsory Heterosexuality and Lesbian Existence (1980)," in *Blood, Bread and Poetry: Selective Prose 1979–1985* (New York: W. W. Norton, 1986), pp. 23–75.

3. Although we have some documented evidence of its use by a physician as early as 1869, the multivolume *Oxford English Dictionary* published in 1933 contains neither the term *homosexual* nor *homosexuality*. See the assessment of this issue by David F. Greenberg in "The Medicalization of Homosexuality," in *The Construction of Homosexuality* (Chicago: University of Chicago Press, 1988), pp. 397–433.

4. There is a tremendously diverse pattern of sexual paraphilias among humans. Some people are sexually attracted to animals (zoophilia), corpses (necrophilia), children (pedophilia), or to various isolated body parts and objects (fetishism).

Many people believe that if we approve of homosexual orientation and behavior, then logically we must approve of all imaginable variations in human sexuality. Thus debates about traditional arguments against homosexuality for these people carry enormous weight. All arguments for sexual restraint of every kind seem to hinge on this test case.

Such fears are unfounded. The conclusion that the acceptance of homosexuality will lead to the acceptance of all other sexual activities (e.g., bestiality) is possible only if one believes that any and all behaviors that produce venereal pleasure for at least one person are morally acceptable. It is not necessary to adopt such an axiom to dismantle heterosexism. Indeed, such a move would be a prime example of "throwing out the baby with the bath water."

5. The use of terminology is not uniform either within or across disciplines dealing with sexuality. This description is close to that provided by Frederick Suppe, "Bisexual and Homosexual Identities," in *Gay Personality and Sexual Labeling*, ed. John P. De Cecco (New York: Harington Park Press, 1985), p. 15. We find it helpful to see orientation as one facet of the broader notion of sexual identity. Although here we emphasize the distinction between orientation and behavior, we also find it accurate and helpful to see behavior as a dimension of orientation rather than a completely separate category. Obviously all of these distinctions are conceptual. In our experience as sexual beings they blend and overlap to form our personal sexual identities.

6. The question of whether such an orientation is by definition lustful or a sinful disorientation is precisely the question under examination. Nevertheless we still do not beg that question when we claim as legitimate, at least in some instances, the fine distinction between sexual attraction in itself and lust per se. See pp. 140–144 for a more detailed discussion of this matter.

7. The 1975 "Declaration on Certain Questions Concerning Sexual Ethics" issued by the Sacred Congregation for the Doctrine of the Faith (CDF) was the first official Roman Catholic document to recognize this distinction. In a later letter on "The Pastoral Care of Homosexual Persons," the CDF teaches that "what is at all costs to be avoided is the unfounded and demeaning assumption that the sexual behavior of homosexual persons is always and totally compulsive and therefore inculpable." See CDF, "The Pastoral Care of Homosexual Persons," *Origins* 16, no. 22 (November 13, 1986): 377, 379–381.

8. See, for example, the data in Eli Coleman, ed., *Psychotherapy with Homosexual Men and Women* (New York: Haworth Press, 1988); Alan P. Bell and Martin S. Weinberg, *Homosexualities: A Study of Diversity Among Men and Women* (New York: Simon and Schuster, 1978); and Alan P. Bell, Martin S. Weinberg, and Sue K. Hammersmith, *Sexual Preference: Its Development in Men and Women* (Bloomington: Indiana University Press, 1981). More recent studies have indicated that neurological differences may exist in gay and straight males. Simon LeVay, a neurobiologist at the Salk Institute in San Diego found that a neuron cluster in the hypothalamus was smaller in gay men. See Denise Grady, "The Brains of Gay Men," *Discover* (January

1992): 29. Researchers make it clear that such differences cannot automatically be considered deficits.

9. See, for example, Frederick L. Witham, "Childhood Indicators of Male Homosexuality," *Archives of Sexual Behavior* 6 (1977): 89–96; "Childhood Predicators of Adult Homosexuality," *Journal of Sex Education and Therapy* 6 (1980): 11–16; and Michael Zent, "A Cross-Cultural Assessment of Early Cross-Gender Behavior and Familiar Factors in Male Homosexuality," *Archives of Sexual Behavior* 13 (1984): 427–439; Joseph Harvey, *Gay Children Grow Up* (New York: Praeger, 1982); and Bell et al., *Sexual Preference*. See also note 11.

10. Through the comparison of 979 homosexual and 477 heterosexual people it became clear that members of the homosexual group evidenced significant gender nonconformity. However, it is not clear whether this is a reflection or cause of homosexuality. See Bell et al., *Sexual Preference*.

11. Richard R. Troiden, *Gay and Lesbian Identity: A Sociological Analysis* (New York: General Hall, 1988), pp. 105–116 provides a useful summary of views and the researchers who support them. As noted previously, there is mounting evidence that genetic influence is significant. Sociobiologists are in the forefront of tracing the complex connections between "nature and nurture" regarding sexuality. See E. O. Wilson, *On Human Nature* (Cambridge, Mass.: Harvard University Press, 1978). The process of natural selection works against genes that decrease a specie's reproductive genes. Although no agreed upon explanation currently exists for the evolution of genes for homosexuality, Wilson's observations about a "kin selection" hypothesis offer one possibility.

12. The use of historical analysis in research and writing on sexuality is represented in a variety of ways by a wealth of scholars. Among those listed in the notes, authors such as Boswell, de Beauvoir, and Greenberg are examples of those who argue from the perspective of historical analysis.

13. Troiden puts the matter clearly: "Even if gender behavior ('masculinity' and 'femininity') and sexual preferences were determined completely by biology, current cultural scenarios would organize and define the meanings of sexuality and genders, the significance of gender behavior and interests, the forms that gender and sexuality should assume, their value, the places where they should occur, and their goals or purposes. Whether a person's place on a Kinsey-like scale of sexual responsiveness and behavior is determined by psychological, social, or biological factors, or by all three, 'the homosexual' is constructed to the extent that position on a spectrum provides the basis for such a classification. This construction transforms a matter of degree into an essential form of being" (*Gay and Lesbian Identity*, p. 129).

14. In a highly select treatment population—prescreened not only for motivation and a cooperative heterosexual partner, but also of whom 87 percent were bisexuals (# 2–4 on the Kinsey scale)—Masters and Johnson admit a "reversion" success rate of only 65 percent. It is never revealed whether any of these clients who "converted" were from among those pre-

dominantly or exclusively homosexual (a 5–6 on the Kinsey scale). See Virginia E. Johnson and William H. Masters, *Homosexuality in Perspective* (Boston: Little, Brown and Co., 1979), pp. 250–254, 334–335, 392, 407.

15. The decision was made by the Board of Trustees in 1973 to amend the second edition of the *Diagnostic and Statistical Manual of Mental Disorders*. The change did not appear in the *DSM* until publication of the third edition.

16. As noted earlier, research on human sexuality reveals that few persons are exclusively heterosexual or homosexual in orientation. Alfred Kinsey in 1948 devised a scale, now widely referred to in research and writing, that sees sexual orientation on a continuum: a person at the #0 would be totally heterosexual in orientation and another person at the #6 would be totally homosexual in orientation. Most people fall between these extreme positions and experience a mix in their sexual orientation.

This means that it is not unusual for a person with a heterosexual identity to experience at some time or another a sexual desire for a person of the same sex. For example, approximately 37 percent of all basically heterosexual men have one or more postpuberty homosexual experience(s) to the point of orgasm before the end of adolescence. Such experiences, though perhaps confusing, do not change the individual's basic sexual orientation.

In studies of men conducted in 1948 and of women in 1953, Kinsey determined that between 7–10 percent of all men and 4–9 percent of all women are either predominantly or exclusively homosexual in orientation (#5–6 on the sexual orientation scale). See Alfred C. Kinsey, Clyde E. Martin, and Wardell B. Pomeroy, *Sexual Behavior in the Human Male* (Philadelphia: W. B. Saunders, 1948), and *Sexual Behavior in the Human Female* (Philadelphia: W. B. Saunders, 1953).

17. In this limited sense Adrienne Rich is correct in arguing that same-sex genital relations are neither necessary nor sufficient conditions for the identification of a lesbian ("Compulsory Heterosexuality and Lesbian Existence (1980)"). Still we include behavior in our broad definition of sexual orientation because ordinarily gay men and lesbians would have some behavioral experience of sexual same-sex relations. Furthermore, for some homosexual people there is no erotic or affectional desire to be with persons of a different sex. They may even find the prospect of such a relationship so repugnant as to make it impossible to closet themselves behind such a facade.

18. The use of typologies in sexual ethics is quite common. Some have organized sexual norms around different theses about the primary purpose of sexuality. Human sexuality is understood to be for (1) reproduction, (2) pleasure or recreation, (3) relationships, or (4) the communication of interpersonal emotions and attitudes. James B. Nelson classifies theological stances toward homosexuality as (1) rejecting-punitive, (2) rejecting-non-punitive, (3) accepting with qualifications, and (4) fully accepting. See *Embodiment: An Approach to Sexuality and Christian Theology* (Minneapolis: Augsburg Publishing, 1978).

19. James C. Dobson's thought on homosexuality as articulated in his column in the March 1991 issue of *Focus on the Family* is representative of this type. See as well William Fitch, *Christian Perspectives on Sex and Marriage* (Grand Rapids, Mich.: Eerdmanns, 1971); Paul D. Meier, *Christian Child-Rearing and Personality Development* (Grand Rapids, Mich.: Baker Book House, 1977); Ruth Tiffany Barnhouse, *Homosexuality: A Symbolic Confusion* (New York: Seabury Press, 1977); and Robert M. Nuermberger, "Good News for the Homosexual," and William Wilson and Robert Abarno, "Christian and Homosexual: A Contradiction," in *Issues in Sexual Ethics*, ed. Martin Duffy (Souderton, Pa.: United Church People for Biblical Witness, 1979), pp. 121–143.

20. Several studies indicate that the opposite is true. Comparing his own data to Kinsey's, Paul Thomas notes that "homosexual individuals, contrary to stereotype, usually relate to the opposite sex with sufficient ease on a social level. Lesbians do not experience repugnance towards men, nor do gay males have contempt for women, at least not as often or as much as non-gay men do!" See Paul K. Thomas, "Gay and Lesbian Ministry During Marital Breakdown and the Annulment Process," in *A Challenge to Love*, ed. Robert Nugent (New York: Crossroad Publishing, 1989), p. 230.

21. Both official Roman Catholic and Lutheran (ELCA) teachings are appropriately classified in this category.

22. In his article "A Pastoral Perspective on Homosexuality," *Word and World* 10, no. 2 (Spring 1990): 131–139, William E. Hulme reports that even in programs like Outposts in Minneapolis-St. Paul, which claim to be able to help individuals change their sexual orientations through prayer and healing services, no client ever "has it made." The repression of homosexual desires is a daily process.

23. In its 1975 declaration the CDF (see note 7 above) counseled life-long sexual abstinence for all homosexual people. Although their individual subjective responsibility for maintaining this lifestyle may be limited due to their particular situation, any and all homosexual behavior is judged by Rome to be objectively sinful.

24. Celibacy is to be distinguished from sexual abstinence. Celibacy is a rare charism of the Spirit given to both homosexual and heterosexual persons. Persons given this gift are enabled to live apart from particular sexual relationships without isolating themselves from others. They are able to enjoy and bear witness to the goodness of their sexuality. Their restraint is purposeful—it is a witness offered for the sake of the Kingdom.

25. See, for example, "The Judgment of Martin Luther on Monastic Vows, 1521," in *Luther's Works* 44: 243–400 (especially pp. 261–264). Further discussion of this matter is scattered throughout Luther's writings. For references, see Ewald M. Plass, ed., *What Luther Says* (St. Louis: Concordia Publishing House, 1959), especially the topic headings, "Celibacy," "Chasteness," "Marriage," and "Monastic Vows."

Roman Catholics are at least more consistent in their judgments about this matter. They either presume that the charism of celibacy is generally available to those who discover themselves to be gay or understand themselves to be commending nothing more than chastity.

26. In his book, *The Limits of Love*, Gilbert Meilaender succinctly explains why this position remains coherent. "Simply to say that one cannot be blamed for a homosexual orientation one did not choose is not to say that such an orientation ought to be affirmed as appropriate or in accord with the Creator's will for human life" (University Park: Pennsylvania State University Press, 1987), p. 128.

27. The CDF used the term *disordered* to describe homosexual orientation in its 1986 letter (see note 7).

28. It is a well-established sociological fact that those who see themselves as normal remain suspicious of even former or reformed deviants. Once labeled *deviant*, a person always remains deviant, even if a different kind of deviant in the eyes of those labeled *normal*.

29. Helmut Thielicke may be one of the earliest modern proponents of this position. In his classic work translated by John W. Doberstein, *The Ethics of Sex* (New York: Harper and Row, 1964), Thielicke argues that because homosexuality is incurable (p. 284), the Church ought to help those willing to sublimate their sexual drive (p. 287) but it should also help others achieve their "optimal ethical potential of sexual self-realization" (p. 285). Another early proponent was Norman Pittenger, who argued in 1967 that the homosexual man "is able to give himself, whole and entire, only to another man" (p. 57). He concluded therefore that permanent unions in love among gay people should be privately blessed by the Church and that gay people should be welcomed into the worship and life of the Church. See W. Norman Pittenger, *Time for Consent: A Christian's Approach to Homosexuality* (London: S.C.M. Press, 1967).

30. It is important to distinguish between ethical positions that commend homosexual behavior as a morally normative practice and those that justify homosexual lifestyles on a case-by-case basis. This distinction between particular acts and general practices informs classic just-war theory. Because of its violence, the practice of war has traditionally been judged evil. However, exceptions can be made to this prohibition, and the just-war theory delineates the criteria by which one may legitimate such exceptions. Though permissible as the lesser of two evils, these justifiable wars are not regarded as holy or commendable practices. They remain ambiguous and morally tragic.

Analogous judgments have been made regarding homosexual behavior. Some have argued that even though homosexual unions are not morally normative or good as a general practice, particular homosexual unions marked by justice, love, and fidelity are justified. This judgment is defended on the grounds that they are the least evil of the sexual alternatives realistically available to those individuals.

31. Proponents of this perspective are many. In his book *Ordinary Saints: An Introduction to the Christian Life* (Philadelphia: Fortress Press,

1988), Robert Benne argues that a life of sexual abstinence is a morally heroic response to homosexuality, out of reach for most gay people. The Church, he argues, should discreetly support loving and faithful gay unions, which are certainly less evil than the promiscuity frequently generated by unrealistic efforts to practice sexual abstinence.

Some Roman Catholic moral theologians have reached similar conclusions. Charles E. Curran, Andre Guindon, Philip S. Keane, S.S., Anthony Kosnik, Daniel Maguire, and Richard A. McCormick, S.J., have all dissented from the official magisterial position on this matter. Though their "modest proposals" (McCormick) vary in significant ways, they share three premises: (1) their limited commendation applies only to "irreversibly homosexual" (McCormick) or "fixated" (Guindon) individuals; (2) the practice of sexual abstinence must prove to be destructive and disintegrating to the individuals; they must be without the gift of celibacy promised to some for the sake of the kingdom; (3) finally this compromise (Curran) is justified not only because it commends a lifestyle less evil than and morally preferable to its only viable alternative (promiscuity), but because it does not violate innocent others or harm society.

32. Daniel Maguire, "The Morality of Homosexual Marriage," in *A Challenge to Love*, ed. Robert Nugent (New York: Crossroad Publishing, 1989), p. 120.

33. Those same-sex relationships may become sources of sexual temptation. Other-sex relationships may create false hopes on the part of the "friend" for a deeper sexual relationship or may tempt the homosexual person to remedy his or her isolation by pursuing a heterosexual relationship.

34. It is of course not unique to us. A task force commissioned by the Catholic Theological Society of America (Anthony Kosnik, chair) came to similar conclusions in its report on *Human Sexuality: New Directions in American Catholic Thought* (New York: Paulist Press, 1977). Homosexual behavior should be evaluated by the same criteria—that of interpersonal affection and responsibility—used to assess heterosexual behavior. John J. McNeil argues that love is the only norm relevant to the evaluation of homosexuality; in *The Church and the Homosexual* (Kansas City, Mo.: Sheed, Andrews and McNeil, 1976).

For the sake of clarity we note that this is our own position and not the official position of Wartburg Theological Seminary, the Evangelical Lutheran Church in America (ELCA), or the Roman Catholic Church.

35. To our knowledge the first to make public use of this analogy in a formal discussion of sexual ethics were British Quakers. See *Toward a Quaker View of Sex* (London: Friends Home Service Committee, 1964), p. 26.

36. In her lecture "Making the Connections" (*New Ways Ministry*, cassette, March 29, 1992) Rosemary Radford Ruether describes human sexual orientation as polymorphous in its potential (see note 16). This explains why dismantling heterosexism threatens so many people. It will affect not just minorities who are "exclusively" homosexual or heterosexual but also

the majority who repress much of their potential attraction to persons of the same sex. Accepting the polymorphous character of our sexuality means that the majority of people, who have refused to honor their same-sex affections, will now be forced to reexamine their sexual identity. This is clearly threatening in a heterosexist world.

37. In contrast, proponents of Positions 1 through 4 in varying ways attribute homosexuality to original sin. Unlike the advocates of Position 5, they do not view it as an inherent part of God's good work of creation. It is seen as not part of the original plan but as originating in the Fall. According to Christian doctrine, original sin results in a corruption that infects all relations constitutive of creation and each creature in its entirety. Like other creatures, human beings are not able to control the power or effects of this infection. In this sense, they are victims of it. But this bondage is not merely the result of the sins of ancestral others. According to Christian doctrine, people are not hapless victims of alienation. They have in some real sense enslaved themselves and continue to do so. Variations in these first four positions reflect in part variations in the degree to which individuals are held to be "at fault" for their "sexual disorientation" and the degree to which it is viewed as a manifestation of this corruption.

38. Episcopal Bishop John Spong reports that "left-handed people were called 'the devil's children.'" See John Shelby Spong, *Living in Sin? A Bishop Rethinks Human Sexuality* (San Francisco: Harper and Row, 1990), p. 38.

39. See Gary David Comstock, *Violence Against Lesbians and Gay Men* (New York: Columbia University Press, 1991), for a current analysis of the crisis such violence represents.

40. Gordon Allport, *The Nature of Prejudice* (Cambridge, Mass.: Addison Wesley, 1954).

41. Rich, "Compulsory Heterosexuality and Lesbian Existence (1980)," p. 29.

CHAPTER 2: EVALUATING HETEROSEXISM

1. We are indebted to the work of Pamela Dickey Young for her description of methodological questions in *Feminist Theology/Christian Theology: In Search of Method* (Minneapolis: Fortress Press, 1990).

2. A review of the origins of the procreative premise behind traditional formulations of Christian sexual ethics reveals that early Christians interpreted the Fall as (in part) the loosening of reason's natural control over human emotions. Virtue was by definition reason's ordering of our passions. It was most appropriate therefore to be suspicious of human sexuality's power to overwhelm the mind. Sex clouded the mind, making it impossible to contemplate God or fight well. Yet far from being distracting, sexuality may harmonize our energies.

Both orgasm and sexual impotence, along with the lust for sexual pleasure, demonstrated that human sexuality could not always be rationally controlled. They revealed the paradigmatic way in which human sexuality was
contaminated by sin. This is the historical foundation for the special association still prevalent in the minds of many Christians between sin in general
and sexual sin. In general the early Christian ideal was to avoid sex altogether. If such activity could not be avoided, it should at least serve its procreative purpose (and those who are so sexually active should try not to
enjoy it!).

The origins of the theory of gender complementarity are ancient as
well, but during the Protestant Reformation with its emphasis on relational-
ity it rose to prominence in traditional Christian sexual ethics. So suspect
was sexuality that its contaminating power could only be restrained. Marriage was the remedy for sexual lust; persons were viewed as partial and
wholeness could be found only through relationship with a person of the
opposite sex.

3. During this century Roman Catholic moral theologians, in contrast to
official teaching, expressed little suspicion of venereal pleasure in their writings, nor did they always argue that procreation is the sole or even primary
norm for human sexuality. But when a discussion of heterosexuality shifts to
homosexuality these concerns reassert themselves, and the significance of the
unitive purpose of sexuality based on new understandings of the totality of
the person fades. Though enjoined in a battle over birth control, the official
magisterium and most moral theologians still agree about the basic procreative framework within which homosexuality should be evaluated.

One should not underestimate the significance of the theological developments fostered by the work of moral theologians in debate with official
teaching. Coupled with the official acceptance of the rhythm method, the
profoundly personalist view of human sexuality expressed in the many writings of John Paul II and the "clear distinction" made between homosexuality, which as such is judged objectively but not subjectively as evil, and
homosexual acts, which may be judged subjectively though never objectively
as good, are hopeful signposts. In her lecture, "Ethical Reality," Margaret A.
Farley argues that one can discern in these subtle shifts a change in the tra-
jectory of the tradition (*New Ways Ministries*, cassette, March 29, 1992).

4. At first glance the answer seems obviously negative. The Roman
Catholic church does not teach that even fertile couples are always obligated
to bear children. Contraception appears not to be the issue. Indeed for a
variety of reasons couples might legitimately practice birth control or
forego having children altogether.

What is at stake is the preservation and upholding of a particular ordering of human sexual activity as normative. Put bluntly, this ordering is vaginal intercourse to the point of ejaculation (in some traditions with the man
above the woman in the so-called missionary position). Nothing may artifi-
cially interfere with the openness of this behavior to procreation.

Here lies the heart of the matter: Why is this particular activity norma-tive? Because sexual intercourse sometimes results in procreation, it is con-cluded that all sexual activity is ordained by God to such generative pur-poses. The biological design for propagating the species is seen as mirroring the love and fecundity of the Godhead that is expressed in the creation of the universe (see CDF, "The Pastoral Care of Homosexual Persons," cited in note 17). Although it may sometimes be justified, nonprocreative sexual activity is less than morally normative. We have come full circle. Despite qualifications to the contrary, this line of reasoning does indeed lead to the conclusion that infertility might well be an impediment to marriage.

5. Most heterosexist moral arguments finally end with the conclusion that nonprocreative sex, when it is a lifestyle choice, represents a selfish decision by heterosexual people and a narcissistic indulgence by homosex-ual people.

6. Anal sex, whether practiced by gay or heterosexual couples, may be judged morally problematic for reasons other than its infecundity or non-procreativity. It may be argued that the health risks it poses are sufficient to make its practice immoral. We discuss implications of this for male homo-sexual relationships in chapter 5.

7. The Roman Catholic church certainly aims for (if it does not always achieve) consistency in matters regarding procreation.

8. Lewis B. Smedes, *Sex for Christians* (Grand Rapids, Mich.: Eerd-manns, 1976), p. 29. See as well Karl Barth, *Church Dogmatics*, vol. 3–4 (Edin-burgh: T. & T. Clark, 1961), p. 166.

9. John McNeill notes ironically that some theologians find "the image of God not in man or woman alone, but only in the heterosexual cou-ple united in marriage. They seem to overlook the fact that this would leave out Jesus, who presumably never married." See John McNeill, "Homosexu-ality, Lesbianism and the Future: The Creative Role of the Gay Community in Building a More Humane Society," in *A Challenge to Love*, ed. Roger Nugent (New York: Crossroad Publishing, 1989), p. 56.

10. Many arguments hinge on this misjudgment. James P. Hannigan argues that "the homosexual couple cannot become a two-in-one flesh unity ritually in the act of sexual intercourse. They can only try to imitate or simu-late the authentic ritual of sexual love." See James P. Hannigan, *Homosexual-ity: The Test Case For Christian Sexual Ethics* (New York: Paulist Press, 1988), p. 100.

11. Of course, female sexual pleasure can be indirectly linked to repro-duction among heterosexuals. Stimulation of the clitoris leads to the secre-tion of vaginal fluids, which makes vaginal intercourse at least comfortable and often desirable, because vaginal intercourse frequently may provide fur-ther stimulation to the clitoris. This loose association of pleasure with vagi-nal intercourse increases the likelihood of its continued practice and in this sense can be said to facilitate reproduction.

12. Although there have been many discussions of this matter, the first

public presentation of the argument was done by Christine E. Gudorf at the 1990 Annual Convention of the Catholic Theological Society of America in San Francisco.

13. In addition to the books and articles cited in chapter 1, we commend John Money, *Gay, Straight and In-Between* (New York: Oxford University Press, 1988), for an analysis of the links between nature and nurture in establishing a person's sexual identity. See also, Edward O. Wilson, *On Human Nature* (Cambridge, Mass.: Harvard University Press, 1978).

14. For a summary of how the broader cultural context supports this challenge to a heterosexist ethos, see Margaret A. Farley, "An Ethic for Same Sex Relations," in *A Challenge to Love*, p. 97.

15. Despite the appearance of some claims to the contrary this is still true for Roman Catholicism. See John Mahoney, *The Making of Moral Theology: A Study of Roman Catholic Tradition* (New York: Oxford University Press, 1987), pp. 325–326, for a summary.

16. A single, definitive treatment of the history of Christian sexual ethics is not available. A number of partial histories are worth study. The following list is by no means comprehensive, but only suggestive of the many valuable studies emerging in the field. See John T. Noonan, Jr., *Contraception* (Cambridge, Mass.: Harvard University Press, 1986); Theodore Mackin, *What Is Marriage?* (New York: Paulist Press, 1982); Beverly Wildung Harrison, *Our Right to Choose* (Boston: Beacon Press, 1983); and John Boswell, *Christianity, Social Tolerance, and Homosexuality* (Chicago: University of Chicago Press, 1980).

17. Sacred Congregation for the Doctrine of the Faith, "The Pastoral Care of Homosexual Persons," *Origins* 16, no. 22 (November 13, 1986). 377, 379–381.

18. For example, "So shall my word be that goes out from my mouth; it shall not return to me empty, but it shall accomplish that which I purpose, and succeed in the thing for which I sent it" (Isa 55:11); "If you continue in my word you are truly my disciples, and you will know the truth, and the truth will make you free" (John 8:31–32).

19. Significant historical differences among Christians mark debate about the place and use of Scripture in moral theology. In, *Protestant and Roman Catholic Ethics* (Chicago: University of Chicago Press, 1978), pp. 21–29, James M. Gustafson comments at length on this historic point of divergence. He also describes the growing significance of Scripture as a source of wisdom for theological ethics among Roman Catholic moral theologians like Bernard Haring and Joseph Fuchs (pp. 98–111).

That the Second Vatican Council called for the renewal of all of Catholic theology, including moral theology, is widely accepted. In large measure this renewal is to be nourished by Scripture. The "Dogmatic Constitution on Divine Revelation," notes that theology will be "strengthened and constantly rejuvenated" by that revelation which together with tradition is its "primary and perpetual foundation" (*Dei verbum*, #24, 127, in Walter M.

Abbott and Joseph Gallagher, eds., *The Documents of Vatican II*, New York: Guild Press, 1966). This charge is made explicitly in reference to *moral* theology in the "Decree on Priestly Formation." There it is argued that "special attention needs to be given to the development of moral theology. Its scientific exposition should be more thoroughly nourished by scriptural teaching" (*Optatam totius*, ibid., #16, 452). This call for the biblical renewal of moral theology was rehearsed in 1966 by Richard A. McCormick in his "Notes on Moral Theology," published in *Theological Studies*, and again in 1984 in his *Readings in Moral Theology #4: The Use of Scripture in Moral Theology*, coedited with Charles E. Curran (New York: Paulist Press, 1984).

The constitution of the Evangelical Lutheran Church in America (ELCA) speaks of Scripture as authority and norm for the church in matters of life and faith. What this means in practical terms for the process and substance of ethical debate has varied in Lutheran history. In its most recent formulation of how the church should engage in moral deliberation, the ELCA approved the following explanation (part of a larger document): "Deliberation in this church gives attention both to God's Word and God's world, as well as to the relationship between them. This church sees the world in light of God's Word, and it grasps God's Word from its context in the world. This church must rely upon God's revelation, God's gift of reason, and the guidance of the Holy Spirit. Scripture is the normative source in this church's deliberation. Through the study of Scripture, Christians seek to know what God requires in the church and the world. Because of the diversity in Scripture, and because of the contemporary world's distance from the biblical world, it is necessary to scrutinize the texts carefully in their own setting and to interpret them faithfully in the context of today. In their witness to God's Word, the ecumenical creeds and the Lutheran confessions guide this church's approach to Scripture, and the Church's history and traditions instruct it in its deliberations." See *The Church in Society: A Lutheran Perspective*; social statement adopted by the Churchwide Assembly of the ELCA meeting in Orlando, Florida, August 28–September 4, 1991 (Chicago: ELCA Department for Studies of the Commission for Church in Society, 1991).

We believe that the Church's dogmatic and ethical formulations need to originate from and come under the constant scrutiny of Scripture. This process may prompt us to rethink and reformulate them. Secular idolatries and presumptions are also persistently challenged by the Bible.

20. For clarification on the question of Scripture's "inspiration" as typically argued on the basis of 2 Tim 3:16–17 and 2 Pet 1:20–21, see Paul T. Achtemeier, *The Inspiration of Scripture* (Philadelphia: Westminster Press, 1980). See also J. Severino Croatto, *Biblical Hermeneutics: Toward a Theory of Reading as the Production of Meaning* (Maryknoll, N.Y.: Orbis Books, 1987), pp. 46–50.

21. We are indebted to the work of many biblical and moral theologians on this question. Two reviews of that literature have proven especially formative for us: the chapter on "The Bible and Ethics: Hermeneutical

Dilemmas," in Lisa Sowle Cahill, *Between the Sexes* (New York: Paulist Press, 1985), pp. 15–44; and Bruce C. Birch and Larry L. Rasmussen, *Bible and Ethics in the Christian Life* (Minneapolis: Augsburg Publishing, 1989).

22. Several other reasons clarify why Scripture, though authoritative and normative, is not the exclusive source of moral wisdom for Christians.

First, the nature of the hermeneutical process itself speaks against such an exclusive reliance. For example, which meaning in the history of the tradition of the text is authoritative? Is the author's intended meaning normative? What about its unintended meanings? What weight should be accorded the interpretation given the text by its original hearers? What is the normative status of interpretations by subsequent though still ancient hearers? Why should the interpretation of contemporary readers be normative? Furthermore the hermeneutical process is dialogical or circular in character. Some scriptural demands are confirmed by their intelligibility. This intelligibility is present on the basis of Scripture's perspicuity, that is, its critical incorporation of worldly wisdom (such as in the Wisdom literature) and its own internal understandability. Its intelligibility also rests in part on its coherence with other sources of wisdom. This cannot be the only criterion, of course. It is essentially conservative and would allow God no prophetic voice that often seems foolish and "crazy."

Second, the ongoing activity of God after the closing of the canon speaks against scriptural positivism. Christians must trust God's promise of the Spirit's guidance not only as they listen to Scripture but in all their unfolding life together.

Third, the very nature of human agency argues against viewing the Bible as our only source of moral wisdom. God created humans for theonomous creativity under the Spirit. This means we were made not for sheer autonomy or freedom, but made to respond to God's call. This call does not demand sheer heteronomy or compliance from us. God did not make us for "blind" obedience. Without understanding, even total compliance with divine commands is not a moral response to God. For this same reason we do not hold very young children, the mentally handicapped, the emotionally disturbed, or the violently coerced morally accountable for their actions. See Franz Bockle, *Fundamental Moral Theology* (New York: Pueblo Publishing, 1980.)

23. A sample of these texts would include the following. Those may abide with God "who do not lend money at interest" (Ps 15:5). "You shall not charge interest on loans to another Israelite, interest on money, interest on provisions, interest on anything that is lent. On loans to a foreigner you may charge interest, but on loans to another Israelite you may not lend upon interest" (Deut 23: 19–20). "But love your enemies, do good, and lend, expecting nothing in return" (Lk 6:35). For more information about this and other instances of "paradigm shifts," see Albert R. Jonsen and Stephen Toulmin, *The Abuse of Casuistry: A History of Moral Reasoning* (Berkeley: University of California Press, 1988), pp. 177–228.

24. Scholars inclined to such faulty reading would do well to remember that this pattern may embody some literalist assumptions they generally deplore.

25. Lisa Sowle Cahill, "Is Catholic Ethics Biblical? The Example of Sex and Gender," *Warren Lecture Series in Catholic Studies*, no. 20 (March 15, 1992): 3.

26. Another example of such diversity emerges in the analysis of material possessions by Luke T. Johnson in his book, *Sharing Possessions* (Philadelphia: Fortress Press, 1981). He reviews three different directives regarding material possessions in that two-volume account of the story of Jesus and the primitive church known as Luke-Acts.

The first is "Wandering Destitution." At certain junctures Jesus demands of his disciples complete renunciation of all possessions. Peter, the sons of Zebedee, and the tax collector Levi "left everything and followed him" (Lk 5). Jesus tells the rich ruler to sell all and follow (Lk 18). The parable of the great banquet ends with "So therefore, none of you can become my disciple if you do not give up all your possessions" (Lk 14:33). Apostles are told to "take nothing for your journey, no staff, nor bag, nor bread, nor money—not even an extra tunic" (Lk 9:3; 10:3-7; see Mark 12:41-44, esp. v. 44, as well).

The second is "Almsgiving and Hospitality." At other junctures the disciples of Jesus are told to give alms to help the poor and to provide hospitality. The woman Tabitha and the centurion Cornelius are commended for their almsgiving in Acts 10. Zacchaeus' promise—to restore what he had stolen, give away half of his possessions, and offer hospitality to Jesus—is upheld (Lk 19). Mary and Martha show Jesus great hospitality yet so far as we know they did not sell their house and follow Jesus (Lk 10). The Apostle Paul was a tentmaker who made enough money to help others more needy than he (Acts 20:18-35). "Day by day, as they spent much time together in the temple, they broke bread at home and ate their food with glad and generous hearts" (Acts 2:46); therefore they must not have abandoned or sold their homes. When the Antiochean church took up a collection to help the Jerusalem community, members contributed "according to their ability" (Acts 11:29). The Apostle Peter is described as the financial administrator of the funds of the community (Acts 6).

The third is "Community of Goods." At still different junctures Christians are described as holding all their possessions in common. "All who believed were together and had all things in common; they would sell their possessions and goods and distribute the proceeds to all, as any had need" (Acts 2:44-45). (It is not clear whether this practice is merely abandoned or clearly rejected in the later chapters of Acts.)

On the level of general principle it is possible to discern amidst this diversity of witness a broad directive. Clearly Jesus' gospel challenges Christians to relate to material resources so as to be dependent on God alone, serve the church's mission, and support those in need. However, on the level of specific instruction the Bible is simply unclear whether Christianity requires that the faithful today in our affluent midwestern context, are to be poor, form communes, or practice charity. Which, if any, of these diverse economic lifestyles applies today? It is equally unclear whether or not pastors should practice radical poverty, be worker priests, or skilled financial administrators.

27. See Willard M. Swartley, *Slavery, Sabbath, War and Women: Case Issues in Biblical Interpretation* (Scottsdale, Pa.: Herald Press, 1983).

28. We believe the texts cited do not in fact "make a case" for slavery because we do not view this portion of the biblical testimony about slavery as authoritative or normative.

29. According to Cahill, *Between the Sexes*, advocates of this position included Brevard Childs, Raymond Brown, and Birch and Rasmussen, to name a few.

30. According to Cahill, ibid., advocates of this view include Paul Ricouer, James Sanders, Paul Hanson, and Joseph Blenkinsopp.

31. James D. G. Dunn, *Unity and Diversity in the New Testament* (Philadelphia: Westminster Press, 1977), pp. 379–387.

32. Phyllis Trible makes a similar claim about the countercultural character of Genesis. She concludes that the Yahwist account of creation in Genesis 2 and 3 is a privileged text about the proper role and status of women in light of which other Old Testament texts should be evaluated. *God and the Rhetoric of Sexuality* (Philadelphia: Fortress Press, 1978). For an analysis of how Christians construct canons within the canon, see Dunn, ibid.

33. Trible, ibid., argues that she did not impose a feminist agenda on her interpretation of the Genesis text. She claims to have merely uncovered this agenda inherent in it. The nonpatriarchal thrust of the text is clearly countercultural. For this reason she believes it should be privileged.

34. Paul Ricouer, "Toward a Hermeneutic of the Idea of Revelation," in *Essays on Biblical Interpretation*, ed. Lewis Mudge (Philadelphia: Fortress Press, 1980).

35. Lisa Sowle Cahill argues that the Congregation for the Doctrine of the Faith in the Roman Catholic church has yet to grapple with biblical wisdom about homosexuality. She views texts cited in their recent instruction regarding the "Pastoral Care of Homosexual Persons" as ornamental to their teaching. This is reflected in their use of neoscholastic rather than biblical terms like *sexual faculty*. See Cahill, "Is Catholic Ethics Biblical? The Example of Sex and Gender," *Warren Lectures Series in Catholic Studies*, no. 20 (March 15, 1992): 2.

36. For a discussion of classic texts, see David Tracy, *Blessed Rage for Order* (New York: Seabury Press, 1975).

37. See Franz Bockle, *Fundamental Moral Theology*, trans. N. D. Smith (New York: Pueblo Publishing Co, 1980); and Joseph Fuchs, *Natural Law: A Theological Investigation*, trans. Helmut Rekter and John A. Dowling (New York: Sheed and Ward, 1965), for an analysis of the biblical basis for the

conviction that there is an objective moral order built into the very fiber of creation.

38. Nontraditional sources of wisdom do challenge traditional interpretations of Scripture. Most mainline Christians have become accustomed to the dialogue between modern physical science and theology. They are comfortable with the heliocentric motion of the planets, for example. Yet Copernican theories were pitted against biblical portrayals of other patterns for centuries. The time has come for a parallel conversation between Christian ethics and the social or human sciences that replaces patterns of silence or mistrust.

39. New Testament texts that speak of and call for a discipleship of equals are many. They include the baptismal reference found in Gal 3:28; references to the equality and reciprocity that should mark marriages in the Lord (1 Cor 7:3–4, 10–16, 32–33; 11:11–12); references to the female leaders of house churches (Lydia in Acts 16:14; Nympha in Col 4:14; Mary, the mother of Mark and John, in Acts 12:12; Priscilla in 1 Cor 16:19; and the reference to Apphia in Philemon 2); references that indicate Paul assumed and accepted that women were praying aloud and prophesying in worship such as 1 Cor 11:5 (even calls for the silencing of women in the later Pastorals indicate that such was the practice); and passages that recognize through leadership titles the presiding and deaconal roles of women (Phoebe in Rom 16:1), and their apostolic missionary activity (Priscilla, Junia, Mary, Tryphana and Tryphosa, and Persis in Rom 16, and Euodia and Syntyche in Phil 4).

New Testament texts that speak of and call for patriarchy are also many. They include passages that dictate that women keep silent (1 Cor 14:33b–36). This passage has received many intriguing interpretations, including that Paul is quoting a slogan of some Corinthian men. Deutero-Pauline passages that rehearse and endorse the patriarchal household codes typical of this era (such as Col 3:18–4:1; 1 Pet 2:11–3:12; Eph 5:21–33); passages in the pastorals that dictate that women not teach men or otherwise preside over them (1 Tim 2:8–15; 3:2; Titus 1:6; 2:3–5); and passages that suggest that women are morally inferior and that they can be saved through childbirth (1 Tim 2:8–15). Except for 1 Cor 14:33b–36, all these patriarchal texts probably reflect a chronologically later time in the development of the New Testament church. See Elizabeth Schussler Fiorenza, *In Memory of Her* (New York: Crossroad Publishing, 1983), for more details.

40. Additional questions also arise. For example, in whose experience should we trust? In *Six Theories of Justice* (Minneapolis: Augsburg Press, 1986), p. 88, Karen Lebacqz argues that Reinhold Niebuhr suggested that a kind of "epistemological privilege" belonged to the oppressed. She notes that he argued this not on the grounds that their point of view was less distortive than the perspective of the oppressor, but because only through a confrontation of perspectives would the truth emerge. So-called objective perspectives are epistemologically impossible. They are not at all politically

neutral, but are inherently conservative. They give advantage to entrenched interests and points of view.

41. According to Fiorenza's argument, *In Memory of Her*, the egalitarian character of the early Jesus movement (the renewal within Judaism) and the early missionary movement (evidenced in the "house church" phenomenon) can be glimpsed through privileged texts that call for a discipleship of equals. The later (post 70 C.E.) patriarchal texts have as their premise the full participation of women in leadership positions. They are treated as analogous to "Keep Off the Grass" signs, which reveal as widespread their "opposite" practice—walking on the grass. Some post 70 C.E. writings, most notably Luke and Matthew, commend nonhierarchical forms of leadership and community.

Furthermore, given Fiorenza's reconstruction, these calls for the repatriarchalization of the church can be comprehended as a survival or coping strategy advocated by some New Testament communities. This compromise was designed to minimize the threat of persecution precipitated by the revolutionary and subversive nature of their egalitarianism. This particular strategy and the Christian communities that adopted it (that is, patriarchal structures) came to dominate the Church as a whole. An alternative response to persecution can be found in the Gospels of Mark and John according to Fiorenza. These communities called their members not to compromise but to an acceptance of the suffering the world would demand of them for the sake of others. Some feminists would question Fiorenza's premise that this response was less patriarchalizing of ecclesial structures in the long run than the former response.

42. There is nothing peculiarly religious about this. All people operate with some kind of "scripture," that is in conversation with a text or source of wisdom indispensable to their deliberations. For some U.S. citizens their Constitution functions as a kind of scripture. In other words, what we are describing from the particular perspective of Christian moral deliberations is a process engaged in by all people because they necessarily stand in a tradition.

43. This particular understanding of the way in which the Bible can function as basis and norm for the reformation of tradition is rooted, like its alternatives in a particular theology of Scripture. See Sandra M. Schneiders, *The Revelatory Text* (San Francisco: Harper, 1991), pp. 43–63, for a helpful discussion of various viewpoints on these matters.

CHAPTER 3: THE BIBLE AND HETEROSEXISM

1. Margaret A. Farley, "An Ethic for Same Sex Relations," in *A Challenge to Love*, ed. Robert Nugent (New York: Crossroad Publishing, 1989), p.99.

2. Although the latter judgment cannot be proven, we believe that it is a reasonable conclusion because there are no words for sexual orientation

in Greek or Hebrew. The concept does not emerge in Western thought until the nineteenth century. The Greek term *homophilia* existed in biblical times but is not used in Scripture.

3. Both the Code of Theodosius and the Code of Justinian commanded death by fire for sodomites and explicitly argued for the necessity of such penalties on the grounds that the state must be protected from the divine wrath that befell Sodom. See George A. Kanoti and Antony R. Kosnik, "Homosexuality: Clinical and Behavioral Aspects," in *Encyclopedia of Bioethics*, vol. 2, ed. Warren T. Reich (New York: The Free Press, 1978), p. 672.

4. We will use the NRSV translation throughout this book. *The New Oxford Annotated Bible*, ed. Bruce M. Metzger and Roland E. Murphy (New York: Oxford University Press, 1991).

5. One of the best texts we have seen on the topic of sexual violence is Marie Marshall Fortune's *Sexual Violence* (New York: Pilgrim Press, 1983), in which she analyzes why we are so prone culturally to confuse sexual activity with sexual violence.

6. The texts of the cited passages are as follows.

"The punishments did not come upon the sinners without prior signs in the violence of thunder, for they justly suffered because of their wicked acts; for they practiced a more bitter hatred of strangers. Others had refused to receive strangers when they came to them, but these made slaves of guests who were their benefactors" (Wis 19:13–14).

"Then he began to reproach the cities in which most of his deeds of power had been done because they did not repent. 'Woe to you, Chorazin! Woe to you, Bethsaida! For if the deeds of power done in you had been done in Tyre and Sidon, they would have repented long ago in sackcloth and ashes. But I tell you, on the day of judgment it will be more tolerable for Tyre and Sidon than for you. And you, Capernaum, will you be exalted to heaven? No, you will be brought down to Hades. For if the deeds of power done in you had been done in Sodom, it would have remained until this day. But I tell you that on the day of judgment it will be more tolerable for the land of Sodom than for you'" (Mt 11:20–24).

"Likewise, just as it was in the days of Lot: they were eating and drinking, buying and selling, planting and building, but on the day that Lot left Sodom, it rained fire and sulfur from heaven and destroyed all of them" (Lk 17:28–29).

"This was the guilt of your sister Sodom: she and her daughters had pride, excess of food, and prosperous ease, but did not aid the poor and needy. They were haughty, and did abominable things before me; therefore I removed them when I saw it" (Ezek 16:49–50).

"But in the prophets of Jerusalem I have seen a more shocking thing: they commit adultery and walk in lies; they strengthen the hands of evildoers, so that no one turns from wickedness; all of them have become like Sodom to me, and its inhabitants like Gomorrah" (Jer 23:14).

"He did not spare the neighbors of Lot, whom he loathed on account of their arrogance" (Sir 16:8).

"The look on their faces bears witness against them; they proclaim their sin like Sodom, they do not hide it" (Isa 3:9).

There are other intrabiblical references to the story of Sodom and Gomorrah. These references do not make any comment about the specific *nature* of the sin of Sodom and Gomorrah. Instead they predict that a destruction, desolation, and intolerable horror analogous to that which fell upon Sodom and Gomorrah will come to others. A comparison is made in these texts to the *consequences* of sin. Such passages include the following.

"If the Lord of hosts had not left us a few survivors, we would have been like Sodom, and become like Gomorrah. Hear the word of the Lord, you rulers of Sodom! Listen to the teaching of our God, you people of Gomorrah! What to me is the multitude of your sacrifices? says the Lord; I have had enough of burnt offerings of rams and the fat of fed beasts; I do not delight in the blood of bulls, or of lambs, or of goats" (Isa 1:9–11).

"And Babylon, the glory of kingdoms, the splendor and pride of the Chaldeans, will be like Sodom and Gomorrah when God overthrew them" (Isa 13:19).

"As when Sodom and Gomorrah and their neighbors were overthrown, says the Lord, no one shall live there, nor shall anyone settle in her" (Jer 49:18).

"As when God overthrew Sodom and Gomorrah and their neighbors, says the Lord, so no one shall live there, nor shall anyone settle in her" (Jer 50:40).

"But whenever you enter a town and they do not welcome you, go out into its streets and say, 'Even the dust of your town that clings to our feet, we wipe off in protest against you. Yet know this: the kingdom of God has come near.' I tell you, on that day it will be more tolerable for Sodom than for that town. Woe to you, Chorazin! Woe to you, Bethsaida! For if the deeds of power done in you had been done in Tyre and Sidon, they would have repented long ago sitting in sackcloth and ashes" (Lk 10:10–13).

7. See the analysis of Gerhard von Rad, *Genesis: A Commentary* (Philadelphia: Westminster Press, 1922), pp. 217–218; and that of Walter Brueggemann, *Genesis* (Atlanta: John Knox Press, 1975).

8. "For if God did not spare the angels when they sinned, but cast them into hell and committed them to chains of deepest darkness to be kept until the judgment; and if he did not spare the ancient world, even though he saved Noah, a herald of righteousness, with seven others, when he brought a flood on a world of the ungodly; and if by turning the cities of Sodom and Gomorrah to ashes he condemned them to extinction and made them an example of what is coming to the ungodly; and if he rescued Lot, a righteous man greatly distressed by the licentiousness of the lawless (for that righteous man, living among them day after day, was tormented in his righteous soul by their lawless deeds that he saw and heard), then the

Lord knows how to rescue the godly from trial, and to keep the unrighteous under punishment until the day of judgment—especially those who indulge their flesh in depraved lust, and who despise authority" (2 Pet 2:4–10).

"And the angels who did not keep their own position but left their proper dwelling, he has kept in eternal chains in deepest darkness for the judgment of the great day. Likewise, Sodom and Gomorrah and the surrounding cities, which, in the same manner as they, indulged in sexual immorality and pursued unnatural lust, serve as an example by undergoing a punishment of eternal fire" (Jude 6–7).

9. The phrases are *indulged their flesh in depraved lust* (NRSV translation of *ekporneusasai*) and *pursued in unnatural lust* (NRSV translation of *apelthousai episo sarkos heteras*). A more literal translation of the latter is "went after strange flesh." See Walter Bauer, *A Greek–English Lexicon of the New Testament and Other Early Christian Literature* (Chicago: University of Chicago Press, 1979), p. 84. It is not clear that this refers to homosexuality. J. N. D. Kelly in *The Epistles of Peter and Jude* (New York: Harper and Row, 1969), p. 258, argues that the Greek cannot support an interpretation of "strange flesh" as homosexuality. Kelly, as well as Richard J. Bauckham in *Jude, 2 Peter* (Waco, Texas: Word Publishing, 1983; Word Biblical Commentary 50) notes that *strange flesh* refers to the (nonhuman) angels in Gen 19:1, and the lust is for them since their flesh is different (*heteras*) from that of other human men.

10. For example, von Rad argues in *Genesis: A Commentary* that the stories of Sodom and Gomorrah in Genesis and that of Gibeah in Judges may be dependent on each other (p. 218). Similarly Claus Westermann suggests in his book, *Genesis 12–36: A Commentary* (Minneapolis: Augsburg Publishing, 1985), that in spite of differences the two stories are about the same issues. For analyses of which story is dependent on the other, see James D. Martin, *The Book of Judges* (Cambridge: Cambridge University Press, 1975) and J. Alberto Soggin, *Judges: A Commentary* (Philadelphia: Westminster Press, 1981). We are indebted to Arland I. Hultgren, "Homosexuality and the Scriptures," in *Perspectives on Homosexuality* (St. Paul, Minn: St. Paul Area Synod, ELCA, 1990), pp. 7–18, for alerting us to these sources.

11. See, for example, John Boswell, *Christianity, Social Tolerance, and Homosexuality* (Chicago: University of Chicago Press, 1980), as well as the analyses of Martin Noth, *Leviticus* (Philadelphia: Westminster Press, 1977), N. H. Snaith, *Leviticus and Numbers* (London: Thomas Nelson and Sons, 1967); and Gordon J. Wenham, *The Book of Leviticus* (Grand Rapids, Mich.: Eerdmanns, 1979).

12. "None of the daughters of Israel shall be a temple prostitute; none of the sons of Israel shall be a temple prostitute" (Deut 23:17); "there were also male temple prostitutes in the land. They committed all the abominations of the nations that the Lord drove out before the people of Israel" (1 Kings 14:24); "He [Asa] put away the male temple prostitutes out of the land, and removed all the idols that his ancestors had made" (1 Kings

15:12); "The remnant of the male temple prostitutes who were still in the land in the days of his father Asa, he exterminated" (1 Kings 22:46).

13. The matter is not so simple as may be implied by our comments here. Clearly, the New Testament dismissed "kasruth" regulations as binding (Mk 7, Rom 14, 1 Cor 8 and 10, Acts 10), but not all of what was covered by these regulations was dispensed with. So in Acts 15:28–29 the Gentiles are to refrain from *porneia*. The critical issue is that the criterion is ethical rather than purity in a narrow sense (that is, fear of contamination from contact with what is anomalous, different, etc.).

14. See Mt 5:43; 5:38–39; 19:19; 22:39; Rom 13:9; Gal 5:14; James 2:8. See as well "Perspectives on Homosexuality: The Report of the Task Force on Issues Related to Homosexuality, Homophobia and the Ordination of Persons of Homosexual Orientation," St. Paul Area Synod, ELCA (April 1990), p. 9.

15. David M. Gunn, "A Fearful Domination: Constructions of Homosexuality in the Hebrew Bible," paper presented at The Society for Biblical Literature annual meeting in Kansas City, 1991.

16. William L. Petersen, in "Can *Arsenokoitai* Be Translated by 'Homosexuals'?" *Vigiliae Christianae* 40 (1986): 187–191, argues that such a translation "violates historical and linguistic fact by attempting to read a modern concept back into antiquity, where no equivalent concept existed" (p. 189).

17. Such translations are found everywhere. For example, see Eileen P. Flynn, *AIDS: A Catholic Call for Compassion* (Kansas City, Mo.: Sheed and Ward, 1985), p. 66.

18. Boswell, *Christianity, Social Tolerance, and Homosexuality*, discusses the linguistic difficulties at length in an appendix, "Lexicography and St. Paul," pp. 335–353. See also Henry G. Liddell and Robert Scott, *A Greek–English Lexicon* (Oxford: Oxford University Press, 1940), p. 1077, for a list of several meanings attested to it in classical sources. The issue of a man remarrying his former wife may not only be a matter of moral weakness (*malakoi*). For example, Philo would have known of Deut. 24:1–4, where this remarrying is called an "abomination," the same word used in the Holiness Code texts already discussed. The word *abomination* is applied to a wide spectrum of human behaviors, ranging from matters now judged to be merely purity concerns to those of grave moral consequence.

19. Boswell, ibid., p. 342.

20. Though the letter is attributed to Paul, most biblical scholars believe it was written by someone else. Variations in language and style, theology and polity, suggest another author.

21. They reached this conclusion by examining the loose parallels between the list found in 1 Timothy and the Ten Commandments. The Greek term, *arsenokoitai*, is sandwiched in between references to persons who are sexually immoral and who are thieves. Thus, some believe the term refers not to sodomy in general but to a type of sexual thievery. See for example, Robin Scroggs, *Homosexuality and the New Testament* (Philadelphia: Fortress Press, 1983).

22. Unlike Calvin and the Reformed traditions, Luther tested Mosaic moral laws for their compatibility with the teachings of the New Testament and natural law. Luther argued that, because they have Christ, he and his contemporaries could make new decalogues, as did Saints Peter and Paul before them. See Martin Luther, "How Christians Should Regard Moses, 1525," *Luther's Works* 35:165, ed. Lewis Spitz (Philadelphia: Muhlenberg Press, 1960), and "Theses Concerning Faith and Law," 1535, *Luther's Works*, 34:112, ed. E. Theodore Bachman (Philadelphia: Muhlenberg Press, 1960).

23. The argument L. William Countryman mounts in this regard is interesting and worthy of serious study, though we were not finally convinced by it. See *Dirt, Greed and Sex* (Philadelphia: Fortress Press, 1988).

24. See Richard B. Hays, "Relations Natural and Unnatural: A Response to John Boswell's Exegesis of Romans 1," *Journal of Religious Ethics* 14, no. 1 (Spring 1986): 184–215. John Boswell's argument regarding this passage can be found in *Christianity, Social Tolerance, and Homosexuality*.

25. See James D. G. Dunn, *Romans* (Dallas: Word Publishing, 1988), for a broader analysis.

26. Such a change in theological position is not without precedent. Jesus himself took such bold moves for profoundly theological reasons, despite the challenge they posed to the Hebrew Scriptures (Mt 5:27ff). The apostles made similar moves; for example, regarding circumcision. We believe the Church universal is called to such boldness in our day regarding heterosexism.

27. In "Perspectives on Homosexuality: The Report of the Task Force on Issues Related to Homosexuality, Homophobia and the Ordination of Persons of Homosexual Orientation," St. Paul Area Synod, ELCA (April 1990), p. 50.

28. To reinterpret a Scripture passage in light of new scientific data that seems to contradict it is not without precedent. Protestants, and eventually even Roman Catholics, accepted the Copernican heliocentric theory of the solar system despite its contradiction of the literal meaning of several passages (e.g., Ps. 45, 78:69; and Eccl. 1:4). Such scientific revolutions in our thinking are not to be feared as long as they do not challenge the gospel, even though they may result in radical reinterpretations of Scripture. (See note 38, chapter 2.)

29. This position is clearly associated with Roman Catholic tradition, but it is also well established in most Protestant traditions. For example, in his defense of the marriage of priests in Article 23 of the *Apology*, Philip Melanchthon argued that in Gen 1:28 God "teaches that men were created to be fruitful and that one sex should have a proper desire for the other. . . . This love of one sex for the other is truly a divine ordinance" (p. 7). In his debate with Rome he noted that "The Word of God did not form the nature of men to be fruitful only at the beginning of creation, but it still does as long as this physical nature of ours exists" (p. 8). He concluded that "the natural desire of one sex for the other is an ordinance of God" (p. 12), and "marriage is necessary for a remedy as well as for procreation" (p. 13).

In his discussion of the sixth commandment (against adultery) in the *Large Catechism*, Martin Luther described marriage "as a divine and blessed estate. Significantly he established it as the first of all institutions, and he created man and woman differently (as is evident) not for lewdness but to be true to each other, be fruitful, beget children and support and bring them up to the glory of God."

For these sources see Theodore Tappert, ed., *The Book of Concord* (Philadelphia: Fortress Press, 1959), pp. 240–241, 393.

30. See Lisa Sowle Cahill, "Is Catholic Ethics Biblical? The Example of Sex and Gender," in *Warren Lecture Series in Catholic Studies*, no. 20 (March 15, 1992): 9–13.

31. See, for example, the diatribe marshalled against the study document prepared by the ELCA Task Force on Human Sexuality entitled "Human Sexuality and the Christian Faith" found in the *Forum Letter* 21, no. 2 (February 3, 1992): 1–3.

32. Although they are weak, arguments from silence are not irrelevant. It is worth questioning why Jesus said nothing about same-sex relationships or behaviors. On the one hand, the Levitical prohibitions were in force so that there may have been little open same-sex activity on which to comment. Still, Jesus and later New Testament writers lived near cities where such behaviors were public enough to cause notice. Christian heterosexists should find it at least peculiar that no ringing condemnation of such activity is ascribed to Jesus.

CHAPTER 4: THE COSTS OF HETEROSEXISM

1. Paul Avis, *Eros and the Sacred* (Harrisburg, Pa.: Morehouse Publishing, 1989), p. 152. Echoing similar concerns the Congregation for the Doctrine of the Faith on July 23, 1992, issued a statement "Some Considerations Concerning the Catholic Response to Legislative Proposals on the Non-Discrimination of Homosexual Persons." In this "background resource" the Vatican contends that some initiatives that would make discrimination based on sexual orientation illegal may have a negative impact on, indeed jeopardize, the family and society. The "background resource" suggests that it may be legitimate to bar gay persons from adopting children, teaching, coaching, or serving in the military. In assessing proposed legislation bishops are told to give priority to their responsibility to promote family life, presumably over their obligation to condemn the violent and malicious treatment of gay persons (which is clearly condemned in the same document). With contrasting emphases in its new (1992) catechism, the Roman Catholic church teaches that while homosexual acts are contrary to natural law, gay persons must be welcomed and unjust discrimination against them must be avoided.

2. See, for example, Alan P. Bell and Martin S. Weinberg, eds., *Homosexuality: An Annotated Bibliography* (New York: Harper and Row, 1972); and the bibliographies published in the *Journal of Homosexuality*.

3. As quoted by Kevin Gordon, in *Homosexuality and Social Justice* (San Francisco: The Consultation on Homosexuality, Social Justice, and Roman Catholic Theology, 1982 and 1986), p. 131.

4. It is crucial that the capacity of this charge to foster violence against lesbians and gay men not be underestimated. In their propaganda campaign against middle-class Jews, the Nazis espoused a uniform family structure, the purity and sanctity of which the Jews were supposedly perverting.

5. Evelyn Hooker's work initiated the reappraisal of the argument that homosexuality was inextricably bound with neuroses or other socially and psychologically debilitating conditions. See, for example, her study, "A Preliminary Analysis of Group Behavior of Homosexuals," *Journal of Psychology* 42 (1956): 217–225, along with her subsequent research.

6. Roger H. Ard, "Why the Conservatives Won in Miami," *The Christian Century* 94 (August 3–12, 1977): 678.

7. Jonathan L. Jenkins, "Review Essay of *The Construction of Homosexuality* by David F. Greenberg," *Lutheran Forum* 39 (Advent 1990): 36, 39.

8. Groups that work to sustain condemnation of gay and lesbian people draw their greatest strength from appealing to fears in this category. One publication, "Some Things You May Not Know About Homosexuality," put it this way: "Compared to heterosexuals, homosexuals are:

- Much more promiscuous—A 1972 study by the U. S. Center for Disease Control revealed that 50% of male homosexuals have had over 500 different sexual partners. For AIDS victims the average is 1,100 different sexual partners.

- Much more pedophilic—In one study, two homosexual researchers found that 73% of male homosexuals have had sex as adults with boys 19 or younger.

- Much more abusive—Data from several studies suggest that, when data from both genders are combined, homosexuals are at least eight to twelve times more likely to molest children than heterosexuals. Another set of data indicates that homosexual teachers are at least five times more likely to make sexual advances toward and at least seven times more likely to have sexual contact with their students than their heterosexual counterparts."

The problem with such assertions is that they present selective data as if it were fact, and offer no information concerning studies that analyze the same issues but with contrasting results. We should be wary of any appeals to fear as the basis for action. What is at stake for those who tender such one-sided analyses of the issue?

9. Virginia Ramey Mollenkott and Letha Scanzoni, *Is the Homosexual My Neighbor? Another Christian View* (San Francisco: Harper and Row, 1978), p. 97.

10. Suzanne Pharr, *Homophobia: A Weapon of Sexism* (Inverness, Calif.: Chardon Press, 1988).

11. Simone de Beauvior perceives lesbians as comprising an underground feminist resistance movement in her classic text *The Second Sex* (New York: Bantam Books, 1953).

12. Rosemary Haughton, "Cultural Imperatives, Taboos and the Gospel Alternative," in *The Vatican and Homosexuality*, ed. Pat Furey and Jeannine Gramick (New York: Crossroad Publishing, 1988), p. 204.

13. Gilbert Meilaender, *The Limits of Love* (University Park: Pennsylvania State University Press, 1987), p. 129.

14. See Edward O. Wilson, *On Human Nature* (Cambridge, Mass.: Harvard University Press, 1978), pp. 121–148.

15. See, for example, the analysis of Carter Heyward, *Touching Our Strength* (San Francisco: Harper and Row, 1989), especially pp. 48–71.

CHAPTER 5: CONFRONTING HETEROSEXISM

1. James R. Zullo and James D. Whitehead, "The Christian Body and Homosexual Maturing," in *A Challenge to Love*, ed. Robert Nugent (New York: Crossroad Publishing, 1987), p. 20.

2. Dorothy Riddle's scale of homophobia names attitudes toward differences in others. Negative levels of attitude, moving from most negative to less negative, are repulsion-pity-tolerance-acceptance. Positive levels move from support, to admiration, to appreciation, to nurturance. Noteworthy in the scale is the inclusion of "acceptance" as a negative attitude. It is an accurate placement, because few of us would be happy for long in a community that merely accepted us.

3. Gregory Baum, "The Homosexual Condition and Political Responsibility," in *A Challenge to Love*, p. 38.

4. This is the argument of Presbyterian theologian Richard Lovelace, *Homosexuality and the Church* (Old Tappan, N.J.: Revell, 1978).

5. This claim is a theological problem only if one equates the baptized community, the visible church as a sociological reality, with the "kingdom of God." In such an equation humanity is divided into the saved (those within the kingdom, in the Church) and the damned (those outside the kingdom, in the world). Such a dichotomy is unbiblical and false, but it persists in many denominations. As we consider the issues of this chapter our presupposition is that the Church does not exist to save people from the world; it exists to save people for the world ("For God so loved *the world* . . ." John 3:16).

6. This is a matter of methodology. See, for example, Evelyn Eaton and James D. Whitehead, *Method in Ministry* (Minneapolis: Seabury Press, 1980); Leonard Swidler, *After the Absolute* (Minneapolis: Fortress Press, 1990); George A. Lindbeck, *The Nature of Doctrine* (Philadelphia: Westminster Press, 1984).

7. For a study of this trend, see Bruce A. Williams, *American Protestantism and Homosexuality: Recent Neo-Traditional Approaches* (Rome: Pontifical University of St. Thomas Aquinas, 1981).

8. This is the argument of Lewis B. Smedes, *Sex for Christians* (Grand Rapids, Mich.: Eerdmanns, 1976), pp. 73–74.

9. Lesslie Newbigin, *The Gospel in A Pluralistic Society* (Grand Rapids, Mich.: Eerdmans, 1989), p. 47.

10. Thomas Kuhn, *The Structure of Scientific Revolutions*, 2d ed. (Chicago: University of Chicago Press, 1970), is the standard text for discussion of paradigm shifts.

11. The assembly did adopt a pastoral letter that set a publication and study process in place, but voted not to *adopt* either the majority or minority report by the more publicized vote of 534–31–1 (93.4 percent of those eligible to vote).

12. A parallel situation exists in the various efforts throughout the country to include sexual orientation in human rights legislation. The efforts have met with limited but significant success. The weight of current statutory evidence, however, stands in stark contrast to these efforts. Sodomy laws are perhaps the best known examples of legislation that emerged within the framework of a paradigm that focuses on sex as sin. For a helpful analysis of legal issues and homosexuality see Richard D. Mohr, *Gays/Justice: A Study of Ethics, Society and Law* (New York: Columbia University Press, 1988). That a need for civil rights legislation exists is amply demonstrated by Gary David Comstock, *Violence Against Lesbians and Gay Men* (New York: Columbia University Press, 1991).

13. Timothy Lull, "Public and Private, Strong and Weak," *Word and World* 10, no. 2 (Spring 1990): 140–146, offers a vision of dialogue where all participants are given voice, including conservative Christians. He draws on Paul's argument (Rom 15:1) about the strong compromising for the sake of the weak. If the situation were not *already* destructive and urgent, an argument for gradual change might be convincing. No one suffered as a consequence of Paul's allowing that not eating meat sacrificed to idols could be followed for the sake of those who were troubled by it. Gay and lesbian people continue to suffer discrimination and violence at the hands of both "weak" and "strong" in Church and society.

14. One could add a third, that the Church never formally declared that being a woman is contrary to the will of God, where it has, of course, said that of homosexuality.

15. Interestingly, however, it was the argument that pregnant women leading worship would make sexuality visible that was most threatening to some. Similarly, with our present prejudices, having an openly gay or lesbian pastor would make our sexuality too visible.

16. We are not arguing that the contemporary situation represents a *status confessionis*, as Lutherans believe was indeed the case in the sixteenth century Reformation. Luther's advice in 1523, seven years prior to the 1530 presentation of the Augsburg Confession, does not demand such a context to be accepted as advice on how to proceed with reform.

17. One must be clear, of course, that these congregations agreed in

their covenants (constitutions) to call as pastors only those approved within the larger (ELCA) church body's understanding of qualifications for ministry. The question is whether they unilaterally declared a different set of qualifications and, if so, whether the case made for doing so is compelling enough to evoke a "spirit rather than letter" of the law response.

CHAPTER 6: DISMANTLING HETEROSEXISM

1. It seems unnecessary to build a case for this assertion. The dichotomies that continue to be used in theological discourse, such as nature-grace, reason-revelation, Scripture-tradition, faith-works, body-spirit, reveal the pervasive influence of dualistic categories. With regard to sexuality, James Nelson has been among the most consistent in pointing out the destructive consequences of body-soul dualism. See his *Embodiment: An Approach to Sexuality and Christian Theology* (Minneapolis: Augsburg, 1978), and *Between Two Gardens* (New York: Pilgrims Press, 1983).

2. See Theodore Mackin, *What Is Marriage?* (New York: Paulist Press, 1982), pp. 127–144; and William S. Babcock, ed., *The Ethics of St. Augustine* (Atlanta: Scholars Press, 1991).

3. We are grateful for Judith Plaskow's essay, "Toward a New Theology of Sexuality," in *Twice Blessed*, ed. Christie Balka and Andy Rose (Boston: Beacon Press, 1989), pp. 141–151, for some of the insights we develop here.

4. Mutuality is essential to but not exhaustive of the content of the sort of inclusive sexual ethic we advocate. Other essential facets of such an ethic would be commitment (fidelity), justice, reproductive responsibility, etc. We cannot at this juncture develop all that we believe is necessary for normative human sexual expression.

5. James B. Nelson, *Between Two Gardens*, p. 5. The reference is to Paul Ricoeur, "Wonder, Eroticism, and Enigma," in *Sexuality and Identity*, ed. Hendrik M. Ruitenbeck (New York: Dell, 1970).

6. Paul Horowitz and Scott Klein, "A Ceremony of Commitment," in Balka and Rose, eds., *Twice Blessed*, p. 129.

7. Richard D. Mohr, *Gays/Justice: A Study of Ethics, Society and the Law* (New York: Columbia University Press, 1988), p. 18.

8. What follows is a description, not a definition. Theodore Mackin, in *What Is Marriage?* (p. 10), points out that not even the Code of Canon Law, nor Vatican II's *Gaudium et spes*, contains a *definition* of marriage. The distinction between description and definition is critical in an analysis of marriage. As a complex personal and social relationship it does not lend itself to reductionistic definition. Protestants would be helped by approaching marriage as a constellation of characteristics that demand constant attention and assessment. Such an approach is enriching and would militate against the sometimes minimalist definitions Protestantism fosters.

9. We realize that some would disagree with the implication that

homosexual people can fulfill the "conditions" of marriage. They argue that homosexual persons are incapable of fidelity because the relationship is intrinsically defective. No substantive evidence exists to support such a view.

10. Heterosexists might argue here that even when the womb is closed, the potential always remains in a marriage of male and female for God to open the womb (for example, the story of Sarah and Abraham). They would argue that this is true no matter what the physiological reason for the infertility (male or female). A nonheterosexist view might see modern reproductive technologies as the means by which God does such miracles (see next note) for homosexual as well as heterosexual couples.

11. Homosexual couples can procreate with the assistance of a third party. For gay men a surrogate mother is needed for artificial insemination with the sperm from one or both of the male partners in the union. For a lesbian couple either or both of the partners can have a child with artificial insemination. These ways of providing children in a same-sex union, unlike adoption, link one partner in the union to the child biologically. This would also be the case if one of the partners brought a child into the union from a previous relationship, although the dimension of mutual consent in the decision to have a child would be different.

Surrogacy is certainly not solely the consequence of modern medicine. The biblical witness on marriage indicates that when wives were infertile other women could and did provide children. The story of Abraham, Sarah, and Hagar is the classic example. The patriarchal framework for such practices obviously raises a different set of ethical concerns than we are treating here.

12. Oliver O'Donovan, "Transsexualism and Christian Marriage," *Journal of Religious Ethics* 11, no. 1 (Spring 1983): 135–162.

13. Ibid., 143.

14. Ibid., 142.

15. O'Donovan's attempt to head off the charge of biologism is unconvincing; ibid., 152.

16. Ibid., 144; emphasis added.

17. Ibid., 152; emphasis added.

18. The Roman Catholic Code of Canon Law states that the two essential properties of a marriage are unity (*unitas*) and indissolubility (*indissolubilitas*) (Canon 1013.2 of the 1917 Code). This does not constitute a definition of marriage in the code, as Theodore Mackin points out in *What Is Marriage?* pp. 10–15, but it focuses on part of the descriptive task in clarifying what marriage is.

19. Mackin, ibid., p. 12.

20. For a survey of the biblical evidence on marriage see O. J. Baab, "Marriage," in *The Interpreter's Dictionary of the Bible* (Nashville: Abingdon, 1962), vol. 3, pp. 278–287.

21. Jeremiah 31:31–33: "The days are surely coming says the Lord, when I will make a new covenant with the house of Israel and the house of

Judah. It will not be like the covenant I made with their ancestors when I took them by the hand to bring them out of the land of Egypt—a covenant that they broke, though I was their husband, says the Lord."

22. Kenneth Stevenson, *Nuptial Blessing*, Alcuin Club Collections (London: SPCK, 1982), p. 64. See pages 3–5, from which the preceding summary is drawn. We also rely heavily on Stevenson for the following discussion of the ritual history of marriage.

23. Ignatius, *To Polycarp*, in Cyril C. Richardson, ed., *Early Christian Fathers*, vol. 1 (Philadelphia: Westminster Press, 1953), p. 119; and Athenagoras, *A Plea*, ibid., p. 337.

24. Tertullian, *To His Wife*, in *Tertullian: Treatises on Marriage and Remarriage, To His Wife, An Exhortation to Chastity, Monogamy*, trans. William P. Le Saint (Westminster, Md.: Newman Press, 1956).

25. Stevenson, *Nuptial Blessing*, p. 18.

26. As noted earlier, this assumes that the procreation is *restricted to the partners* in the marriage. Surrogacy in any form obviously qualifies the stated conclusion. In his discussion of Canon 1013.1 of the 1917 Code of Canon Law, Mackin, in *What Is Marriage?*, argues that because the *finis* (end) of marriage is described by the canon as procreation and the nurture of children, homosexual marriage is impossible. To make this case, however, he must link canon 1013.1's description of the *finis* of marriage with Canon 1013.2's definition of the *essential* properties or characteristics of a marriage. He explains the connection as follows.

"*There is a sense in which a marriage's primary end is also one of its essential properties*. For if procreation and nurture were not marriage's primary end, it would be some other kind of relationship—sexually realized, perhaps, but not marriage *in exactly the same sense* as that intended by the canon. And because there is no known way in which two men or two women can together conceive a child, this definition voids even the possibility of a homosexual marriage" (p. 34, n. 5; emphasis added). The logic of his first sentence represents a confusion of categories. It is not self-evident that an "end" toward which something moves is by virtue of that an "essential property" of it. This could be true only if the end of marriage was presumed uniform. That is precisely the premise under examination. And it is obviously the case that a nonheterosexist view of marriage would not be understood "in *exactly* the same sense" as the canon's.

27. See Stevenson, *Nuptual Blessing*, pp. 70–71, for citation and discussion.

28. Ibid., p. 68.

29. Ibid., p. 75; cited text is from J. B. Molin and P. Mutembe, *Le rituel du Marriage en France du XIIe au XVIe siècle* (Paris, 1974), p. 106.

30. Ibid., pp. 135–136.

31. See Mackin, *What Is Marriage?*, for a detailed historical analysis of these issues.

32. Mackin, ibid., points out that not until the twelfth century was mar-

riage accepted by the Roman Catholic church as a "saving sacrament." That is, it was not only a sacred sign (Augustine's definition) but also a personally sanctifying sacred sign (p. 31). Protestants traditionally have avoided speaking of sacraments in this way. This is due to a larger debate rooted in different understandings of the relationship of grace and nature.

33. Ibid., p. 21. A difficulty with Mackin's example here is his focus on the first "good" of marriage, "offspring" (note his use of the singular "good" in this quote as compared with the "goods" of marriage, of which procreation-offspring is but one). Again this illustrates a heterocentric bias in reading the evidence.

34. "Pastoral Constitution on the Church in the Modern World," Part II, Chapter 1.50, in *The Documents of Vatican II*, ed. Walter M. Abbott and Joseph Gallagher (Chicago: Follet Publishing Co., 1966), pp. 253–254.

35. *Apology of the Augsburg Confession*, Article XXIII: 11–13, in *The Book of Concord*, ed. Theodore Tappert (Philadelphia: Fortress Press, 1959), p. 241.

36. See, for example, Martin Luther's comments on the sixth commandment ("you shall not commit adultery") in *The Large Catechism*, ibid., pp. 392–395.

37. *Code of Canon Law* (Washington, D.C.: Canon Law Society of America, 1983), p. 387.

38. For some Protestants the restriction of the covenant to a man and a woman rests more on a theory of gender complementarity that is signed by procreative potential.

39. Theodore Mackin, "How to Understand the Sacrament of Marriage," in *Commitment to Partnership*, ed. William P. Roberts (New York: Paulist Press, 1987), p. 53. The observations of the following paragraphs are based on the arguments of Mackin's article.

40. Ibid., p. 56.

41. Ibid.

42. We are indebted to O'Donovan, "Transsexualism and Christian Marriage," for exploring the unique ethical questions raised here. Transgender people identify themselves with the sex other than the one to which they belong biologically. Modern surgical procedures allow them to adapt their bodies to their self-perceived gender identity. The male-to-female transition in such surgery is more successful physiologically than the female-to-male one. Surgeons can replicate female genitalia so that a male-to-female patient can engage in sexual intercourse. To date, however, it is impossible to construct artificial male genitalia so that a female-to-male patient can sustain a spontaneous erection. In either case the person remains chromosomally a member of his or her original sex and cannot be fertile in the new gender role.

After surgery a transgender person is a member of the assumed sex both psychologically and physiologically. But for legal purposes is the postoperative transgender person a member of the original birth sex or of the assumed sex? For example, should their birth certificate be changed? If the person marries, the heterocentric bias of our culture assumes that it will be to a member of the opposite sex. Yet a transgender person might choose to be in a same-sex union. The intuition of belonging to the other sex is distinct from but related to the issue of sexual orientation. If the person was in a heterosexual marriage prior to surgery, does their new sexual status result in a dissolution of the original marriage? If so, on what grounds? The legal ramifications of such technologies are less than clear to say the least.

CHAPTER 7: MOVING BEYOND HETEROSEXISM

1. This is not to say that sexual authenticity is not a moral problem for heterosexual people. For example, many who are married habitually fail to identify themselves as such in their workday lives. Additionally it is not always clear who should be told about one's sexual attractions, or whether all sexual attractions should be named. Discerning what is prudent to reveal about one's sexual feelings in various contexts is difficult. Sometimes naming an attraction will decrease the possibility of being swept away by it. Other times it makes awkwardly and palpably real what might have been a passing fantasy.

2. According to the study by Bell and Weinberg, nearly 20 percent of all homosexual persons have been married at least once. This is probably a conservative estimate, because those still married would not have been likely to participate in their survey. See Alan P. Bell, Sue K. Hammersmith, and Martin S. Weinberg, *Sexual Preference: Its Development in Men and Women* (Bloomington: Indiana University Press, 1981).

3. Watergate was not only illicit but scandalous in precisely this sense. Not only was the break-in illegal, harmful to the individuals violated and the politicians involved in the cover up, but it had negative effects on our respect for the *office* of the president of the United States.

4. Researchers are divided about whether or not gay and lesbian teenagers are especially at risk regarding suicide. Although it is perhaps premature to reach a definitive conclusion in this matter, a 1989 U. S. Department of Health and Human Services study reported that homosexual teens were three times more likely to attempt suicide than heterosexual teens.

5. William Carroll, "God as Unloving Father," *The Christian Century* 108, no. 8 (March 6, 1991): 255.

6. For more details, see "The Christian Body and Homosexual Maturing," by James R. Zullo and James D. Whitehead, in *A Challenge to Love*, ed. Robert Nugent (New York: Crossroad Publishing, 1989), pp. 20–37.

7. Adrienne Rich, *On Lies, Secrets and Silences* (New York: W. W. Norton and Company, 1979), p. 186.

8. Stuart Byron, "The Closet Syndrome," in *Out of the Closets*, ed. Karla Jay and Allen Young (New York: Pyramid Books, 1974), p. 59.

9. Rich, *On Lies, Secrets and Silences,* p. 188.

10. Timothy F. Lull, "Public and Private, Strong and Weak," *Word and World* 10, no. 2 (Spring 1990): 142.

11. Rich, *On Lies, Secrets and Silences,* p. 186.

12. Ibid., 192.

13. In a brief editorial, James H. Burtness notes that the ELCA bishops jumped to this conclusion on the basis that it was not *explicitly* forbidden in the teaching statements on human sexuality of their predecessor body churches. He points out "the fact that the predecessor bodies had not made a *practice* of ordaining publicly declared homosexuals" (emphasis ours). See James H. Burtness, "The Bishops Say Yes and No," *Dialog* 27, no. 3 (Summer 1988): 167.

14. Lull notes that this option has received implicit approval through candidacy and roster screening processes that "did not probe private lives too deeply." See "Public and Private, Strong and Weak," p. 141.

15. Carroll, "God as Unloving Father," p. 256.

16. Ibid., p. 256.

17. Ibid., p. 256.

18. This is the definition of sexuality that dominates the PCUSA study of human sexuality. See *Keeping Body and Soul Together: Sexuality, Spirituality and Social Justice* (PCUSA, printed in U.S.A., 1991), p. 16.

19. Margaret A. Farley, "An Ethic for Same-Sex Relations," in *A Challenge to Love*, p. 93.

20. John McNeill, "Homosexuality, Lesbianism and the Future: The Creative Role of the Gay Community in Building a More Humane Society," in ibid., pp. 52–64.

21. Farley, "An Ethic for Same-Sex Relations," p. 105.

22. Mary E. Hunt, "Lovingly Lesbian: Toward a Feminist Theology of Friendship," in *A Challenge to Love*, pp. 135–156.

23. Most lesbians (between 58 and 71 percent) have only two to fourteen sexual partners. This is not drastically different from a comparable control group among the straight population. In contrast, 14 to 15 percent of all gay men reported having between 500 to 999 partners, and between and 19 and 28 percent of gay men in the Bay area report having over 1,000 sexual partners. Even if these statistics prove to be idiosyncratic to the San Francisco gay community rather than generally representative, and even if one of the impacts of AIDS has been a reduction in such casual coupling, the general pattern of indiscriminate sexual relationships may hold true.

24. Bertrand Russell in his book, *Marriage and Morals* (New York: Liveright, 1929) argued that sexual fidelity really makes sense only for those who parent. He claimed that children need such stability; lovers do not.

25. Wendel Berry, "The Body and the Earth," in *Recollected Essays* (Berkeley, Calif.: North Point Press, 1981), p. 302.

26. "Perspectives on Homosexuality: The Task Force on Issues Related to Homosexuality, Homophobia and the Ordination of Persons of Homosexual Orientation," St. Paul Area Synod, ELCA (April 1990), p. 51.

27. John B. Cobb, Jr., *Matters of Love and Death* (Louisville, Ky.: Westminster–John Knox Press, 1991), p. 101.

POSTSCRIPT

1. Lisa Sowle Cahill, *Women and Sexuality* (New York: Paulist Press, 1992), p. 7.

2. Mary Midgely, "On Not Being Afraid of Natural Sex Differences," in *Feminist Perspectives in Philosophy*, ed. Norwena Griffiths and Margaret Whitford (Bloomington: Indiana University Press, 1988), p. 35.

3. Ann Ferguson, Jacquelyn N. Zila, and Kathyrn Pyne Addelson, "On 'Compulsory Heterosexuality and Lesbian Experience': Defining the Issues," in *Feminist Theory: A Critique of Ideology*, ed. Nanner O. Keohane, Barbara C. Gelpi, and Michelle Z. Rosaldo (Chicago: University of Chicago Press, 1981), pp. 178–180.

4. Cahill, *Women and Sexuality*, p. 8.

5. John Mahoney, *The Making of Moral Theology. A Study of Roman Catholic Tradition* (New York: Oxford University Press, 1987), p. 328.

6. Ibid., p. 330.

7. Gerald J. Hughes, "Is Ethics One or Many?" in *Catholic Perspectives on Medical Morals*, ed. John P. Hangan, John Collins Harvey, and Edmund D. Pellegrino (Dordrecht: Kluwer Academic Publishing, 1989), p. 192.

Bibliography

Abbott, Walter M., and Gallagher, Joseph, eds. The Documents of Vatican II. New York: Guild Press, 1966.

Achtemeier, Paul T. The Inspiration of Scripture. Philadelphia: Westminster Press, 1980.

Allport, Gordon. The Nature of Prejudice. Cambridge, Mass.: Addison-Wesley, 1954.

Ard, Roger H. "Why the Conservatives Won in Miami," The Christian Century 94 (August 1977): 678.

Avis, Paul. Eros and the Sacred. Harrisburg, Pa.: Morehouse Publishing, 1989.

Babcock, William S., ed. The Ethics of St. Augustine. Atlanta: Scholars Press, 1991.

Balka, Christie, and Rose, Andy, eds. Twice Blessed. Boston: Beacon Press, 1989.

Barnhouse, Ruth Tiffany. Homosexuality: A Symbolic Confusion. New York: Seabury Press, 1977.

Barth, Karl. Church Dogmatics, vol. 3–4. Edinburgh: T & T Clark, 1961.

Bauckham, Richard J. Jude, 2 Peter. Waco, Texas: Word Publishing, 1983.

Bauer, Walter. A Greek-English Lexicon of the New Testament and Other Early Christian Literature. Chicago: University of Chicago Press, 1979.

Bell, Alan P., and Weinberg, Martin S., eds. Homosexuality: An Annotated Bibliography. New York: Harper and Row, 1972.

Bell, Alan P., and Weinberg, Martin S. Homosexualities: A Study of Diversity Among Men and Women. New York: Simon and Schuster, 1978.

Bell, Alan P., Hammersmith, Sue K., and Weinberg, Martin S. Sexual Preference: Its Development in Men and Women. Bloomington: Indiana University Press, 1981.

Benne, Robert. *Ordinary Saints: An Introduction to the Christian Life.* Philadelphia: Fortress Press, 1988.

Berry, Wendel. *Recollected Essays.* Berkeley, Calif.: North Point Press, 1981.

Birch, Bruce C., and Rasmussen, Larry L. *Bible and Ethics in the Christian Life.* Minneapolis: Augsburg Publishing, 1989.

Bockle, Franz. *Fundamental Moral Theology.* New York: Pueblo Publishing, 1980.

Boswell, John. *Christianity, Social Tolerance, and Homosexuality.* Chicago: University of Chicago Press, 1980.

Brueggemann, Walter. *Genesis.* Atlanta: John Knox Press, 1975.

Burtness, James H. "The Bishops Say Yes and No." *Dialog* 27, no. 3 (Summer 1988): 167.

Buttrick, George A. *The Interpreter's Dictionary of the Bible.* Vol. 3. Nashville: Abingdon, 1962.

Cahill, Lisa Sowle. *Between the Sexes.* New York: Paulist Press, 1985.

———. "Is Catholic Ethics Biblical? The Example of Sex and Gender." *Warren Lecture Series in Catholic Studies,* no. 20 (March 1992): 2, 3, 9–14.

———. *Women and Sexuality.* New York: Paulist Press, 1992.

Carroll, William. "God as Unloving Father." *The Christian Century* 108, no. 9 (March 6, 1991): 225.

Catholic Theological Society of America. *Human Sexuality: New Directions in American Catholic Thought.* New York: Paulist Press, 1977.

The Church in Society: A Lutheran Perspective. Chicago: ELCA Department for Studies of the Commission for Church in Society, 1991.

Cobb, John B., Jr. *Matters of Love and Death.* Louisville, Ky.: Westminster–John Knox Press, 1991.

Code of Canon Law. Washington, D.C.: Canon Law Society of America, 1983.

Coleman, Eli, ed. *Psychotherapy With Homosexual Men and Women.* New York: Haworth Press, 1988.

Comstock, Gary David. *Violence Against Lesbians and Gay Men.* New York: Columbia University Press, 1991.

Congregation for the Doctrine of the Faith. "The Pastoral Care of Homosexual Persons." *Origins* 16, no. 22 (November 1986): 377, 379–381.

Countryman, L. William. *Dirt, Greed and Sex.* Philadelphia: Fortress Press, 1988.

Croatto, J. Severino. *Biblical Hermeneutics: Toward a Theory of Reading as the Production of Meaning.* Maryknoll, N.Y.: Orbis Books, 1987.

De Beauvoir, Simone. *The Second Sex.* New York: Bantam Books, 1953.

De Cecco, John P., ed. *Gay Personality and Sexual Labeling.* New York: Harington Park Press, 1985.

Dobson, James C. *Focus on the Family* (March 1991).

Duffy, Martin, ed. *Issues in Sexual Ethics.* Souderton, Pa.: United Church People for Biblical Witness, 1979.

Dunn, James D. G. *Romans.* Dallas: Word Publishing, 1988.

———. *Unity and Diversity in the New Testament.* Philadelphia: Westminster Press, 1977.

ELCA Task Force on Human Sexuality. "Human Sexuality and the Christian Faith." *Forum Letter* 21, no. 2 (February 1991): 1–3.

Fiorenza, Elizabeth Schussler. *In Memory of Her.* New York: Crossroads Publishing, 1983.

Fitch, William. *Christian Perspectives on Sex and Marriage.* Grand Rapids, Mich.: Eerdmans, 1971.

Flynn, Eileen P. *AIDS: A Catholic Call for Compassion.* Kansas City, Mo.: Sheed and Ward, 1985.

Fortunato, John. "The Last Committee on Sexuality (Ever)." *Christianity and Crisis* 51, no. 2 (February 1991): 34–35.

Fortune, Marie Marshall. *Sexual Violence.* New York: Pilgrim Press, 1983.

Fuchs, Joseph. *Natural Law: A Theological Investigation*, trans. Helmut Rekter and John A. Dowling. New York: Sheed and Ward, 1965.

Furey, Pat, and Gramick, Jeannine, eds. *The Vatican and Homosexuality.* New York: Crossroad Publishing, 1988.

Gelpi, Barbara C., Keohane, Nanner O., and Rosaldo, Michelle Z., eds. *Feminist Theory: A Critique of Ideology.* Chicago: University of Chicago Press, 1981.

Gordon, Kevin. *Homosexuality and Social Justice.* San Francisco: The Consultation on Homosexuality, Social Justice, and Roman Catholic Theology, 1982 and 1986.

Grady, Denise. "The Brains of Gay Men." *Discover* (January 1992): 29.

Greenberg, David F. *The Construction of Homosexuality*. Chicago: University of Chicago Press, 1988.

Griffiths, Norwena, and Whitford, Margaret, eds. *Feminist Perspectives in Philosophy*. Bloomington: Indiana University Press, 1988.

Gunn, David M. "A Fearful Domination: Constructions of Homosexuality in the Hebrew Bible." Paper presented at the Society for Biblical Literature, Kansas City, 1991.

Gustafson, James M. *Protestant and Roman Catholic Ethics*. Chicago: University of Chicago Press, 1978.

Hangan, John P., Harvey, John Collins, and Pellegrino, Edmund D., eds. *Catholic Perspectives on Medical Morals*. Dodrecht: Kluwer Academic Publishing, 1989.

Hannigan, James P. *Homosexuality: The Test Case for Christian Sexual Ethics*. New York: Paulist Press, 1988.

Harrison, Beverly Wildung. *Our Right to Choose*. Boston: Beacon Press, 1983.

Harvey, Joseph. *Gay Children Grow Up*. New York: Praeger, 1982.

Hays, Richard B. "Relations Natural and Unnatural: A Response to John Boswell's Exegesis of Romans l." *Journal of Religious Ethics* 14, no. 1 (Spring 1986): 184–215.

Heyward, Carter. *Touching Our Strength*. San Francisco: Harper and Row, 1989.

Hooker, Evelyn. "A Preliminary Analysis of Group Behavior of Homosexuals." *Journal of Psychology* 42 (1956): 217–225.

Hulme, William E. "A Pastoral Perspective on Homosexuality." *Word and World* 10, no. 2 (Spring 1990): 131–139.

Jay, Karla, and Young, Allen, eds. *Out of the Closets*. New York: Pyramid Books, 1974.

Jenkins, Jonathan L. "Review Essay of *The Construction of Homosexuality* by David F. Greenberg." *Lutheran Forum* 39 (Advent 1990): 36, 39.

Johnson, Luke T. *Sharing Possessions*. Philadelphia: Fortress Press, 1981.

Johnson, Virginia, and Masters, William H. *Homosexuality in Perspective*. Boston: Little, Brown and Co., 1979.

Jonson, Albert R. and Toulmin, Stephen. *The Abuse of Casuistry: A History of Moral Reasoning*. Berkeley: University of California Press, 1988.

Keeping Body and Soul Together: Sexuality, Spirituality and Social Justice. Presbyterian Church U.S.A., Printed in the U.S.A., 1991, p. 16.

Kelly, J. N. D. *The Epistles of Peter and Jude.* New York: Harper and Row, 1969.

Kinsey, Alfred C., Martin, Clyde E., and Pomeroy, Wardell B. *Sexual Behavior in the Human Male.* Philadelphia: W. B. Saunders, 1948.

Kuhn, Thomas. *The Structure of Scientific Revolutions,* 2d ed. Chicago: University of Chicago Press, 1970.

Lebacqz, Karen. *Six Theories of Justice.* Minneapolis: Augsburg Press, 1986.

Liddell, Henry G., and Scott, Robert. *A Greek-English Lexicon.* Oxford: Oxford University Press, 1940.

Lindbeck, George A. *The Nature of Doctrine.* Philadelphia: Westminster Press, 1984.

Lovelace, Richard. *Homosexuality and the Church.* Old Tappan, N.J.: Revell, 1978.

Lull, Timothy. "Public and Private, Strong and Weak." *Word and World* 10, no. 2 (Spring 1990): 140–146.

Luther, Martin, "How Christians Should Regard Moses, 1525," in *Luther's Works* 35, ed. E. Theodore Bachmann; and "Theses Concerning Faith and Law, 1535," in *Luther's Works* 34, ed. Lewis Spitz. Philadelphia: Muhlenberg Press, 1960.

Mackin, Theodore. *What Is Marriage?* New York: Paulist Press, 1982.

Mackin, Theodore. "How to Understand the Sacrament of Marriage." *Commitment to Partnership,* ed. William P. Robert. New York. Paulist Press, 1987.

Mahoney, John. *The Making of Moral Theology: A Study of Roman Catholic Tradition.* New York: Oxford University Press, 1987.

Martin, James D. *The Book of Judges.* Cambridge: Cambridge University Press, 1975.

McCormick, Richard A. "Notes on Moral Theology." *Theological Studies* 27, no. 4 (December 1966): 607–654.

——, and Curran, Charles, C., eds. *Readings in Moral Theology #4: The Use of Scripture in Moral Theology.* New York: Paulist Press, 1984.

McNeil, John J. *The Church and the Homosexual.* Kansas City, Mo.: Sheed, Andrews and McNeil, 1976.

Meier, Paul D. *Christian Child-Rearing and Personality Development.* Grand Rapids, Mich.: Baker Book House, 1977.

Meilaender, Gilbert. *The Limits of Love*. University Park: Pennsylvania State University Press, 1987.

Metzger, Bruce M., and Murphy, Roland E., eds. *The New Oxford Annotated Bible*. New York: Oxford University Press, 1991.

Mohr, Richard D. *Gays/Justice: A Study of Ethics, Society and the Law*. New York: Columbia University Press, 1988.

Mollenkot, Virginia Ramey and Scanzoni, Letha. *Is the Homosexual My Neighbor? Another Christian View*. San Francisco: Harper and Row, 1978.

Money, John. *Gay, Straight and In-Between*. New York: Oxford University Press, 1988.

Mudge, Lewis, ed. *Essays on Biblical Interpretation*. Philadelphia: Fortress Press, 1980.

Nelson, James B. *Between Two Gardens*. New York: Pilgrims Press: 1983.

——. *Embodiment: An Approach to Sexuality and Christian Theology*. Minneapolis: Augsburg Publishing, 1978.

Newbigin, Lesslie. *The Gospel in a Pluralistic Society*. Grand Rapids, Mich.: Eerdmans, 1989.

Noonan, John T., Jr. *Contraception*. Cambridge, Mass.: Harvard University Press, 1986.

Noth, Martin. *Leviticus*. Philadelphia: Westminster Press, 1977.

Nugent, Robert, ed. *A Challenge to Love*. New York: Crossroad Publishing, 1989.

O'Donovan, Oliver. "Transsexualism and Christian Marriage." *Journal of Religious Ethics* 11, no. 1 (Spring 1983): 135–162.

"Perspectives on Homosexuality." St. Paul Area Synod, ELCA (April 1990).

Peterson, William L. "Can *Arsenokoitai* Be Translated by 'Homosexuals'?" *Vigiliae Christianae* 40 (1986): 187–191.

Pharr, Suzanne. *Homophobia: A Weapon of Sexism*. Inverness, Calif.: Chardon Press, 1988.

Pittenger, W. Norman. *Time for Consent: A Christian Approach to Homosexuality*. London: S.C.M. Press, 1967.

Plass, Ewald M., ed. *What Luther Says*. St. Louis: Concordia Publishing House, 1959.

Reich, Warren T., ed. *Encyclopedia of Bioethics*, vol. 2. New York: The Free Press, 1978.

Rich, Adrienne. "Compulsory Heterosexuality and Lesbian Exis tence (1980)." *Blood, Bread and Poetry: Selective Prose 1979–1985*. New York: W. W. Norton, 1986.

———. *On Lies, Secrets and Silences*. New York: W. W. Norton, 1979.

Richardson, Cyril C., ed. *Early Christian Fathers*, vol. 1. Philadelphia: Westminster Press, 1953.

Ruitenbeck, Hendrik M., ed. *Sexuality and Identity*. New York: Dell, 1970.

Russell, Bertrand. *Marriage and Morals*. New York: Liveright, 1929.

Scheiders, Sandra M. *The Revelatory Text*. San Francisco: Harper, 1991.

Scroggs, Robin. *Homosexuality and the New Testament*. Philadelphia: Fortress Press, 1983.

Smedes, Lewis B. *Sex for Christians*. Grand Rapids, Mich.: Eerdmans, 1976.

Snaith, N. H. *Leviticus and Numbers*. London: Thomas Nelson and Sons, 1967.

Soggin, James Alberto. *Judges: A Commentary*. Philadelphia: Westminster Press, 1981.

Spong, John Shelby. *Living in Sin? A Bishop Rethinks Human Sexuality*. San Francisco: Harper and Row, 1990.

Stevenson, Kenneth. *Nuptial Blessing*. London: SPCK, 1982.

Swartley, Willard M. *Slavery, Sabbath, War and Women: Case Issues in Biblical Interpretation*. Scottsdale, Pa.: Herald Press, 1983.

Swindler, Leonard. *After the Absolute*. Minneapolis: Fortress Press, 1990.

Tappet, Theodore, ed. *The Book of Concord*. Philadelphia: Fortress Press, 1959.

Tertullian. *Tertullian: Treatises on Marriage and Remarriage, To His Wife, An Exhortation to Chastity, Monogamy*, trans. William P. Le Saint. Westminster, Md.: Newman Press, 1956.

Thielicke, Helmut. *The Ethics of Sex*, trans. John W. Doberstein. New York: Harper and Row, 1964.

Toward a Quaker View of Sex. London: Friends Home Service Committee, 1964.

Tracy, David. *Blessed Rage for Order*. New York: Seabury Press, 1975.

Trible, Phyllis. *God and the Rhetoric of Sexuality*. Philadelphia: Fortress Press, 1978.

Troiden, Richard R. *Gay and Lesbian Identity: A Sociological Analysis.* New York: General Hall, 1988.

Von Rad, Gerhard. *Genesis: A Commentary.* Philadelphia: Westminster Press, 1922.

Wenham, Gordon J. *The Book of Leviticus.* Grand Rapids, Mich.: Eerdmans, 1979.

Westermann, Claus. *Genesis 12–36: A Commentary.* Minneapolis: Augsburg Press, 1985.

Whitehead, Evelyn Eaton, and Whitehead, James D. *Method in Ministry.* Minneapolis: Seabury Press, 1980.

Williams, Bruce A. *American Protestantism and Homosexuality: Recent Neo-Traditional Approaches.* Rome: Pontifical University of St. Thomas Aquinas, 1981.

Wilson, Edward O. *On Human Nature.* Cambridge, Mass.: Harvard University Press, 1978.

Witham, Frederick L. "Childhood Indicators of Male Homosexuality." *Archives of Sexual Behavior* 6 (1977): 89–96.

———. "A Cross-Cultural Assessment of Early Cross-Gender Behavior and Familiar Factors in Male Homosexuality." *Archives of Sexual Behavior* 13 (1984): 437–439.

Young, Pamela Dickey. *Feminist Theology/Christian Theology: In Search of Method.* Minneapolis: Fortress Press, 1990.

Index